Bodybuilding Meal Prep Cookbook

Easy and Macro-Friendly Meals to Cook, Prep, Grab, and Go| With 5 Foolproof Step-by-step Bulking and Cutting Meal Prepping Guide.

George B. Allen

Copyright© 2021 By George B. Allen All Rights Reserved

This book is copyright protected. It is only for personal use. You cannot amend, distribute, sell, use, quote or paraphrase any part of the content within this book, without the consent of the author or publisher.

Under no circumstances will any blame or legal responsibility be held against the publisher, or author, for any damages, reparation, or monetary loss due to the information contained within this book, either directly or indirectly.

Disclaimer Notice:

Please note the information contained within this document is for educational and entertainment purposes only. All effort has been executed to present accurate, up to date, reliable, complete information. No warranties of any kind are declared or implied. Readers acknowledge that the author is not engaged in the rendering of legal, financial, medical or professional advice. The content within this book has been derived from various sources. Please consult a licensed professional before attempting any techniques outlined in this book.

By reading this document, the reader agrees that under no circumstances is the author responsible for any losses, direct or indirect, that are incurred as a result of the use of the information contained within this document, including, but not limited to, errors, omissions, or inaccuracies.

Table of Contents

Introduction 1
    The Ultimate Goal 3
    Build Good Habits 3
    The Dirt on Bulking 4

Chapter 1 It's All in The Mind 6
    The Growth Mindset 6
    Stop the Excuses 7
    Commit to Your Goal 7
    Recipe to Success 8
    Making Mistakes 10

Chapter 2 Eat Big to Get Big 13
    Ectomorph 13
    Mesomorph 14
    Endomorph 14
    In-Betweeners 14
    Undereating 14
    The Mystery of Appetite 16
    Breaking Down Your Bulking Macros 18
    What and How to Eat to Bulk Up 21

Chapter 3 The Role of Exercise 31
    Weight Training and Weight Gaining ... 31
    Exercise Selection 31
    Compartmentalize Your Body Parts 36
    Guide to Working Out without a Gym ... 37

Chapter 4 Supplements 39
    Do Hardgainers Need Supplements? 39
    Best of the Best 39
    In the Bulking Bad Bin 42
    Citrulline Malate 42
    Beta-Alanine 42

    Ashwagandha 42
    What About Our Vegan Friends? 43

Chapter 5 Meal Prep Basics 44
    What is Meal Prepping 44
    Why Meal Prep? 44
    Meal Prep Principles 44
    The Art of Storage 45
    Food Storage Guidelines 46
    How to Thaw Safely 47
    Safe Reheating Guidelines 47

Chapter 6 Step-By-Step Meal Plans 49
    Bulking Meal Plan-1 (Calorie Goal: 3500-4000) . 49
    Bulking Meal Plan-2 (Calorie Goal: 3000-3500) . 54
    Bulking Meal Plan-3 (Calorie Goal: 2500-3000) . 60
    Cutting Meal Plan-1 (Calorie Goal: 2000-2500) . 65
    Cutting Meal Plan-2 (Calorie Goal: 1500-2000) . 71

Chapter 7 Fast Carb Pre-Workout Meals ... 76
    Perfect Fluffy Basmati Rice 76
    Black Beans and White Quinoa 76
    Fluffy Brown Rice Pilaf 77
    Tangy Kale Salad 77
    Sushi Bowl with Vegetable 77
    Tofu and Brown Rice Bowl 78
    Beans and Spinach Rice Bowl 78
    Soya Mince Brown Rice Noodle Bowl 78
    Classic Scotcheroos 79
    Veggie Quinoa Bowl with Basil Pesto ... 79
    Baked Mango Quinoa Bowl with Tempeh .. 79
    Quinoa with Peas and Red Cabbage 80

Chapter 8 Preworkout Smoothies........ 81
- Vanilla Fruity Spinach Smoothie 81
- Tropical Fruits Smoothie 81
- Citrus Julius Smoothie 82
- Sunny Orange Smoothie............. 82
- Banana-Almond Milk Smoothie 82
- Creamy Banana and Blueberry Smoothie 83
- Apple and Coconut Milk Smoothie 83
- Citrus Strawberry-Banana Smoothie 83
- Mango and Blueberry Smoothie 84
- Banana, Raisins, and Oats Smoothie 84

Chapter 9 Post-Workout Meals 85
- Avocado, Veggie, and Eggs on Toast 85
- Cantaloupe and Cottage Cheese Bowl......... 85
- Macadamia and Coconut French Toast 85
- Egg Rice Skillet 86
- Cuban Swiss Sandwich Quesadilla 86
- Speedy Chocolate Protein Snack Mug 86
- Balsamic Melon and Cottage Cheese 87
- Matcha Green Tea Fudge Bars............... 87
- Protein Salad with Buttermilk Dressing......... 87
- Chicken Breast Salad 88

Chapter 10 Breakfast................ 89
- Honey Greek Yogurt Parfait 89
- French Toast with Cottage Cheese 89
- Baked Sweet Potatoes with Cottage Cheese...... 90
- Cinnamon Apple Flapjacks 90
- Banana, Blueberry, and Peach Smoothie Bowl ... 90
- Breakfast in A Jar.................91
- Ham and Cheese Quiche 91
- Turkey Sausage-Egg Scramble.........91
- Baby Spinach and Tomato Frittata........... 92
- Banana and Oat Protein Bars 92
- Blueberry-Oat Muffins 92
- Breakfast Turkey Hash.............. 93
- Breakfast Skillet................. 93
- Egg and Canadian Bacon Cups 93
- Chicken Breast and Polenta Pizza 94
- Thyme Crustless Quiche 94
- Eggs Benedict with Hollandaise-Mustard Sauce .. 94
- Cinnamon Sweet Potato Pancakes........... 95
- Polenta Squares with Blueberry Sauce and Banana 95
- Eggs and Cheery Tomato Breakfast Melts 95

Chapter 11 Meats................. 96
- Vietnamese Beef and Rice Noodle Bowl 96
- Beef Burgers................. 96
- Flank Steak with Brussels Sprouts 97
- Bison and Portobello Buns............ 97
- Steak with Coffee-Rub 98
- Ginger Beef Sirloin and Bok Choy 98
- Southern Pork Medallions 98
- Muscle-Building Beef Meatloaf........ 99
- Sirloin Steak................. 99
- Adobo Sirloin Steak 99
- Cheesy Beef Stroganoff 100
- Beef and Chicken Sausage Stuffed Peppers 100
- Chinese Plum Sauce-Glazed Pork Chops 100
- Mustard Sage-Coated Pork Tenderloin 101
- Cajun Pork Chops with Tomatoes 101
- Parmesan Breaded Pork Chops 101
- Stir Fried Pork and Bok Choy Noodle 102
- Easy Eye Round Steak 102
- Roasted Coffee-Rubbed Pork Tenderloin........102

Chapter 12 Vegetables and Sides 103
- Vegan Buddha Bowl 103
- Maple Butternut Squash 103
- Asparagus with Shiitake Mushrooms Stir-Fry ... 104
- Maple Syrup-Glazed Carrots........... 104
- Cauliflower Purée with Fresh Thyme 104
- Parmesan Zucchini Fries.............105
- Twice-Baked Potatoes with Cheddar 105
- Cauliflower Rice 105
- Coconut Milk-Smashed Sweet Potatoes........ 106
- Fresh Vegetable Stir Fry.............. 106
- Hasselback Sweet Potato............ 106
- Roasted Vegetables with Herb......... 107
- Black Bean and Corn Quesadilla 107
- Stir-Fried Butternut Squash and Broccoli........107
- Mozzarella Butternut Squash 108
- Yummy Chile Relleno Casserole 108
- Breaded Squash Fries............. 108
- Curried Cauliflower and Potatoes 109
- Zucchini and Baby Spinach Sauté 109
- Teriyaki Sweet Potato and Broccoli Bowl 109

Chapter 13 Fish and Seafood 110
- Red Snapper En Papillote 110
- Tamari Salmon Fillet and Zucchini 110

Parmesan Tilapia Fillet with Asparagus 111
Blackened Baked Tilapia Fillet 111
Cod Fillet with Charred Tomatillo Salsa 111
Fresh Snapper with Broccoli 112
Creamy Fettucine with Sea Scallops 112
Marinated Halibut Fillet with Leeks 112
Graham Cracker-Crusted Tilapia Fillet 113
Mahi-Mahi Fillet with Fruity Salsa 113
Almond-Crusted Baked Cod Fillet 113
Tuna Melt Stuffed Tomatoes 114
Dijon Mustard Baked Scallops 114

Chapter 14 Poultry 115
Homemade Shepherd's Pie 115
Chicken Breast Burrito Bowl 115
Salsa Chicken with Red Kale 116
Chicken Breast with Tomato-Corn Salad 116
Stuffed Chicken Breast with Broiled Tomatoes . . . 117
Mustard Almond-Crusted Chicken Breast 117
Roasted Whole Chicken with Apple 118
Greek Chicken Skewers 118
Traditional Chicken Cacciatore 118
Chicken Hobo 119
Jerk Chicken Breast Grill 119
Aussie Chicken Breast 119
Chicken and Broccoli with Red Wine 120
Nice Chicken Cacciatore 120
Chicken Fettuccine with Shiitake Mushrooms . . 120
Chicken Breast Pesto Pasta 121
Japanese Chicken Yakitori 121
Cheddar Chicken Quesadilla 121
Curried Chicken 122

Chapter 15 Salads 123
Greek Chicken Breast Salad 123
Turkey, Walnut, and Fruit Salad 123
Tuna and Avocado Salad 124
Egg Salad on Rice Crackers 124
Rotisserie Chicken Cobb Salad 124
Lemony Tuna Nicoise Salad 125
Orange Kale Salad 125
Coconut-Crusted Chicken Breast Salad 125
Hot Santa Fe Taco Salad 126
Chickpea and Baby Spinach Salad 126
Black Bean and Corn Salad 127
Baby Spinach Caprese Salad 127

Lime Cucumber Salad 127
Easy Tuna Salad 127
Chicken and Chickpeas Pasta Salad 128

Chapter 16 Snacks and Power Bars 129
Nuts Energy Balls 129
Cinnamon Peanut Butter and Banana Nice Cream 129
Quick Lemon Drop Energy Balls 130
Cherry and Nuts Energy Bites 130
Beef Cheeseburger Bites 130
Protein Pumpkin and Oat Bars 131
Honey Lean Rice Crispy Treats 131
Oats and Almond Milk Bars 131
Iced Pumpkin and Pecan Bars 132
Simple Dough Oats 132
Avocado and Strawberry Toast 132
Pistachio Energy Balls 133
Coconut Lemon Protein Balls 133

Chapter 17 Desserts and Shakes 134
Oat and Chia Seeds Muffins 134
Banana-Peanut Butter Mug Muffins 134
Blueberry-Almond Milk Shake 135
Carrot and Banana Shake 135
Chocolate Mousse 135
Cloud Bread Bake 136
Chocolate Almond Shake 136
Citrus Creamsicle Shake 136
Elvis Milkshake 137
Orange and Beet Protein Shake 137
Banana-Chai Tea Protein Shake 137
Baked Protein Swirl Brownies 138
Almond-Soy Protein Shake 138
Oatmeal-Almond Protein Shake 138
Fruit Crisp 139
Chocolate Cranberry Quinoa Bars 139

Chapter 18 Soup 140
Curry Red Lentil Soup 140
Carrot-Coconut Milk Soup 140
Hearty Spicy Chili 141
Cheesy Chicken Enchilada Soup 141
Green Split Pea Soup 142
Carrot, Tomato, and Spinach Soup 142
Red Lentils and Asparagus Soup 142

- Lush Minestrone Soup 143
- Potato and Brown Lentil Soup 143
- White Bean Soup with Turkey Sausage 143

Chapter 19 Sandwich and Wraps 144
- Breakfast Burritos 144
- Egg and Avocado Sandwiches 144
- Turkey Lettuce Wraps 145
- Italian-Style Sloppy Joe 145
- Spiced Turkey Taco Lettuce Wraps 145
- Classic French Dip Sandwiches 146
- Perfect Vegan BLT Sandwich 146
- Chickpea Mustard Salad Sandwich 147
- Speedy Tofu Club Wrap 147

Chapter 20 Sauces, Dressings and Rub 148
- Lime Avocado Dressing 148
- Light Ranch Salad Dressing 148
- Tangy Maple-Tahini Sauce 148
- Best Guacamole 149
- Easy Homemade Hummus 149
- Fresh Berry Sauce 149
- Low-Fat Tzatziki Sauce 150
- Spicy Cilantro Dressing 150
- Green Salsa Verde 150
- Strawberry-Peach Vinaigrette 151
- Pine Nuts-Basil Pesto Sauce 151
- Maple Peanut Butter Sauce 151
- Balsamic Raspberry Dressing 151
- The Best Beef Rub 152

Appendix : Measurement Conversion Chart 153

Introduction

I'm going to start off by saying I almost gave up. It is just extremely difficult for some of us to gain weight. It took me years to figure out what I was doing wrong and find out the correct ways to approach healthy weight gain. A lot of people will tell you to "just eat more." If only it were that easy! Thinking about it, it's exactly the same as saying to someone who has been struggling with obesity their whole lives to "just eat less." If it were as simple as that, the US would not be smack-bam in the middle of an obesity crisis at the moment (Centers for Disease Control and Prevention, 2018).

I wasted years and a lot of money on bulking supplements, expensive gym memberships, nutritional programs, and who knows what else all to gain weight and muscle. I remember standing in front of a mirror in the men's locker room after a grueling 45 minutes in spinning class and thinking to myself that I would never get the body I dreamt of—my genetics wouldn't allow it. By chance, a buff guy walked past, and he must have noticed the look of disappointment on my face.

It turns out he knew exactly what I was going through. After chatting with him for a while and getting inspired by his transformation photos, I decided to give it one more shot. I tossed everything I thought I knew about nutrition and exercise out the window and started redefining how I assumed the human body worked.

The bottom line is—anyone can pick up weight and pack on muscle. It doesn't matter if you're a man or woman. As long as you make a few fundamental changes, you'll be able to move from a small to large T-shirt size in no time!

It's been years since I fell down the rabbit hole of gaining weight the healthy way—and with weight I don't mean fat but lean muscle mass. I am proud to say that I achieved the body I always wanted and have maintained it. Now, I want to share my knowledge with you to motivate you never to give up. I know it isn't easy; focusing on eating right and working out for months on end only to find that you haven't gained a pound can be very off-putting. After reading this book, you'll have all the know-how to put on muscle and keep it on successfully.

Eating will play a big part in your transformation because, let's face it, if you're not gaining weight, you're not eating enough. But please don't misinterpret what I'm saying and think that I'm now joining the "just eat more" club. Yes, technically they are correct, but it's more complicated than that. For example, how much more should you eat—2,000, 3,000 calories? And what types of food? What about exercise? Supplements?

The basic principle of gaining weight may be that you have to consume more calories than your body needs for fuel, but the type of calories matter. You also need to consider the effect exercise has on your weight gain.

Here's an example of how the various elements work together—either in your favor or against you.

If you weigh 122 pounds and you're not very active, you will need to eat close to 2,400 calories to maintain your current weight. Eating anything above 2,400 calories will lead to weight gain. In this case, 3,000 calories a day should do the trick, but then again, what if you have bad genetics, a stubborn body, or a slow metabolism? Then you'll have to consume even more calories! You'll have to consider any changes in activity and compensate accordingly.

As you can see, it's easy to say you should eat more and you'll gain weight fast, but there are so many variables when it comes to eating that it is not as simple as it sounds.

I also don't want the book's title to mislead you. Although I'll be focusing on how to gain weight in seven days, you'll need more than a week to see significant change. The last thing I want you to do is set unrealistic goals, so let me set the record straight before we move on. There is no magic pill or quick fix that will give you muscles overnight—you will have to train and eat healthily for three to five years to reach the upper limit of your muscle size. That is a lot of hard work. There is no way that you'll gain close to 30 pounds of lean muscle in a month; it doesn't matter how hard you exercise or how much you eat.

Arnold Schwarzenegger, who is arguably one of the most influential bodybuilders in history, got excited about gaining 25 pounds in 12 months. In his book, Arnold: The Education of a Bodybuilder (2013), he wrote: "Many people regret having to serve in the army. But it was not a waste of time for me. When I came out, I weighed 225 pounds. I'd gone from 200 to 225. Up to that time, this was the biggest change I'd ever made in a single year."

Now, if someone like Schwarzenegger, who has mastered the art of body transformation, says gaining 25 pounds in one year is an achievement, you better believe it.

I chose seven days and not weeks, months, or years because you only need to use the methods mentioned for a short period to understand the basics. Afterward, you'll feel confident enough to apply your knowledge to reach your ideal weight and maintain it.

Ultimately, I will help you change your mindset from thinking like a discouraged skinny guy with a high metabolism who can't gain weight to an attitude of confidence in your ability to pack on healthy weight. This will fundamentally be your secret to success.

There will also be a focus on nutrition, exercise, and supplementation—I want this book to be your go-to manual whenever you're not sure about something. Call it a bulking bible, if you will!

I think it is time we get started.

The Ultimate Goal

I know how it goes. You amp yourself up to build some muscle, join the gym and go five times a week, you follow a clean diet, and break the bank on supplements that promise you gains galore. Then, a few weeks later, the scale still reads exactly the same, or maybe your weight even dropped. That wasn't your goal, was it? No, you wanted to bulk and fill out a t-shirt for once.

Your friends and family may say you lacked the willpower and motivation, but you and I know that wasn't the case—the disappointment got the best of you, and you decided to throw in the towel.

I know this story all too well because I lived it. But what separates those who succeed from those who don't? The way you recover from failing. If you see failure as the end, then you're not going to get anywhere. But, if you approach it as a learning curve, you can adjust what went wrong and move on toward better results.

Actually, I suggest you stop calling it 'failure,' but think of it as a process—a journey toward your goals. If you can do this, you'll be able to analyze each part of the process objectively. If something in your routine or diet is not working, then you'll be able to find the missing piece and adapt your approach. You'll also be able to identify the parts that are working, and this is how you will, in time, develop a lifestyle that works for you. Gradually, your routine will become a habit, and soon, you'll find yourself automatically making choices that lead to gaining and maintaining your muscle.

I know this all is easier said than done—rewiring your brain and body is not so straightforward. For this reason, I include some tips that helped to get and keep me on track, and I'm sure they'll be of benefit to you too.

Build Good Habits

As soon as your actions become habits, they no longer stress you out—they are something you do on autopilot. Now, I know this doesn't sound very sexy. I mean, you want a magic supplement or revolutionary workout that will make you look like a superhero in two days, right? Well, no such luck—even superman has to train several hours a day and eat a massive calorie surplus. That being said, remember that as a skinny guy, you have a few genetic advantages that will help you bulk up sooner than the average Joe. Yes, you will need to work hard but may be able to get away with just three challenging workouts a week—not five.

I'm not saying it's going to be easy, but it is manageable and, above all, realistic.

Here are some tips to help you consciously create a new habit.

1. Define a realistic and reachable goal. You're only going to feel disappointed if you don't gain twenty pounds of muscle in one month.
2. Forget about willpower and motivation; those come and go. Instead, focus on discipline.
3. Stay honest and accountable to yourself.
4. Don't be too rigid—adjust your plan if and when needed.

But how much muscle can you build, and how long will it take? Before you can set a reachable goal, you probably need to know the answer to this question. After all, it's not enough to just say, "I want to build muscle." You need to know how much so that you can come up

Introduction • 3

with a detailed plan. For example, if you say you want to gain 30 pounds in 30 weeks, then you will need to gain a pound a week to reach your goal. This is measurable and can be adjusted–if you see you gained less than a pound, then you know you should eat more calories the coming week. As soon as your goal is vague ("I want to get strong"), you will not be able to measure your progress and won't be able to reevaluate as you go along. That is an easy way to lose motivation—you won't be able to reward yourself for small victories or a job well done.

Also, keep in mind that the average man can only expect to gain between one to two pounds of muscle per month. So, although you may see a one-pound difference on the scale in a week, don't get too happy. It is usually a combination of fat, water, and glycogen.

What I want you to take away from this section of the book is that your road to muscle gains is not "all or nothing." If you've failed, then it's not a reason to give up, but one to try again—this time taking what you learned to get you a step closer to where you want to be.

To summarize, here's what you can do to reach your goal:

- Be realistic. Don't set yourself up for failure by aiming to gain 30 pounds in 10 weeks.
- Make the changes gradually. Start working out three times a week and see how that works. You can bump it up to five times once you're used to going to the gym. If you jump into the deep end with your exercise and diet, you're going to burn out and set yourself back.
- Make changes in your environment if you find it hard to stick to your goals. Dump all the unhealthy food, get yourself some protein powder, and do what you need to ensure your environment is in line with what you're trying to achieve.
- Sleep enough.
- Turn your actions into bulking habits.
- Hold yourself accountable. I used to bet on myself. I would give a friend of mine $30 every time I skipped the gym. When I found that I didn't reach my calorie goals daily, I gave another friend $20.
- Celebrate all victories. It doesn't matter if you're lifting 10 pounds more than the previous week, gained one inch on your upper thigh, or put on a few pounds—everything is worth celebrating. You worked hard for this.

The Dirt on Bulking

If you're as desperate to put on weight as I was a few years ago, I am sure you've considered dirty bulking—if you haven't already tried it. Personally, I tried it more than once and hated it both times. Don't get me wrong. Living off of junk food, sweets, soda, and everything else unhealthy was delicious—in the beginning, but then the negative effects started to kick in, and I didn't feel so great. Hang on; I am getting ahead of myself. Let's first look at bulking in general.

Bulking includes regular weight training, following a whole food diet consisting of a good deal of protein, sleeping enough, and consequently gaining muscle mass. Done correctly, bulking is incredibly healthy. It is especially beneficial to those who are underweight. The important thing is to keep body-fat percentages within the healthy range (under 20% for men and just above 30% for women). When bulking leads to you gaining excess weight or becoming obese, then you should reconsider your strategy.

In general, bulking includes some type of weight training. Hypertrophy training has the best results, and it is also the safest. The reason why I recommend hypertrophy training (we'll discuss this more in-depth later) is because:

- It is done in moderate rep ranges (8-20 reps). This is good for both muscle mass and cardiovascular fitness.
- You can choose what exercises best suit your body. If you want to go for a lift with lower injury risk (goblet squats and front squat instead of low-bar back squats), you're more than welcome to.
- It improves body composition, and this is great for your general health.
- In combination with hypertrophy training, bulking also involves following a healthy diet. Some healthy bulking foods you'll eat include oats, grains, rice, nuts, fruit, milk,

protein powder, ground meat, etc. You'll be consuming more nutrients, which will boost your energy and help you build muscle, and strengthen your bones.
- Lastly, during the bulking process, you'll make a number of healthy lifestyle changes like sleeping more and taking time to relax. All of this will improve your health, which is why this type of bulking is considered 'clean.'

Dirty bulking is when you don't care how you put on weight—you'll eat whatever you want, whenever you want. Some people even call it a "see-food" diet because you're 'allowed' to eat anything in sight—pizza, sweets, doughnuts, chicken wings, or a third helping of dessert. It's all there for the taking.

This type of bulking was made famous by a specific group of powerlifters (Westside Barbell, n.d.). They used to eat more than one McDonald burger and hash browns for lunch, followed by a pizza as a snack later in the afternoon. As you can imagine, these guys didn't just become strong; they also became fat. The health issues that go with being overweight soon caught up with them, and they had to make an effort to lose weight and turn things around.

Personally, I believe dirty bulking should be avoided at all costs. You may think my aversion stems from my own negative experience, and this would be partly true. But, science agrees. Here are some of the reasons why this type of bulking may not be the best choice.

- Processed food can make you gain fat because it is so high in dietary fat (Horton et al., 1995).
- Processed food usually contains a lot of saturated fat, which can lead to obesity and heart disease (Rosqvist et al., 2014).
- An excessive amount of sugar intake can lead to obesity.
- Your digestive system will suffer since processed foods usually don't contain enough fiber and probiotics and prebiotics found in whole, natural foods.

- Your immune system will get weaker since the food you eat doesn't contain a lot of nutrients and immune-boosting vitamins and minerals.
- The fat you gain will most probably be visceral fat, which is harmful to your health in the long run (Pollock et al., 2012).

Although I'm not a fan of dirty bulking, I want you to have all the information so that you can make an informed decision. This means I would be amiss if I didn't tell you that the harm dirty bulking can do can be offset by cardio. It comes down to burning visceral fat for energy, as well as increasing your metabolism. If you keep that in mind, dirty bulking may be appropriate for you if you're very active and have a difficult time eating enough calories when clean bulking.

Now that we have covered what it means to be a hardgainer and established that it isn't all that bad, and examined the difference between clean and dirty bulking, I think it is time to focus on your mindset. You'll be surprised what a massive impact your thoughts can have on your muscle-building process. Let's get you amped and ready!

Chapter 1 It's All in The Mind

You may believe that the biggest obstacle you face on your bulking journey is your genes. But, it's not always our physical 'limitations' that hold us back—a lot of the time, it is our mindset.

I know after trying over and over again to get the scale to budge, but nothing happens, a person gets frustrated and unmotivated. The constant failure can be a real downer, so much so that we start to believe we won't ever be able to reach our goals. It is this belief that may be holding you back.

If you've been doing things right and you still struggle with being skinny, then you may want to look at your attitude. You'd be surprised to find out that your psychology can change your physiology (Ng, 2018).

Just before the year 2000, a group of powerlifters competing at the national level formed part of a study (Constantinos, Collins & Sharp, 1999). Considering that these lifters were already at the top of their game and very close to their genetic potential, you may not believe that a mindset shift would make much of a difference. Well, as soon as they believed they were given steroids, they were able to add between 50 and 100 pounds to their weights over the course of their training. What's even more interesting is that these results were better than steroids could ever have produced! The next phase of the study saw researchers coming clean: they told the powerlifters they were given placebo pills. Guess what happened? Their performance regressed as their mindset shifted.

It should be clear to you now that your mindset is more powerful than you think, and it may be the only thing stopping you from growing.

Who would've thought that steroid-like gains are only a mind shift away?

Having the right attitude makes life easier—you'll be able to stick to your plan, overcome setbacks, and make consistent progress.

But how do you change your way of thinking—how do you get yourself into a "growth mindset"?

The Growth Mindset

When I decided to focus on gaining weight, it soon became evident that my mindset was not aligned with my goal—I didn't think it was possible for me to fill out. There is a big likelihood that you will face your own struggle, but I want you to remember a few things.

It wasn't your choice to be skinny, just as instantly burning every calorie you eat wasn't. You got this body, and now you have to work with it. If you think back to the previous chapter, you'll remember that your genetics aren't so much of a setback as you've been led to believe—it can actually be used to your advantage.

So, if genetics aren't standing in your way of building an impressive physique then it must be your mind. At first, I didn't believe this. After accepting that bulking was possible by following the right diet and exercise program and not the bogus advice that floods the internet, I saw results. This is the growth mindset.

Carol Dweck (2007) defines this as follows: "the growth mindset is based on the belief that your basic qualities are things you can cultivate through your effort. Although people may differ in every which way…everyone can change and grow through application and experience."

But this positive type of outlook also has a counterpart—the fixed mindset—an "either you have it or you don't" attitude. As you can imagine, this mindset leaves no room for growth—literally.

Let's look at two fictitious skinny guys, one with a growth mindset and the other with a fixed one. How will this affect their results?

Guy number one believes that skinny guys can build muscle if they eat correctly, follow the right training program, get enough rest, etc. This belief motivates him to try his best, and he is enthusiastic about what lies ahead. Furthermore, he sees failure as nothing but an opportunity to improve, which ultimately brings him closer to his goal.

Guy number two, on the other hand, loses all motivation even before he starts. He finds excuse after excuse about why he won't ever be able to get the body of his dreams. He blames his lack of progress on all the challenges skinny guys face.

Although both these guys have the same body type and face the same obstacles, their approach is entirely different due to their mindset. For example, if the guy with the growth mindset realizes eating 2,500 calories a day isn't enough, he'll simply try to eat more. The guy with the fixed mindset will be so blinded by being a "skinny guy" that he'll use his fast metabolism as a reason to throw in the towel. This, in turn, only feeds into the narrative in his head: skinny guys can't build muscle.

So, one guy's attitude is geared toward growth and success, while the other focuses on obstacles and not possibilities.

Stop the Excuses

I am ashamed to say that I was much like guy two in the above scenario—I had so many excuses.

- I'm a hardgainer.
- I'm an ectomorph.
- My metabolism is too fast.
- My stomach isn't big enough to handle all the food.

I also told myself that I was too old to change my body for the better. I want to focus on this excuse in this section because I don't want anyone to miss out on the body of their dreams because they believe their time has passed.

Although it is easier when you're younger, there is no rule that says you can't bulk up in your 30s, 40s, or 50s. But it's easy to use your age as an excuse, isn't it? So, if you believe that it only gets harder to build muscle as you get older, what are you waiting for? The longer you put it off, the more difficult it will become, right? Not entirely.

Scientists studied men between 18 and 40 and found no difference in their ability to build muscle (Hubal et al., 2005). Researchers conjectured that only after the age of 60 would the ability to gain muscle diminish. But in 2018, Greg Nuckols, powerlifter extraordinaire with a BS in Exercise and Sport Science and a Master's in Exercise Physiology, found the age to be closer to 80-years-old (Stronger by Science, n.d.).

When I first learned this, I realized that instead of creating imaginary obstacles, all I had to do was research everything I thought was true to find out if it was, in fact, reality. A lot of the time, it wasn't, and it quickly dawned on me that I could do this! What's more, it motivated me so much that even real obstacles didn't scare me anymore.

Commit to Your Goal

There are skinny people out there who reach their goals in two or three months. If you're naturally lean, you can gain up to one pound a week. Other people may be lucky enough to gain as much as two pounds a week. Still, even if you only gain half a pound per week, that's over 25 pounds a year! It is vital that you keep the perspective—delays happen. Maybe you get a stomach bug, or you go away on vacation, and there's no gym to go to. During this time, you may not see the scale move up, and you will have to adjust a few things to get yourself back on the gain train.

The truth is, I can't tell you exactly how long it will take you to get to where you want to be, and neither can you. The best you can do is to commit to your goal to such a degree that setbacks won't derail you completely. If you're able to answer why you want to build muscle, why you think it will improve your life, and why you believe it is worth doing, then you'll be inspired to push through when things don't go right.

Yes, it's best to avoid any setbacks, but as the saying goes, life happens. The aim is to stay calm and figure out how soon you can get back on track.

Recipe to Success

Changing your lifestyle in order to change your body consists of juggling a lot of balls. Another way to think of it is like baking a cake: you need to follow a recipe that calls for specific ingredients and must follow a sequence of steps. In this section, I will break down some of the critical components of your bulking recipe.

Willpower, Motivation, Discipline

Most people just 'fall' into habits. A study found that humans spend almost half of their day following one routine or another—regular things we didn't set out to do and don't even think about (Neal, Wood & Quinn, 2006).

We so mindlessly fall into a habit of limiting the number of daily decisions we have to make. This frees up a lot of decision-making power, as well as willpower. But willpower can only carry you so far—you will need to be motivated and disciplined to reach your goals.

Motivation

If it wasn't for motivation, you wouldn't be attempting to make your dreams of a buff body come through. It doesn't matter if your motivation is going from a small t-shirt to a large or if you want a six-pack. Motivation gives you purpose. Humans won't achieve anything without this important life skill.

To stay motivated, try the following.

- Review your goals and progress on a regular basis. Gaining an inch on your biceps is a great motivator and will just push you to continue.
- Set new goals as you go. I always have goals within my goal. For example, my main goal may be to build muscle, but a subgoal can be breaking my personal best weight on the bench press.
- Find a more experienced gym buddy to help keep you motivated. Support is paramount, and if you can find it from someone who's been where you are now, all the better.
- Keep your circle positive. If your friends and family are upbeat and cheering for you, it will enhance your positive self-talk, which will keep you motivated to smash your goals.

If you lose motivation along the way, don't worry; there are ways you can get it back.

- Make sure your goals are realistic in the timeframe you set. If you find you've been a little too overambitious, break your main goal down into smaller chunks.
- Remember why you set the specific goal—what motivated you in the first place?
- Look for inspiration from others who've had a similar goal and made it. Their success will motivate you.
- Take a break. Sometimes you need to stop, get focused, and start afresh.

Discipline

When it comes down to it, discipline is going to be your key to success. Yes, motivation is on the list too, but the fact of the matter is, you're not always going to be motivated. Some days you're going to get up, and the last thing you'll want to do is go to the gym. Other days you won't be in the mood to follow your diet—who wants to cook when you can get take out? It's during these times where self-discipline will help you stay focused on your goals. Discipline will make it possible for you to push through any obstacles and discomfort and smash your gym goals even on days where you'd much rather pick up a beer than a barbell.

Then, after you're a size you're happy with, you'll need to keep going to the gym to maintain your new gains. But, by this time, going to the gym will come automatic—it will be one of those habits you do on autopilot.

When you get to this point, it will generally be hard to break the habit. This is especially true if you built in 'cues' to tell your body it is time to lift some weights. These cues include location, time, people, emotional state, etc. For example, you may enjoy a cup of coffee every time before hitting the gym—that's a cue. Or maybe you pack your gym bag the night before and place it in your line of sight for when you wake up—another cue.

To make the habit stick even further, reward yourself. As time goes on, the workout itself will become the reward—the energy you'll have, your elevated mood, looking better, being stronger, etc. It is the starting part that is difficult, especially when you feel tired from the exercise, have to deal with sore muscles, and lose time out of your day where you could be doing something less taxing. So, having a reward in the beginning will keep you going when you badly want to give up.

Here are some things I rewarded myself with while I was getting into the habit of regularly going to the gym.

- Enjoying my favorite snack.
- Watching a movie.
- Relaxing in a bath.
- Playing on a gaming console for an hour.

Consistency

Nothing builds momentum like consistently doing something. It shows that you dedicated yourself to reaching a goal, and you chase it day after day. One excellent thing about always working toward something is you turn tasks into habits, which is desirable. Remember, you're going to have to maintain your body once you get it where you want it to be. It's going to be much easier to do when you're in the habit of eating healthy and hitting the gym. A habit can be described as a "neurological craving," and we all know how powerful cravings can be!

Patience

You're not going to wake up with a buff body after only a few sessions at the gym. Patience is important to keep your mind focused on the end goal. It is especially important considering the amount of frustration you're sure to face on this journey. If you're not in a rush, you'll be able to take any setbacks (and there will be setbacks) in stride.

I want to take a moment to discuss, as a skinny guy, just how much muscle you can expect to gain and how fast. We touched on it briefly earlier, but I feel it is important to drive the point home. I don't want you to lose motivation and feel discouraged because your expectations are too high.

As a newbie, I gained 14 pounds in five weeks. Now, according to the experts, that's unheard of; some may even call it scientifically impossible. If you talk to anybody in the bodybuilding business, they'll tell you that if the muscle-building stars are aligned in your favor, you'll be able to gain just under 10 pounds in three months.

What does "muscle-building stars" mean? Well, if you follow the right training program, train four to five times a week, eat enough nutritious food, get enough sleep, have no stress, and are still in your twenties, then everything is in place for some significant gains. Eight or nine pounds of gains, that is. But why then do some of us put on a lot of weight so quickly?

Firstly, it is clear that some beginners are able to gain muscle three times faster than others. Secondly, other beginners don't gain muscle at all. This phenomenon is known as 'non-responders.'

Now, you may immediately jump to the conclusion that you're a non-responder because you have a hard time gaining weight. But let me remind you of hardgainers or ectomorphs who have a hard time gaining weight, not muscle.

Remember, skinny guys actually have the ability to build muscle faster than others. After all, we tend to have less muscle on our bones than the bulky guys out there, so there's a lot of room for growth.

But let's get back to the claim that skinny guys can only gain eight to nine pounds in three months.

Various studies debunk this.

- A study found that it was possible to gain nine pounds of muscle in just eight weeks (Tarnopolsky, et al., 2001).

- In another study, untrained beginners gained an average of 12 pounds in 10 weeks (Willoughby, Stou, & Wilborn, 2007).
- One group of beginners who took part in another study gained 15 pounds of muscle in 12 weeks (Hartman, et al., 2007).

As you can see, we are capable of gaining more muscle and at a faster rate than at first believed. It's all about consistently training and implementing some dietary interventions. But what should also be clear is that slow and steady wins the race. Each of these studies was just under three months long, so don't expect you'll look all buff in a week.

Structure

As I mentioned earlier, there is a 'recipe'—or structure—when building a new body. If your approach is organized, then there won't be any confusion about what you have to do when. You'll have an idea of what tasks you need to complete each day to reach your goal. For example, get up at a set time, exercise for a specific amount of time, eat certain foods, then your day will be structured around one goal: bulking up. That will be your main focus, which will minimize your chances of getting distracted and falling off the weight-gain wagon. Approaching this journey without structure will only make you feel unmotivated. That being said, don't be too rigid in your approach—be flexible when you need to be.

Making Mistakes

I can't tell you how many mistakes I made when I first started. We experience missteps during our bulking journey because mainstream advice is geared toward weight loss—the last thing we want. Most bulking programs include some form of weight loss, even if not evident at first glance. As I mentioned earlier, as hardgainers, we have to reverse all the advice out there. Of course, I didn't know this when I first attempted to build muscle; thus, I made mistakes.

Before I look at the most common mistakes you want to avoid, let's have a quick pep talk—something I needed a few years back but wasn't lucky enough to get.

The most important thing to remember is: messing up is natural. If you don't make mistakes in life, you'll never learn anything. The key is to accept what happened, bounce back, and turn your slipups into successes. The last thing you want to do is beat yourself up over it.

Here are some tips I learned that taught me how to deal with mistakes.

You're not your mistake: Don't jump to conclusions. I know it's easy to think, "I'm such a failure," when you struggle to gain weight. But that is just frustration talking—mistakes do not define you as a person.

Own it: You may be looking for an easy way out. "I have bad genetics" is a good example of making an excuse when mistakes happen. Realize that you're the one at fault—maybe you didn't do enough research on what you should eat as a hardgainer, or perhaps you chose the wrong exercise plan. By owning your mistake, you can figure out how to move forward.

Recognize your mistakes: If you don't know what you've done wrong, you won't be able to change it. This means you'll probably keep making the same mistake, and it will frustrate you. Educate yourself as much as possible so that you'll be able to figure out what you can change when you don't see the scale moving. I suggest you find someone who is going through the same as you or has already conquered any skinny-guy obstacles. They'll be able to point out what you should change.

Fix it: This builds on the previous point—problems usually have solutions; you just have to think about how you can improve the situation. Fixing your mistakes may even be easier than you thought. The mantra I want you to repeat over and over is: there are no mistakes, only lessons.

Now, what are the top mistakes newbies make?

Mistake 1: Overeating At Each Meal

I know as ectomorphs with superfast metabolisms, we have to eat more than the average person if we want muscle gains. You do, however, have to find what your limit is. Eating too many calories at one sitting will be a waste considering that your body only uses a certain amount of nutrition at a time. I recommend you eat smaller meals more frequently throughout the day. This will promote protein synthesis and prevent a boost of fat-storing enzymes and hormones.

Mistake 2: Not Knowing The Best Meal Times

If you want to build muscle, breakfast and your post-workout meal are the most important. You should eat more carbohydrates, protein, and fat during these meals. When you eat a high-calorie breakfast, you boost muscle-building (anabolic) hormones, which will suppress catabolic hormones that are responsible for the breakdown of muscle tissue. When it comes to post-workout meals, your muscles will suck up all nutrients, and this will promote muscle growth and block your body from storing fat.

I also recommend a pre-workout meal to stop your muscles from using their own energy stores. Thirty minutes before you hit the gym, eat 20 grams of protein (you can also drink whey protein) and 40 grams of carbohydrates. This will trigger your body's anabolic processes sooner, and your muscle-building efforts will be more effective.

When you neglect these vital meal times, you compromise your recovery, and you won't be able to return to the gym as frequently as necessary for those muscle gains.

Mistake 3: Skimping On Carbs

Although protein is the most important when it comes to muscle growth, carbs also play a vital role—especially after hitting the gym. What's more, it will be difficult for you to meet your daily calories if you hold back the carbs. Since building body mass is your main goal, you want to eat two to three grams per pound of body weight. This will reduce your cortisol level, which is a good thing considering that cortisol may reduce the testosterone in your body, and this is the last thing you want when you're attempting to build muscle (Brownlee, Moore & Hackney, 2005). Without testosterone, your muscles will deteriorate. I recommend you include between 80 and 100 grams of fast-digesting carbs post-workout. This will spike insulin, which plays a role in delivering glucose, amino acids, and any supplements you may be taking to your muscle cells.

Mistake 4: Neglecting Your Aminos

Three amino acids are essential when you're bulking: branched-chain amino acids (BCAAs) including leucine, isoleucine, and valine. When you take BCAAs before and after exercise, your muscles won't be catabolized and burned. All bodybuilders dread this muscle breakdown state, but luckily amino acids can help prevent it. Leucine seems to play the most important role since it stimulates insulin and, more importantly, stimulates the messengers in muscle cells, promoting growth.

Mistake 5: Pushing Yourself Past Your Limit

I know you're desperate to show off your biceps but remember, you're only human, and our bodies need time to repair. Even if you follow a diet filled with nutrients, you still stand a chance of burning out or, worse, injuring yourself if you go too hard. Know your limits and pace yourself—you can't lift weights when you're injured.

Mistake 6: Not Giving Yourself Time To Recover

This goes hand-in-hand with mistake five—you have to take a rest day or two. If you rest, catabolic hormones wane, and as you can recall, this is a good thing for muscle gains. I know some bodybuilders feel that a good eating plan will make up for hardcore training, but even the best nutrition plan won't override your need for proper rest. Yes, a nutritious diet also suppresses catabolic hormones, but its effectiveness is limited—rest does most of the work.

Mistake 7: Forgetting Your Midnight Snack

By now, we know that meeting your daily calories is vital when you want to bulk, but it goes further than that. The secret is keeping your body in an anabolic state. Your muscles will then have constant access to amino acids, which promote growth. However, during sleep, your body won't be able to stay in this state. One way to work around this is to eat a midnight snack. I drink a protein shake with some added arginine (an amino acid that supports growth-hormone production) nightly. This ensures that my muscles have around-the-clock delivery of amino acids. Making gains while you sleep—who would say no to that?

Mistake 8: Being Inconsistent

It's all about taking small steps every single day. If you consistently miss the gym or deviate from your eating plan, you're not going to make any gains. Well, not the type you're looking for—you'll probably gain fat. I've covered forming habits already, so I won't hammer on—but just remember, you'll get where you want to be by putting in the effort day after day. As a side note, if you do miss a day or even a few days due to unforeseen circumstances, don't beat yourself up too much. Yes, you'll lose muscle during this time, but you'll gain it back when you get back to your program.

Now that we've covered the importance of a positive mindset, it is time to get down to the two most weighty (pardon the pun) aspects when it comes to building muscle: diet and exercise. In Chapter 3, we'll look at nutrition, and after that, Chapter 4 will deal with getting active.

Chapter 2 Eat Big to Get Big

What you eat plays a vital role for your body. It doesn't matter if you're trying to bulk or not; what you fuel your body with will impact your physical well-being and health. So, you can imagine that your nutritional plan can make or break your bulking progress.

We've already established that most skinny people are ectomorphs. The specific body types—ectomorph, mesomorph, and endomorph—each look and run somewhat differently. Before you start your training and diet, you need to figure out your body type—that will guide your way forward.

I do have to mention that body types aren't considered a reality in the scientific community. You will, however, hear it said a lot by bodybuilders.

So, to better tailor your muscle gaining plan to your body and make your goals more realistic and attainable, let's look at the three body types, and you can select which one you think you are. Also, keep in mind that you're not bound to one category forever—you can change it over time. After all, that's your aim.

Although most people tend to lean toward one group or the other, your lifestyle, genetics, and training style play a part in how you look.

Ectomorph

You already know the basics of the ectomorph body type but let's recap. If you're an ectomorph, you tend to be skinny and struggle to gain weight—it doesn't matter if it is fat or muscle. People whose biggest goal is to gain muscle but struggle to do so are known as 'hardgainers.'

The ectomorph body shape is lean with long limbs and small muscles. They will usually continue to look skinny in the calves and forearms even when they manage to put on weight. Of course, working those muscles in the gym will make a difference!

Ectomorphs' main challenge is the amount of food they need to eat to gain weight. But, it isn't impossible for them to be every bit as fit as someone with another body type who is large and muscular.

As an ectomorph, you should eat a lot of protein and carbohydrates, lift heavy weights on a regular basis, and limit cardio.

I will cover ectomorph-specific nutrition throughout this book because most of you reading this are most likely to have this body type.

Here are some things to consider with our small appetites, fast metabolism, and high-calorie goals.

- We don't need to focus on nutrient-dense foods too much. It's all about eating more of the good stuff and less of the bad food.
- Skipping breakfast is not a good idea. In fact, you want to eat a lot throughout the day—breakfast, second breakfast, lunch, snack, dinner, and don't forget your midnight fueling!
- We thrive on higher-calorie foods like nuts, cheese, dried fruit, banana, rice, muesli, and trail mix. If you've been doing some research, you'll know that other body types are told to avoid these types of foods.
- "Do not drink your calories" is not something that applies to ectomorphs. Since we have to consume much more calories than we're used to, it counts in our favor to

consume liquid calories that aren't so filling. They're digested quickly, making space for more food.

Mesomorph

With this body type, you have the best of both worlds. Mesomorphs usually have wide shoulders, a slender waist, thin joints, and a muscular belly (albeit a little round). They tend to be naturally fit, but this doesn't mean they're free to eat what they want and lead a sedentary lifestyle. What gives mesomorphs an edge over other body types is the fact that they're able to bounce back easily from being out of shape.

Mesomorphs should lift moderately heavy weights and do cardio activities on a regular basis. They're best for bodybuilding since they're naturally strong.

When it comes to eating, this body type requires slightly higher calories than others because they have more muscle mass. They respond better to high-protein diets.

Endomorph

Endomorphs have wide hips, a thick rib cage, and short limbs. Their muscle mass may be higher than the other two body types, but unfortunately, this usually goes with high amounts of body fat. Gaining weight may come easily, but they have to keep a close eye on what they eat to prevent putting on fat. Their main struggle comes when they try to lean out—they'll have to work harder than the other two body types.

When it comes to exercise, lifting moderate weights and focusing on fast-paced training work best. If they work out but still gain weight in the form of fat, the problem usually lies in the kitchen. Cutting out refined carbs should be their primary focus.

In-Betweeners

It often happens that you're a little bit of this mixed with a little bit of that. This may make it challenging for you to find a workout program that best suits your body type. For example, an ectomorph may have large arms yet identify as a mesomorph with hardgainer features. What do you do then? Well, the right program will be a mix where the basic rules for an ectomorph body type are followed, but any training of the upper arms will be limited.

Since in-betweeners find it problematic to distinguish their body type, they may end up favoring the body type they want to be. In this case, they will most likely follow the wrong program and get the wrong results.

If you're not sure what body type you have, there is a quiz you can do that may steer you in the right direction (Bodybuilding.com, n.d.).

Undereating

The people who have been telling you to "just eat more" may be right to some degree. Since an ectomorph's stomach is smaller than that of others, we often don't eat the number of calories our body actually needs. No wonder we can't gain weight; we may even lose weight due to undereating.

One of the key drivers of building muscle is creating a caloric surplus—without this, you can only dream about getting bigger. The upside of this obstacle is that we usually have smaller stomachs (unless you're skinny-fat) than the average person, which means seeing your abs isn't too far off in the future.

To help you eat enough calories, you need a diet designed around calorie-rich foods. If you eat foods with a high-calorie density, then you'll be able to eat more and get yourself in a caloric surplus. This is the only way you can feed your body the energy it burns per day and then some. The relationship between calories and meeting your body's needs is called an energy balance.

This balancing act can go three ways:

1. Gaining weight: You eat a surplus.
2. Losing weight: You create a negative energy balance (calorie deficit).
3. Maintaining weight: You eat just enough calories to cover the energy your body burns every day.

In all three of these scenarios, you have to think of your basal metabolic rate (BMR) and add any physical activities or exercise.

Your BMR

What is BMR, I hear you ask. This is the amount of energy you spend when doing nothing—you can be sitting on the couch watching TV, and you'd be busy burning energy. It is when your body has nothing to do other than run itself. Your digestive system should also be on a break during this time—it usually takes 12 hours for the digestive process to become inactive.

Think of BMR as trying to figure out how much gas your car will use while parked and idling. It's about finding out how much energy your body needs to maintain the heart, kidneys, lungs, nervous systems, liver, intestines, muscles, and skin. In general, 70% of a person's total energy use is for this upkeep—20% goes to physical activity and the remaining 10% to food digestion.

Your BMR is usually measured under restrictive circumstances, but since not all of us have access to a team of experts who can give us an exact number, we can use nifty programs found on the internet (Calculator.net, n.d.).

To give you an idea, on average, competitive bodybuilders take in 3,800 calories for men and 3,200 for women (Spendlove, et al., 2015). Compare this to 2,400 and 1,200 calories these men and women consume during the cutting phase.

Newbies will be able to gain strength when lifting during a calorie deficit, but if you're an experienced lifter who has been doing this for a while, you are going to experience some loss of strength.

To understand why a caloric surplus is absolutely necessary, let's look at the downsides of a calorie deficit.

- It makes it difficult for your body to synthesize muscle proteins (Zito, et al., 2007).
- It reduces anabolic hormone levels while increasing catabolic hormones. This reduces testosterone and increases cortisol, which hampers your body's ability to build muscle (Tomiyama, et al., 2010).
- It reduces your ability to perform during workouts.
- To recap:
- Your stomach can be six times smaller than someone who would be classified as obese. This makes it hard for you to eat more calories—you'll feel bloated, tired, and may suffer from acid reflux when you try to force-feed yourself. You have to choose foods that increase your ability to overeat (more on that later).
- If you do succeed in getting yourself into a calorie surplus, your metabolism may throw a wrench in the works. As an ectomorph, you may burn 1,300 extra calories per day—doing nothing.
- You have less fat in your body, and this improves your testosterone and cortisol levels (Gates, et al., 2013). Furthermore, this low-fat percentage improves your body's ability to clear glucose from your blood, making it less likely that you'll store fat (Horton, et al., 1995).
- You're further away from your genetic potential, so you can, in actual fact, build muscle faster than the average person.

Tracking Your Progress

We play by the same rules as the other body types, but our methods are quite different considering the above. Furthermore, our goals are usually poles apart from the general man on the street—we want to gain weight, not lose it.

For us, it takes a lot of smart planning, more effort, and time to gain weight and muscle. Unfortunately, we can't just do what comes naturally—we're built to be skinny, so we have to work around our genetics. The good news is, when we reach our goal, our new weight and body shape will become our new normal.

To know how things are going on the diet and exercise front, you have to measure your weight each week. Get yourself a digital scale; mechanical ones are less accurate. Then get into the habit of weighing yourself once a week right after waking up and going to the toilet. You can also weigh yourself daily, add the numbers, and then divide it by seven at the end of the week.

The number on the scale depends on the food in your system, if you're retaining water, etc., so getting your average weight loss at the end of the week may give you a better idea of where you're at. Of course, daily weigh-ins may demotivate you. You know yourself the best and will be able to select a method that won't have too much of a negative impact on your mindset.

If you don't see the number on the scale budge after a week's dieting and exercise, don't panic. This will happen a few times on your journey to bigger muscles. You will need to adjust some things to get back on the gain train. First, increase your calorie intake by 200 calories—the surplus you initially created is clearly not enough. Input everything you ate during the day into a calorie tracker app to make sure you're not undereating (MyFitnessPal, n.d.). As time goes on, you'll get better at knowing which foods will lead to gains, and you'll be able to eyeball your calorie intake.

Then, consider reevaluating your exercise program; are you perhaps doing too many cardio-based exercises and not lifting enough weights? The next chapter will break down the best exercises for muscle building and guide you in creating an exercise program that will build muscle.

I want to pause and talk about sustainability. It doesn't matter if you're doing everything right in the beginning; if your program is not sustainable, you're wasting your time. Remember, your motivation will be high in the beginning and you'll be able to force yourself through the more challenging parts. However, in time, things may happen that frustrate and demotivate you. Maybe you get a cold, you break up a long-term relationship, or you lose your job—all this can throw your best intentions out of the window.

Be realistic and realize that you will encounter things along the way that will knock you off your plan. The only advice I can give you to get through these times is to create a plan that doesn't include too many difficult challenges. I'm not saying you shouldn't push yourself at times, just not all the time.

If you find yourself falling off the wagon for whatever reason, try sticking to the following to minimize the impact.

- Eat enough food, even if it is not the healthiest.
- Consistently focus on eating enough protein.
- Lift weights. If you can't go five days (if that is what your program calls for), then try to go for three days. If that isn't possible, what about lifting one day a week? If that is still not possible, try to get active in other ways—but avoid cardio as it will increase weight loss.

There's a saying in the fitness world: 20% of what you're doing will give you 80% of your results. In other words, every bit helps.

The Mystery of Appetite

The other thing to keep in mind is our appetite as hardgainers. One of the big reasons we don't gain weight is that we struggle to eat enough to gain weight. This happens because our appetite switches off as soon as we've consumed enough food to keep our bodies running. As you read earlier, ectomorphs have higher insulin sensitivity, and while it is a good thing to help us build muscle faster, it counts against us when it comes to our appetite.

Luckily for us, there are ways to increase our appetites. Training, for example. Hardgainers burn more calories than the average Joe, if you recall. However, if you work out, these calories will be invested into building muscles and won't just disappear into thin air. Furthermore, your muscles' need for extra calories will boost your appetite.

Consistently pushing your muscles to depletion will signal your brain that building muscle is a high priority. Our appetites will increase to make muscle growth possible.

This will not last forever—your body will find a new baseline. For the first few months of your weight training, you will have a big appetite. But, after gaining five, ten, or twenty pounds, your body will probably have had enough of the overeating, and your appetite will reach a new set point–one where you can maintain your gains but not make new ones.

A word of caution, though: too many excess calories will go toward fat gain. Although you will get pretty wide, especially when your training and diet are on point, aim to cap any weight gain at a pound per week. If you do gain more, a good look in the mirror will indicate if you're gaining flab or some firm guns.

Then there are some things to consider when it comes to appetite: stress and exercise may count against you.

Stress and Appetite

Even on a good day, our tiny stomachs, fast metabolism, and insulin sensitivity make it hard for us to consume enough calories. If we get tired, busy, or stressed, our appetites will suffer. For ordinary people, the worse their lifestyles, e.g., the more stress, bad sleeping habits, etc., the more weight they gain. Hardgainers experience the opposite.

Most people turn to food when they go through a stressful period. This is due to the dopamine release—our bodies associate eating with pleasure, so giving into cravings creates a surge of this feel-good hormone.

When you're skinny, things work a little differently. Firstly, we don't reach for ice cream or comfort food when we're going through a hard time—we entirely forget to eat (Born, et al.). Our hedonistic response to food is lower. For example, when you break up with your girlfriend, she may run to the fridge as a source of comfort, whereas you will completely forget you own a fridge! Hardgainers do not seek food out for pleasure. If only we did, that would make gaining weight so much easier.

Add to that our insulin sensitivity, and we'll struggle with our appetites even when we give in to the comfort food cravings.

Furthermore, stressful situations always lead to a loss of appetite. It comes down to prioritizing your needs. When your stress levels are high, the last thing you need is to eat and for your body to digest food—it's all about short-term survival, and unfortunately for us hardgainers, that doesn't include eating. Think of it this way: if a lion is chasing you, you're not going to stop to eat. Our bodies experience stress at such an extreme that our whole digestive system may shut down.

But as with everything, there are things you can do to lower stress and boost your appetite. The most apparent relaxation methods are by meditating, doing yoga, or taking supplements that combat stress (Ashwagandha and Rhodiola Rosea come to mind). However, when your ultimate goal is to build muscle, you'll be happy to know that two of the things you'll be doing a lot will beat your anxiety—getting active, especially hypertrophy training, as well as getting a good night's sleep, lowers stress.

What's interesting is that moderate rep ranges have the biggest stress-busting effect (Strickland & Smith, 2014). Coincidentally, hypertrophy training has the same rep range—twelve reps per set, to be exact. By exercising regularly—cardio and lifting weights—not only helps reduce stress but helps you recover after those hectic lifting workouts. I recommend you do hypertrophy training, as well as some relaxing cardio for 30 minutes, two to four times a week. My favorite cardio activity is going for a morning walk—nothing like some sunshine to wash away the stress.

Improving your sleep is also an excellent way to ease your anxiety. Not only will you build muscle 30% faster, but you'll be calmer during the day. On the nights that we don't sleep well, the stress hormone cortisol gets released, and this elevated level will lead to more stress (Leproult et al., 1997). Bye-bye appetite! So, if you want to be able to eat for gains, get some good shut-eye—it will also improve your training performance, make you gain less fat, and boost your willpower.

What is significant is that all these stress-busting methods work together. You lift weights or get active in general, and this makes you sleep better. The next morning when you wake up, you'll have more energy to work out, and your muscles will grow faster; this, in turn, will improve your training. The benefits just multiply.

Now you will have to let me contradict myself for a second: lifting weights can also stifle your appetite.

Physical stress has the ability to make you less hungry (Hopkins, King & Blundell, 2010). Again it is a case of most guys getting ravenous after hypertrophy training, but we're not most guys, are we? Personally, I lost my appetite after strenuous exercise. This led to me consuming fewer calories than I was supposed to, and I lost weight. Not at all an ideal situation when you're trying hard to bulk up.

In general, most bodies will automatically upregulate how much fuel they need as soon as a person starts exercising—this facilitates muscle growth. But why then are some guys unlucky? Well, it seems the type of exercise plays a role too. If you're partaking in very strenuous exercise, the more likely it is that you'll lose your appetite. Remember the analogy I used of being chased by a lion? The same applies here. Your body experiences so much physical stress during intense exercise that the last thing it will worry about is food. So, it makes sense that more moderate activity will cause a lower stress response, and your appetite will remain the same.

It's also good to note that intense exercise will only negatively affect your appetite for around an hour. As soon as the cortisol levels in your blood regulate, your appetite will come back—and with a vengeance. I suggest you try to eat even though you're not hungry; otherwise, by the time your appetite picks up again, you'll already lag behind with your daily calories. A mid-workout shake may be just what you need to stay ahead of things. To skip gorging yourself and feeling sick afterward, mix yourself a carb and protein shake and sip on it during your workout. It is an easy way to get enough calories, and it will boost your performance in the gym.

Just keep in mind that your digestion won't run as smoothly while you're exercising. For this reason, don't eat foods—before or during your workout—that are hard to digest.

The best workout shake is mixing protein with maltodextrin. This turns your shake into a mass gainer that is packed with high-density calories, carbs, and protein. You can sip on this during your workout or right after. Research shows that consuming calories right after your workout—the time when your muscles are extra insulin sensitive—will help you build muscle (Aragon & Schoenfeld, 2013). This is known as the "post-workout anabolic window" and is a hotly-debated topic. One school of thought exaggerates the importance of taking in calories during this time, while others say the benefits aren't significant enough.

Speaking from personal experience, I would pay attention to the post-workout anabolic window if I were you. Eating/drinking carbs and protein right after a workout is beneficial if you're an ectomorph who loses your appetite after working out. It will make it less likely that you'll fall behind on your calories.

Of course, you don't have to mix yourself an elaborate shake made of various supplements—chocolate milk will work just as well. I will cover supplements in Chapter 5, but I want you to know mass builders or weight-gainer shakes are all about an influx of calories—how you get those calories in your body is up to you.

Breaking Down Your Bulking Macros

If you're new to nutrition, figuring out the right macronutrients (protein, carbohydrates, and fat) for bulking may seem like an impossible task. There are three key elements when working out your macros.

1. Research which macros help to build.
2. Find out which macros avoid fat gain.
3. Learn which macros will easily get you into a calorie surplus.

If you're like me, it may be about more than pure bulking—you probably want to improve your general health as well. If that is the case, then you can add a fourth element to the above: research which macros have the best impact on your health as you gain muscle.

Let's break down the recommended macros if you're a skinny guy or ectomorph who is trying to gain some mass.

Protein

I'm going to start off by saying protein is much more critical when you're trying to build muscle than carbohydrates are. You will see a lot of back and forth about the essential role carbs play in bulking, especially for skinny guys. But if you consider that our muscles are made of protein, then it's clear to see that without protein, you can't build muscle.

So, how much protein do you need to boost your gains? Research shows that 0.8 grams of protein per pound of body weight is the secret to success, but some studies do point out that a slightly higher intake (1 gram instead of 0.8 grams) will lead to better results (Iraki et al., 2019).

I tend to take a "more is better" approach and recommend you aim for 1 gram per pound of body weight per day. The reason why I think a little extra is beneficial is that it adds some breathing space. Some nutrition labels may exaggerate their protein content, which means you will miscalculate your daily protein intake and may not be eating enough to build muscle.

Since the protein recommendations for weight lifters are twice as high as for a sedentary person, it makes sense that eating enough protein is a problem for beginners, vegetarians, and vegans. One will often find that those who struggle to build muscle may still gain weight but in the form of fat. This is a problem if you're skinny-fat.

When it comes to your protein intake, you need to keep in mind that consuming more protein than your maximum requirements for muscle building will be of no benefit to you. You will get the calories from the protein, but that's about it. Researchers discovered this when they gave participants 550% more protein than the recommended amount, and they didn't gain extra muscle (Antonio, et al., 2014).

This is important because a high-protein diet has a satiating effect, making it difficult for you to eat enough calories. You're already struggling to eat enough calories, so don't make it harder by overeating protein. Furthermore, our bodies produce heat as we digest food, and this raises our metabolism—again, something hardgainers want to avoid. Diet-induced thermogenesis (DIT), as the experts call it, looks at how many calories your body burns as heat after eating specific foods (Westerterp, 2004).

Let's look at DIT after eating 1,000 calories of each macro:

- Fat – 15 calories
- Carbohydrates – 75 calories
- Protein – 250 calories

As you can see, protein is significantly higher than the other macros, which makes gaining weight on a high-protein diet somewhat tricky. Hardgainers should get any extra calories from fat or carbs.

Carbohydrates

Eating enough calories is one of the most crucial aspects when you're trying to bulk. I already covered why getting any extra calories from protein may not be a good idea, so as soon as you've figured out how much protein you're supposed to eat, it's time to move on. But don't worry, you'll like where we're going: carb land.

You've seen it everywhere, "carbohydrates are bad for you," or, "don't eat carbs, they're poison." I can go on and on. Well, luckily for us, carbs are some of our best friends—it's much easier to meet your daily calorie requirements if you eat more carbs and fats. We'll get to why in a moment. First, let's look at how many carbs you should aim for on a bulking diet.

If we look at bodybuilding research, we'll see that getting between 40-65% of our calories from carbs will help us build muscle, increase our performance when lifting weights, and is excellent for our overall health (Iraki, et al., 2019).

Although some people may opt for a more low-carb approach, it's not ideal for bulking. Diets with low carbohydrate macros will work better if you're trying to lose a few pounds—the opposite of what our goal is.

I find that an eating plan built around 50% carbohydrates of your daily calories per day works best. This translates to 3 grams of carbs per pound of body weight. You may think that 50% is a lot but don't worry, there will be more than enough space on your plate for protein and fat.

Also, the leaner you are, the higher your carb tolerance will be, and you may have to bump up your carb intake to 60%.

Let's break down the numbers to give you a better idea. If you weigh 150 pounds and you're bulking on 20 times your body weight in calories per day, i.e., 3,000 calories, then you'll eat 450 grams of carbs a day (3 grams of carbs per pound of body weight). If you then decide to give 60% of your overall calories to carbs, it will work out to 1,600 calories.

But don't ectomorphs need more carbs?
Ectomorphs and Carbs
We don't need to eat more carbs than the general person, per se, but it does make it more comfortable for us to consume enough calories.

Here's why carbs help us bulk up:

- They are not as filling as protein, so ectomorphs are able to eat more calories (Holt, et al., 1995).
- We have higher carb tolerance (Gokulakrishnan, et al., 2011).
- Lifting weights increases our ability to handle high-carb diets.
- Increased muscle mass further helps improve our carb tolerance.

One study found that overweight participants who lifted weights while following a low-carb diet lost fat and muscle. The other group who consumed more carbohydrates gained more muscle (Perissiou, et al., 2020).

I know with all the anti-carb propaganda out there, you may not be convinced that carbohydrates will help you reach your goal. It is true that carbs cause weight gain—but isn't that precisely what you're aiming for? What counts in your favor is that you're lean and more insulin sensitive than the average person. Add to that a good weight lifting program, and you're in a unique position to benefit from increasing your carbs.

The advantages of following a bulking diet high in carbs include:

- It increases glycogen in your muscles.
- You'll see an improvement in performance during your workout.
- Muscles grow more rapidly.
- Carbs lower your protein oxidation, which allows you to use any protein you eat more efficiently.
- It increases the testosterone levels in your body and also reduces the stress hormone, cortisol.
- You'll be less likely to get sick because carbohydrates boost your immune system.
- It's affordable and easy to make.

Carbs Vs. Fat

We've established eating carbohydrates has various benefits when you're trying to gain muscle. All in all, high-carb diets are good when you're trying to bulk, especially if you're naturally skinny. But then, why are low-carb and keto diets so popular, and why won't they work for us?

Firstly, some ectomorphs successfully gained muscle following low-carb diets—it probably

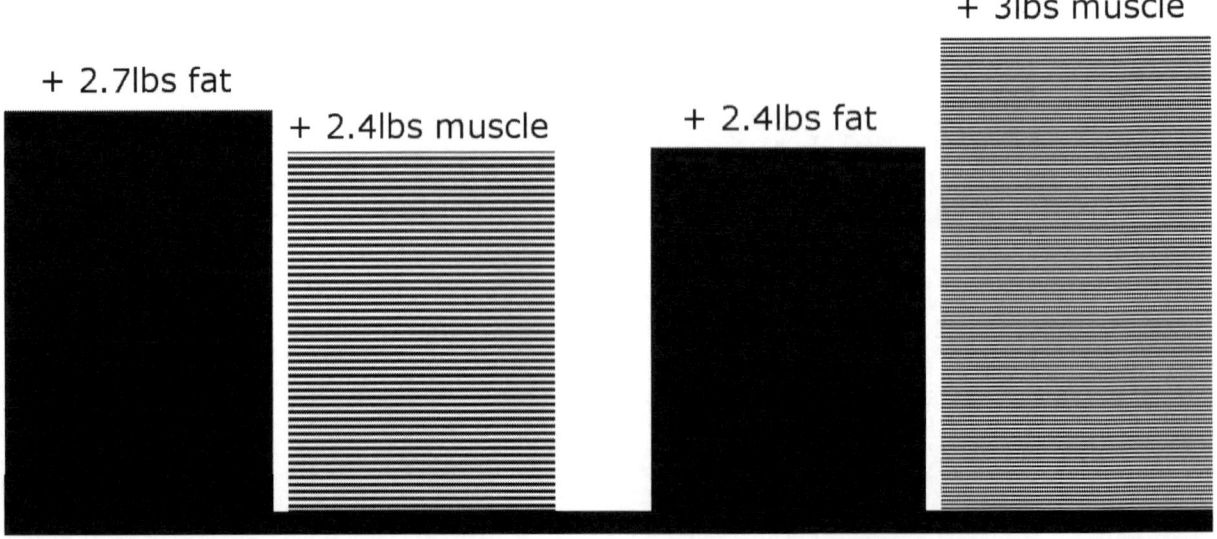

Fat Overfeeding Carb Overfeeding

20 • Chapter 2 Eat Big to Get Big

just took them longer to reach their goal. So, if you want to go the low-carb, high-fat route, you're more than welcome to. Just remember that dietary fat is stored as body fat with no difficulty at all—opening up the door to becoming skinny-fat.

Comparing skinny and overweight people, a study looked at whether participants responded better to carbs or fat (Horton, et al., 1995). The heavy-set group gained around 33% muscle and 67% fat. This ratio is often cited as the muscle-fat-ratio of obese people who don't exercise.

On the other hand, the lean group had different results—they gained more muscle than fat. But it didn't stop there. The lean group was split into two, where the first group overate carbohydrates and the second, fat. Both of these groups didn't lift weights or exercise at all. Unsurprisingly, eating fat caused more fat gain and less muscle growth—53% fat and 47% muscle. The group who got their calorie surplus from carbs had significantly more muscle growth and less fat gain—56% muscle and 47% fat.

These findings suggest that for people who aren't overweight, eating more carbs reduces fat storage.

In another study, bodybuilders who followed a rigorous program added 1,800 carbohydrates to their diet (Rozenek, et al., 2002). It was discovered that not only did the extra carbs lead to rapid muscle growth, but these men also lost fat at the same time! No doubt that eating enough protein, following a good training routine, and catching some *zzz*'s also played a role, but it is clear that carbs aren't the devil they're made out to be. Well, not for us hardgainers.

Fat

We've covered protein and carbs; all that is left to do is fill the remaining calories with fat.

I'm not going to bore you with good fats and bad fats or lecture you to avoid all saturated and trans fats. However, I do want to caution you not to go all out and drive your saturated fat consumption up too high. You'll recall that I mentioned a lot of us aren't just doing this to fill out a T-shirt; some of us want to live healthier. Saturated and trans fats aren't on the road to health when consumed in large quantities. You will hear about some guys who will drown themselves in whole milk to bulk up, and yes, the number on the scale will grow, but unfortunately, it will most likely be fat.

It's best to eat a mix of fats. By all means, enjoy your eggs, eat red meat, and drink whole milk, but don't neglect sources of polyunsaturated and monounsaturated fats, as well as omega-3 fatty acids. Aim for a balance of fats.

Let's break down the macros one last time:
- Protein: 20% (1 gram of protein per pound of body weight per day)
- Carbs: 50-60% (3 grams of carbs per pound of body weight per day)
- Fat: 20-30%

What and How to Eat to Bulk Up

We're starting to get down to the nitty-gritty now: what to eat and how to eat. Before we jump into what makes the perfect bulking diet, let's take a moment to distinguish between some of the terms I've been throwing around.

Bulking: Eating more than what your body requires with the aim of growing muscles.

Lean bulking: Bulking but with a focus on minimizing fat gain during the process.

Aggressive bulking: Bulking, but the goal is to maximize muscle growth.

Dreamer bulking: Your attempt to bulk accidentally leads to weight gain.

Throughout this book, whenever I talk about bulking, I generally mean lean bulking—building muscle while preventing fat gain.

Okay, I think it is time to address that small stomach of yours and how you can meet your daily calorie needs without bursting at the seams.

Focus on Food

To guarantee your success on the diet front, you'll need to focus on foods that are high in calories yet not very filling. Junk food may pop into your mind—and you wouldn't be wrong. These highly-processed and fatty foods are high in calories and easy to digest, making them an excellent choice for gaining weight. Right? Yes and no. The benefits you get from the high-calorie count are outweighed by the fact that these are what we call empty calories. So yeah, you'll be able to reach your calorie target and feel full while doing it, but you'll get limited nutritional value. Furthermore, junk food usually contains a lot of saturated fat and sugar, and research has shown that it is more likely to be stored as visceral fat than muscle (Rosqvist, et al., 2014).

Lucky for us, there are bulking foods that are healthy, good for muscle growth, wonderful for your digestion, yet high in calories! Needless to say, a bulking diet is more complicated than just eating wholesome food. You will notice that the best bulking nutrition programs focus on foods that break down into glucose. Starches low in fiber (white rice and pasta) will be star players on your plate. This may be confusing in the beginning as it is the polar opposite of most mainstream diets.

So what characteristics do great bulking foods have? They:

- are high in calories, in other words, calorie-dense.
- help stimulate muscle growth.
- are healthy in general.
- won't easily be stored as fat.

You're going to search far and wide for a single food that ticks all these boxes. Take spinach as an example; it has great health benefits, promotes muscle building, but isn't high in calories. Then we have white rice; it basically contains no micronutrients but is very high in easily digestible calories. Since these calories come entirely from glucose, it is near impossible to be stored as body fat because it goes straight to the muscles.

The secret to a great bulking diet is combining different foods in order to end up with a nutrition plan that's great for muscle growth in general.

Thanks to The Satiety Index of Common Foods, we're able to get our hands on a list of foods that are filling yet low in calories (Holt, et al., 1995). We can then turn this list on its head and use the information to find out how we can eat more calories.

Here is some important information we gleaned from the index.

The more you process whole foods, the less filling they become. The refining process removes fiber and water, and breaks everything down into smaller particles. This means processed foods are very efficient at delivering calories—no wonder junk food plays such a significant role in obesity.

If you want to lose weight, eat potatoes. The index explains that you'll feel 300% fuller after eating a potato than you would a banana. That's not good news when you're trying to fill a tiny stomach with as much food as possible to meet your daily calorie goal. That being said, deep-frying potatoes puts another spin on things. If you cut the potato up, coat it in olive oil, and bake it, you'll be eating more healthy calories (thanks to the oil), and also make the potato less filling (a lot of the water will be cooked out).

You'll be excited to learn that you can cook a steak to be less filling too. I'll get to that in a second; first, let's discuss why some foods are more filling than others.

Researchers concluded that foods high in protein, fiber, or water were the most filling. Furthermore, foods that are difficult to chew also fill you up quicker (Mourao, et al., 2007). For example, overcooked chicken breast beats shredded chicken when it comes to satiety.

There are a lot of foods out there perfect for a bulking diet: low in protein, low in fiber, don't contain a lot of water, are flavorsome, and easy to chew. Doritos, anyone? But the fact that this food ticks all the boxes of foods that aren't filling doesn't mean it's suitable for building muscle. Foods may end up lacking vitamins and minerals, be too low in protein and fiber, be too high in saturated fat, and may play havoc on your digestive system.

The ideal is to find foods that are high in calories but still good for your body and bulking. If that isn't possible, then we'll cheat the system.

Plan B for Bulking

We now know foods that are hard to chew are very filling. That takes steak and chicken breast off the plate. But don't worry, we still have some options that will make us meet our macros without ruining our appetite.

Protein

Drink your protein. I know that doesn't sound too appetizing: liquidized chicken—I think not. But, whey protein shakes, milk, and yogurt are good sources of liquid protein.

Go for the high-calorie protein sources. Chicken thighs are high in protein and healthy fat. Even better, they are a softer cut of meat, so you won't be chewing too much. Salmon is also a good choice when you're looking for protein high in calories.

Cook meat the right way. There are various ways you can cook meat to make it less satiating and quicker to digest. If the meat is soft and in small pieces, you're on the right track. I often grab ground meat and leave the steak for special occasions.

Fiber

Don't overthink your fiber intake. You really don't need that much when you're bulking. Aim for 10 grams for every thousand calories—no more. Remember, you're eating a lot of food, and you don't want to put extra strain on your digestive system by adding to the already fibrous content.

Still, here are ways you can reduce your fiber intake but stay your healthy self.

Leave the brown rice alone. White rice is lower in fiber, less filling, easier to digest, quicker to prepare, and cheaper.

Choose fruit over vegetables. I know you've been told veggies are healthier than fruit. Actually, they're both equally healthy—both contain phytonutrients and are high in fiber. The only reason fruit has been dubbed 'bad' is that it is high in calories and contains many natural sugars. This leads to weight gain—something which may be a problem for the general public, but not for us hardgainers!

Blend high-fiber foods. There's no argument here: leafy greens are superfoods. However, when you have a small stomach, they can fill you up quickly since they're everything you don't want in a food. They take long to chew, they're high in fiber, contain a lot of water, and are super low in calories. To get around this, throw them in the blender. This pulverized mix will take up much less space in your tummy and will digest faster.

Water

If you're in the habit of drinking water with your meals, I suggest you put an end to it if you want to gain weight. A 12-week study found that drinking water with meals could cause weight loss of just under five pounds (Dennis, et al., 2010). That's a lot of weight for a skinny guy.

If you're desperate for something to drink during a meal, reach for some milk or fruit juice—you'll end up consuming close to 15% more calories (Daniels & Popkin, 2010). That translates to 375 calories per day when you're following a 2,500-calorie diet. You'll be able to gain more than half a pound a week just by enjoying a nice beverage during your meal—not to mention during the day.

Some other things to consider when it comes to fluids:

Drink water between meals. You don't want something that contains no calories to take up any space in your stomach at mealtime—space should be reserved for high-calorie food. If you do feel like having water with your meal, have a glass of milk or some juice instead.

Try dried fruit. A raisin is 1/10th the size of a grape but contains the same calories and nutrient values. To give yourself a nutrient boost without filling yourself up too much, choose dried fruit over regular fruit whenever possible. Dried mangoes are my favorite, and they're really great as a snack.

Don't stress. I know water is essential, but keep in mind that a lot of the foods you eat also contain water. Unless your urine is very dark, you're most probably getting enough water from your diet. I'm not saying don't drink water, but I suggest limiting it to between meals to ensure your stomach has enough space for food.

The Buffet Effect

I'm sure I'm not the only one who magically finds place in my stomach when spoiled for choice. This phenomenon is known as the buffet effect—where people end up eating more because there is a greater variety of foods to select (Johnson & Wardle, 2014).

Researchers believe the reason behind this spectacle is that our bodies crave an assortment of nutrients from different sources. You may just have eaten a dinner rich in iron but without much vitamin C. Then, when you're given a choice to eat a fruity dessert, your stomach will eagerly make space for it. Of course, the buffet effect is all good and well, until you start to binge on junk food. A lot of obese people will jump from sweets to salty chips and then to something sweet again. This behavior will activate the buffet effect, but their bodies won't get any nutrients—it's called junk food for a reason.

However, if you're bulking, you can kickstart this effect by switching between different types of nutritious foods. Not only will it help you consume more calories, but the variety of nutrients you'll be eating will also prevent any deficiencies.

Best Bulking Foods

It's finally that time: where I list the best foods that will help you gain muscle. Nonetheless, I want you to keep in mind that this isn't a comprehensive list. You should look at it as more of a guideline and add or remove foods as you see fit. You've been given the knowledge to distinguish if a food is bulk-friendly or not.

Bulking diets are flexible, and although you should pay close attention to what you eat, eat food that you enjoy and can afford. Also, give your body time to adjust. You may feel lethargic at times, be extra thirsty at others, or need to get up and go to the toilet during the night—it's your digestive system that is adapting to the new diet. For this reason, don't make drastic changes overnight. If you want to have a smoothie from breakfast instead of a full bacon and egg breakfast, go for it. But change only that for the day—tomorrow you can make another change.

Milk

By far, milk is the most famous liquid in the world of muscle gains—next to whey protein, of course. The reason why milk is so popular is that it isn't very filling yet is an easy source of calories and protein.

To give you an idea, one quart of whole milk contains:

- 630 calories
- 32 grams of protein
- 49 grams of carbohydrates
- 34 grams of fat

Just by adding a quart of milk to your diet, you can gain a pound per week.

But the benefits don't stop there; milk contains a lot of vitamins and minerals that help with bulking:

- It's high in zinc, selenium, and magnesium.
- It's amino acid profile is balanced.
- It's usually fortified with vitamin D.
- It's rich in calcium.
- It contains casein protein.
- It's anabolic.

On the last point, researchers have no idea which property of milk boosts muscle growth, but the fact that it does can't be denied (Hartman, et al., 2007).

Olive Oil

If you're looking for a calorie-dense food that beats the rest, look no further. One tablespoon of olive oil contains a whopping 120 calories. With such a high-calorie count, olive oil is great when you're in a pinch and realize ten minutes before bedtime that you've eaten 230 too few calories for the day. Nothing a shot of olive oil can't fix!

In fact, I drink some olive oil every night before I go to bed. It is the simplest way to get yourself into a calorie surplus—and it's healthy. Olive oil is a powerful antioxidant, so you'll get a lot of health benefits from consuming it daily (Tripoli, et al., 2005).

You will experience similar benefits from flaxseed, avocado, walnut, fish, and krill oils.

Fish and krill oils specifically have some exceptional bulking benefits. According to the experts, just one tablespoon of fish oil a day will boost your body's muscle-building capabilities (Lewis, Radonic & Wolever, 2015).

If you're not sure about the best fats, always go for minimally processed oils—they're higher in monounsaturated and polyunsaturated fats. Again, I'm not saying avoid saturated oils like coconut oil or butter like the plague. It's all about moderation and the fact that they aren't the best bulking oils.

Nuts and Nut Butters

Nuts pack a lot of calorie punch for their small size, and this makes them great while you're bulking up. They contain healthy fat, fiber, minerals, and even protein. The magnesium in most nuts is excellent for a testosterone boost and subsequent muscle growth.

Specific nuts like almonds and brazil nuts are hyped up for their muscle-building benefits, and although these claims may be true, whole foods, in general, have numerous comparable benefits. The bottom line is real food is good for us, so the most successful bulking diets will contain a wide variety of wholesome foods.

Trail Mix

I doubt you'll ever see a bodybuilder without trail mix somewhere on their body or tucked away in a gym bag. This combination of nuts, dried fruits, and muesli has the capability to take your diet to the next level. A friend of mine added trail mix (450 calories) as a snack between lunch and dinner and later added another snack between breakfast and lunch. This may seem like a small change, but he gained 15 pounds in four months just by adding this one thing to his diet.

If you add some oats and grains, you have a blend of healthy bulking foods: muesli. I usually mix in some milk or yogurt and eat it like cereal.

Dark Chocolate

Even the healthiest among us need chocolate at times, and if you reach for dark chocolate, you can do so without feeling guilty. Not only is it a great source of healthy fats, high in minerals, and a powerful antioxidant, it's also high in calories and easy to digest. If we're looking at bulking-specific benefits, the epicatechin in chocolate needs a moment in the spotlight. This compound helps dilate blood vessels and improves blood flow—the popular pre-workout supplement L-citrulline does the same. Prunes, beets, and spinach also have this effect, and if you follow a diet rich in these foods, your workout performance will improve dramatically.

I like adding dark chocolate chips to my trail mix or muesli for a calorie kick.

Protein

What would a bodybuilder be without his protein shake? I can't explain how great it is to be able to drink your protein, especially for guys with small stomachs. It has happened to me countless times where my meal just doesn't make the protein cut, and I have to think of ways to up my protein intake. Having a protein shake simplifies my life drastically.

If you want some extra calories and protein, mix your shake with milk and not water.

White Rice

If you're eating on a budget, then white rice will help stretch your money—it's the cheapest bulking food you'll find. Better still, there are roughly 200 calories in one cup of cooked rice, and since those calories come from starch, it will be transformed into glucose in no time. Not only will the glucose fuel your muscles, the chances of it being stored as fat is improbable.

The only time I'd pick brown rice over white is when I need a fiber or protein boost.

Oats

Just as white rice does, oats will break down into glucose in a jiffy. Oats, however, are much more filling than white rice, so are used in different ways. For example, you can add ground oats to your workout shake or blend it into a smoothie. Just keep in mind that oats can be a little hard on your stomach and may make you feel bloated or uncomfortable during your workout. Another reason why oats are popular among bodybuilders is their fiber beta-glucan content, which is excellent for your heart health. Also, you may be consuming more cholesterol and saturated fats while on a bulking diet. Oats will balance things out and keep you healthy.

Smoothies

Your blender will soon become your best friend. Drinking your calories opens up so many delicious doors.

Blending foods make them:

- Calorically dense.
- Less filling.
- Easy to digest.

And the food won't lose any of its nutritional value!

When I'm in the mood for a smoothie, there is one recipe I keep going back to:

- Baby spinach
- Handful of nuts
- Handful of oats
- A scoop of whey protein
- Mixed berries
- Yogurt
- Water or milk

It may not sound tasty, but when you're trying to gain weight you may have to take one for the team every now and again and try out recipes that aren't the greatest. I like this smoothie because it is the ultimate when it comes to fueling muscle growth.

Cheese

High in calories and protein, cheese is ideal for adding to meals to make them more flavorsome. Some cheese also contains a high amount of probiotics, which is excellent for your digestive health—parmesan is a great example.

Raw Eggs

Eggs contain a lot of vitamins and minerals, as well as protein, good fats, and calories. No wonder bodybuilders are known for downing a raw egg or two when they're trying to bulk up. I've done it myself, but that doesn't mean you should too. There's a risk of salmonella poisoning, so if you do decide to give this a shot, make sure you choose high-quality eggs and get your general practitioner's permission. It's not worth the risk, especially considering that cooked eggs are just as nutritious and actually easier to digest.

Ground Meat

Earlier, you read that the more you chew, the fuller you get. Steak may sound like a more delicious option, but ground meat has other things that count in its favor. It's easier to chew, less filling, digests quicker, and isn't as chewy as other meats.

Salmon

You don't have to eat salmon on a daily basis if you're not a fish lover. Twice a week is more than enough to reap all the benefits. However, it's a delicious and healthy option to boost your calories and protein. Since it is easy to chew and digest, salmon is one of the least filling yet most nutritional sources of protein.

Non-Starchy Vegetables

Spinach, beet, and leafy greens rank as some of the top bulking foods, but why? It's not like they contain any calories. Veggies, especially leafy green ones, are great for your general health; they promote a healthy immune system and heal your digestive system. So, in the long run, they'll definitely help keep us healthy. But what about the here and now and your bulking goals?

You'll be happy to find out that foods that contain nitrates improve the 'pump' you get when weight lifting. The pump is important because it indicates increased blood flow to the muscles, and that means extra muscle-building nutrients to help the bulking process along.

Stoke the Metabolic Fire: How Many Times Should You Eat?

You've most probably seen videos where bodybuilders share their eating patterns with viewers. Cooking and eating often takes up most of their day unless they're smart enough to meal prep for the week! Eating six or seven meals a day is no joke, especially not if you're a hardgainer with a small stomach. But is it essential to eat so many times or will three meals a day do?

If you ask the guys who eat a lot throughout the day, they will tell you it's to keep their metabolisms going, avoid any blood sugar drops, and prevent their muscles from catabolizing. One of them may even tell you that eating seven times a day is vital to keep your body from going into starvation mode. That's a lot to worry about, and I don't know about you, but as a hardgainer, we have enough on our plate (quite literally).

But is what they're saying true at all? For the most part, no. As intermittent fasting grows more popular, the science behind mini-meals throughout the day is fast becoming obsolete. Research now shows that fasting throughout the day limits fat gain—but then again, it also slows down muscle growth.

So, what's the ideal? It's clear that there are a lot of myths when it comes to meal frequency. Let's see what is true and what isn't.

1. Frequent meals will affect your metabolism positively. This is due to what is known as the thermic effect of food (TEF). That being said, eating, in general, will boost your metabolism. The only difference is how big the increase is. For example, if you eat small meals throughout the day, your metabolism will only go up by small amounts. The same applies to eating bigger meals less frequently. However, when researchers looked into the effects of meal frequency on healthy male participants, they found that a person's metabolism is higher when eating three solid meals instead of 14 small ones (Munsters & Saris, 2012).
2. It will take days after your last meal for muscle catabolism to kick in—if you stimulate your muscles. This is good news for the bodybuilders who force themselves to eat throughout the day because they are scared of muscle loss. It's exercise that matters most, not how frequently one eats. Still, I do recommend you enjoy a post-workout snack. It may not be necessary, but it will benefit your muscles.
3. If you're healthy, your blood sugar levels will be stable. Researchers found that only after 48 hours or more without food will you notice a difference in a healthy adult's blood sugar level (Lieberman, et al., 2008). The Munsters & Saris study mentioned in point one also established that insulin sensitivity is better when meals are limited to three a day.
4. Eating enough protein (even if just once a day) will supply you with enough amino acids to last you all day long. Also, since your body can make most of the 27 amino acids, there's no reason for you to constantly attempt to supply it with some.
5. Your body will only go into starvation mode after 60 hours without food (Nair, et al., 1987). I'm explicitly citing such an old study to show just how gullible we are. Scientists have known for years that "starvation mode" won't happen when you skip a meal or two, but still, we fell for the myth, hook, line, and sinker.

Why then do bodybuilders still eat numerous times a day if most of these myths have been debunked? Primarily because the studies they use as proof are correlation studies. Since eating six times a day became so fashionable under the super fit, there is a correlation between fit people and frequent eating.

It's also easy to believe these myths because frequent eaters will feel and hear their stomach grumble, which, to them, means their body is hungry. The interaction of hormones in an empty stomach may indeed create some interesting sound effects, but the reason behind it isn't hunger as much as it is habitual. Your body gets used to eating X amount of times, and when you skip a meal, your body is just a little confused. It is, however, entirely possible to train your body to expect food less frequently.

Okay, all this is very interesting, but I still haven't answered your question. How many meals should you eat per day?

Well, you have to consider two factors:

1. How much can you comfortably consume in one meal? You may find it easy to eat a healthy 1,200-calorie meal. If that is the case, you won't have a problem sticking to three big meals a day. But then there are those

among us who'll get indigestion, feel tired, and just generally unwell after just looking at 1,200 calories. These guys will have to eat smaller meals throughout the day, as well as a snack or two. Flip back to the section where I discuss meals that are calorie-dense and not very filling.

2. How much time do you have to eat? It isn't easy when you have a fast-paced job to take breaks every so often to eat a meal. Even if you have a desk job, there's no guarantee that your boss will be happy with so many mini lunch breaks. You have to consider how many meals you can fit into your schedule, and then you can size your meals appropriately.

As an ectomorph, you'll most likely do just fine eating three or four meals a day with a snack in between. I like to stick to breakfast, lunch, dinner, and throw in a snack just before bedtime. But that's just me; you may prefer eating breakfast, brunch, lunch, and a six-course dinner, ending the day off with another late-night meal. The bottom line is, there is no right or wrong answer when it comes to meal frequency—it's all about making it work for you and your body.

Let me remind you that stress is not good when you're trying to build muscle. The last thing you want to do is add unnecessary anxiety to your day because you forgot to eat meal number four, and now your muscles are slowly fading away. Relax and grab yourself a snack.

Success Lies in Snacking

You may have conveniently forgotten that as skinny guys, our stomachs can be six times smaller than regular guys. No wonder they can gobble up giant meals and flush them down with thick, milky drinks. We can't even get close to eating as much as they do, and when we try, we end up feeling lethargic and unwell. Acid reflux is common among ectomorphs who try to eat meals that are too big for their stomachs.

Following a bulking diet isn't going to make things easier on you. Yes, by selecting smart foods, you'll be able to consume all the calories you need without being uncomfortably stuffed, but I'm not going to believe you when you tell me you're not going to try to eat more than you can handle.

I was there—the risk of getting acid reflux and feeling like you want to sleep for a week getting clouded by muscle gains. "The muscle growth will be worth suffering through acid reflux," was one of my mantras when I tried to stuff my face with as many calories as possible. This was a decision I would regret immediately after taking the last bite.

So, I changed my approach. Instead of focusing on eating a lot of calories during meals, I started to add snacks. Now, I am one of the biggest snack advocates you'll ever find. The main reason why I'm such a fan is that your body isn't very good at tracking calories when you snack (Douglas, et al., 2012). If you eat a 300-calorie snack after lunch, you'll end up eating 100 fewer calories for dinner. This results in 200 extra calories, which your stomach and appetite hardly noticed.

Now you see why snacking is possibly one of the best ways to up your calorie intake. You won't experience the discomfort you do when trying to eat a big meal.

But there's more to it than our tiny stomachs. What you snack on can also make a huge difference to your bulking success. If you snack on high-protein foods, then you're stimulating muscle growth, and you'll effectively be increasing how much muscle your body builds during the day. What's more, the gains you make will be leaner since you're building muscle without drastically increasing your calorie intake. Win-win!

To make your life more comfortable, try working in a 250-calorie snack between meals. You'll thank me later.

Healthy is the Name of the Game

Two of the most common complaints you'll hear ectomorphs make are:

I feel tired, bloated, and full of gas after eating.

I'm full for too long after eating and can't eat enough.

I know how it feels to fall behind on calories because we just feel too physically ill to eat any more. During this time, I'm all for eating smaller meals throughout the day—if only to avoid having to eat a huge meal to make up the calories we lack.

I've also found that I tend to reach for unhealthy food when I still have a lot of calories to get through. Processed foods high in saturated fats, additives, and sugar come to my rescue. But I pay a different price after eating these foods. I may not feel bloated and stuffed to the brim, but I feel shaky and lethargic.

This is something I am trying to avoid as much as possible. The fact is junk food has been linked with numerous digestive issues—some only mildly uncomfortable, others severe and painful like inflammatory bowel disease (IBD). For this reason, it is crucial to make healthy choices whenever you can, or 80% of the time at least. I'm not saying you should become a health fanatic who puts your nose up at anything other than celery. It's all about balance, and ice cream and pizza are part of that balance.

So what's the take-home if you're an ectomorph looking to bulk? Think whole foods jam-packed with vitamins, minerals, pre- and probiotics, phytonutrients. But it's a little more complicated, isn't it? We also have to pay attention to the types of whole foods we eat: they should be high in calories (preferably), should take up too much space in our stomachs, and be easily digestible. A tall order, I know. As we read earlier, not all foods will tick all the boxes at once (spinach, with its low-calorie content, comes to mind), but if you mix and match, you'll have a diet that considers your ectomorph physique.

Here are some things you need to remember when building a perfect ectomorph bulking diet.

1. It's not about cutting bad foods out; it's about adding the right foods. Any diet that is too constrictive is going to make your life difficult at some time or another. You should make your diet as simple as possible, and one way to do that is to limit the number of foods you're not allowed to have and instead add some healthier options to the menu. Fruit juice, nuts, trail mix, dried fruits, protein powder, etc., will all make your bulking journey easier to stomach—literally.

2. Don't focus on big meals; instead, add snacks. I know I don't have to repeat it, but you have a smaller than average stomach, and you have to find a way to compensate for its size. The best way I've found to eat enough calories without suffering some nasty side effects is to add a snack between main meals.

3. Always choose calorie-dense foods. This is why trail mix is one of my top bulking foods—it is very high in calories but also nutrients. Nuts and dried fruit on their own are also good options, especially when the day is over and you realize you still have to find 250 calories somewhere.

4. Low-fiber foods are best. Stick to eating 10 grams of fiber per 1,000 calories. Too much will make it near impossible for you to eat enough, and you'll end up lagging behind your daily calories. You'll have to make up for this deficit some time or another, and it usually involves eating a huge meal that leaves you feeling sick afterward.

5. Earlier in this book, I said your blender is going to be your best friend. I still stand by that statement. Food that requires little to no chewing won't be as filling, and your digestive system won't have a hard time breaking it down. Choose ground meat over steak, drink a smoothie instead of eating vegetables, and find ways to blend, grind, or cook your food that will make it easier to process.

6. Drink your calories. There's nothing like filling up on calories that clear out of your stomach faster. You may not even feel like you ate anything and will be brave enough to eat a meal or snack—extra calories are always welcome. Milk, fruit juice, smoothies, and whey protein are great options when you're growing muscle.

7. Take care of your digestive system. Foods like onion, garlic, banana, and yogurt make the digestion of calories more manageable. Together with a healthy diet, I also supplement with pre- and probiotics to keep my digestive system healthy and strong.

8. Spice up your life. Don't be boring—there's more to life than chicken, white rice, and broccoli. And even if this is one of your favorite meals, there's no need for it to be bland. Remember, you're trying to gain weight, so it should be high up your agenda to boost your appetite. If you spice your food and make it taste better, you'll actually want to eat more of it. It's just your stomach size that will hold you back once you get a taste of something you like!

That covers everything you need to know to create your own muscle building nutrition plan. With some digging, you'll be able to find some great plans designed by fellow hardgainers. But since bulking is such a personal thing, with so many variables—and I'm not even talking about the universal ones we share—you need to be able to sit down and plan your own diet. After reading this chapter, you should be able to figure out what foods are conducive to building muscle and why.

Time to move on to the second most important aspect of building muscle: your training program.

Chapter 3 The Role of Exercise

Gaining weight safely is very important; otherwise, you are as likely to lose your gains as quickly as you put the weight on. Normally, a slightly more extended period at a steady pace proves to yield the best results if you want to keep packing on the bulk and maintain it. After all, nothing is worse than doing all the work only to watch it all melt away again, right? In this chapter, I will cover different approaches to optimal, safe weight gain that will make you proud!

Weight Training and Weight Gaining

Especially at the beginning stages of weight training, many guys still think that the number on the scale is an accurate show of proper weight gain. However, this is by no means the correct way to gauge your progress because the scale merely shows us our body's weight, not our body composition (fat to muscle ratio). What you want to do is put on muscle specifically; therefore, the scale can not effectively show you how much of that weight gain is actually muscle mass. For all you know, it could be water weight or even fat, which is not ideal.

It is all about accumulating the correct kind of weight, not just packing on pounds for the scale's sake. It is a well-known fact in exercise physiology that muscle is far more dense than fat. This is where weight training or general resistance training plays a pivotal role in safe gains—only a gradual increase in resistance forces our muscles to develop and grow bigger. If your body is forced to work harder, it is forced to increase in strength. This, in turn, will cause your body to need more food, not only to accommodate the increase in muscle mass but to ultimately manage the heavier lifts: more muscle, more weight–the basic principle.

Exercise Selection

For sufficient weight gain in the shortest time, you should employ exercises that work best for your fitness level, body type, and time management. Some people have better results with combination training, while others gain better on generic weight training regimes. You should select exercises that cover most of the body, perhaps combining different disciplines. Not only are these exercises efficient in yielding results, but they will also elevate your fitness level along with the changes in body composition you might need to pack on the bulk.

Here is a list of workouts that usually benefits most people overall, regardless of their preferences or fitness levels, and still remain the most effective basic exercises. I will break some of these exercises down in further detail later on in this chapter.

Deadlifts: Arguably, deadlifts are the best overall strength building exercise that targets all the major muscle groups. In other words, with every rep, your entire body works, where most other activities focus on a specific muscle group.

Back squat: Much like the deadlift, the barbell back squat employs all the major muscle groups with the added bonus of increasing explosive power, such as higher jumps or faster sprints.

Pull-ups: Where squats and deadlifts significantly promote tone and size to the lower body, there is no question that pull-ups are the upper body equivalent of a beast builder. Not only do they give you impressive shoulders and a broad chiseled back, but the development of the latissimus dorsi (lats) and deltoid muscles encourage solid weight gain. Even the abdominal muscles are fully engaged during a pull-up, so you can work on that six-pack at the same time.

Rows: Do not underestimate the efficacy of changing the center of gravity of any exercise. Whereas generic rows are good for cardio or toning, exercises such as inverted rows consistently improve the posture and significantly strengthen one's lower back and deltoids.

Crunches: Depending on your current core strength, there are many variations of abdominal exercises that you can use. Yes, there are no excuses when you know what to use to get that core rock hard! You can use basic crunches if you have a weak back or do a combination of ab exercises to suit you. Leg lifts, bicycle treads, and hanging leg raises are great for stabilization and strength.

Bench press: We all know it is the gym rat's favorite measuring contest—how much you can bench—but on the scientific side, the bench press is tried and tested as one of the best exercises for strength increase and muscle growth. Not only does it increase size in the arms and chest, but the angle of the bench during your workout also determines which side of the pectoral muscle you hit. This is advantageous for maximum growth and esthetics of the chest when it comes to definition.

Creating Hypertrophy

Hypertrophy, by definition, is the increase of muscle size through weight training (or a similarly effective resistance regime). Although we know that weight training for this purpose is ideal, there are other methods of resistance training to use, such as calisthenics. Calisthenics is the use of only one's body weight to increase flexibility, strength, and endurance.

When trying to stack up that muscle size for weight gain, you can use techniques and exercises for optimal hypertrophy in the shortest possible time. There has been a lot of debate on the most effective hypertrophy methods in weight training, for instance, the use of pyramid sets. Some people prefer to start with low, heavy rep sets, gradually increasing in reps as they use lighter reps to achieve failure. Others might disagree, but once again, let me reiterate that you should choose your own training methods according to what works best for your progress and, of course, what you enjoy more!

Compound exercises (deadlifts, squats, kettlebell swings) are always the best rule of thumb since they utilize the entire body's muscle groups with every rep. This way, you achieve more in the same amount of time than you would have by just your regular isolation exercises (such as bicep curls or leg extensions). Keep in mind that you can split your training days in several ways, alternating between weights and machines, high reps, and low, but try to do workouts that involve the entire body. Why?

Because full-body workouts release more anabolic hormones and therefore promote muscle growth much faster and efficiently. Free weights are preferable to machines in that free weights employ more muscle recruitment and activation than static devices.

It is not just your training technique that helps build muscle mass faster, but various other factors, such as intensity, velocity, and volume. For optimal gains, you can choose a different approach to someone who wants to add endurance to size. In other words, lighter weight/higher reps usually stimulate muscle endurance as much as tone, whereas heavier weight at lower reps is best for just bulking. If the latter is what you are looking for, calculate your load at 70% 1RM (1 Rep Maximum—the heaviest you can lift for only one rep), which is an excellent way to measure your load weight.

Ultimately, when using weights for hypertrophy, you should remember to juggle your intensity, load, reps, sets, and methods to keep your body guessing; otherwise, you will hit a plateau. Do not be afraid to play around with your workouts to whip those muscle fibers.

Calisthenics

On the subject of juggling reps, methods, and intensity, it is crucial to adapt to the technique when it comes to calisthenics for hypertrophy. Calisthenics use body weight, so you have to change the way you train to bulk on these exercises. Don't be too concerned with high repetition training, no matter at what speed, because it is far more important to do your repetitions in a full range of motion and to do compound exercises with correct form.

Calisthenics should include workouts like push-ups, dips, pull-ups, leg raises, and squats. You should try to avoid calisthenics that need stabilization. Such exercises hardly encourage hypertrophy. Keep it simple and do it properly, rather than take on moves that divide the muscles' work. Just like weight training, calisthenics should be alternated in volume and technique to keep the body guessing. For instance, use a wider grip on your pull-up.

The most critical component is to work right down the middle. Too heavy, too much, or too little, anything that has a 'too' in front of it, is counterproductive. Overdoing reps or loading too heavy will guarantee injury or prolonged recovery that will negatively impact your progress and hold up your muscle growth.

Compound Exercises

As I mentioned before, compound exercises are exercises that combine work from all the major muscle groups in the body at the same time. We also know that these testosterone-boosting workouts promote strength and explosiveness and elevate fat burning potential while enhancing muscle growth and mass gain.

Testosterone is the wonder hormone for strength, size, and power, and it is straightforward to naturally elevate your testosterone levels. Most anabolic training releases testosterone to manage the body's workload, forcing the muscles to adapt accordingly—bulk is the name of the game. Needless to say, most of the well-known, time-tested compound exercises covered here boost testosterone in the best way. Shall we have a look at the list and how to do these exercises correctly?

Squats

The barbell squat is probably the best-known compound exercise, where you use your entire body to push the weight upward into a standing position. The University of Texas conducted a study where they found that squats synthesize more human growth hormone and testosterone than a session of leg presses, regardless of the amount of weight involved.

To do your squat: Place a barbell across your shoulders (and start with a comfortable weight so as not to injure yourself.) Make sure your feet are shoulder-width apart and get a firm grip on the barbell with your hands at a similar distance. Bend your knees and sink as if you are sitting down on a chair, keeping your heels firmly on the floor and your spine aligned. Use your heels to press upward when you stand up again in a controlled movement that will employ your hip and knee joints.

Clean and Press

Recruiting as much muscle as possible in one go is the secret to boosting testosterone, which is why compound moves are the best. Make sure that you are well-versed in the fundamental forms of squats and deadlifts before you attempt cleans, especially clean and press. It is a more advanced exercise that requires proper form while hitting the glutes, quads, core, back, and arms, so make sure you do it correctly.

To do your clean and press: Put your barbell in front of you on the floor. Step up to it and keep feet shoulder-width apart. Make sure you have a good grip (not too wide) on the barbell. The clean and press is a swift, three-stage movement.

1. Like with a deadlift, lift the barbell.
2. Use your back and arms in a swift motion to bring the barbell to rest onto your chest while you squat. Take care to keep your back straight; otherwise, you could be injured.
3. From your squat, push up into a standing position and lift the barbell above your head (barbell press). Bring the barbell back down to your chest and set it down in the same position as you started.

Deadlift

The deadlift is a simple and beneficial exercise to elevate testosterone levels, primarily because it elicits significant muscle groups as a compound move. Along with huge legs, the deadlift creates an amazing back and strengthens the core. You can do deadlifts at your own pace, playing around with various loads of weight and speed of execution.

To do your deadlift: Place your barbell in front of you on the floor and spread your feet shoulder-width apart. Your hands should be a comfortable distance away from each other. You can use various grips in order to exercise different sides of the forearm muscles, over or under, or a combination of both. Never lock your elbows—you will injure your joints!

Lift the barbell with your spine aligned and your back straight until you are in a standing position. Make sure that your movements are controlled throughout until you set the barbell down again, making sure that you stay in the correct posture.

Military Press

The standing military press looks so easy that it is hard to believe that it is beneficial in muscle mass growth stimulation. Just raising a barbell from your chest above your head and back seems redundant, but it is far from pointless. Doing this exercise slowly is super effective in chewing at those stabilizing muscle groups while increasing the size of your back, arms, chest, and shoulders. The standing military press utilizes the entire body to bear the barbell's overhead weight, forcing all major muscle groups to keep the core in place and stabilize the barbell.

To do the military press: Start by holding a barbell in front of your chest and then push the weight up above your head. Keep your knees soft and your body straight, especially if the weight is substantial.

Pull-up

The pull-up is, without a doubt, the most popular calisthenics exercise for a full-body workout. Not only does it boast the most effective muscle engagement for upper body strength and definition, but it also benefits different muscle groups with even the smallest handgrip change! Over the bar grip hits the back, shoulders, and arms while reverse grip adds some serious abdominal and bicep hell that will leave you pumped. Not to mention the width at which you place your hands. Wide grip or narrow grip, each hits different muscle groups for isolation, definition, and overall growth.

To do the pull-up: You don't need any free weights or gyms to do this exercise. Just mount a beam in a doorway or any variation of a bar fixture, and you are set!

Importance of Proper Form

Muscle injuries and tears can occur easily if you do your exercises with incorrect form. The tiniest mistake could cost you days of inactivity that will significantly mar your progress, so it is imperative to make sure that you have the correct form for each individual exercise. Not only is proper form essential to avoid hurting yourself, but it will also help you utilize a full range of motion. Employing all the relevant muscle groups and controlling the movement is of utmost importance to get the best results.

Your ego can also get in the way of proper form, and there are few things as embarrassing as watching an ego-driven weight lifter loading as much weight as possible just to impress others. Ego is the antithesis of discipline, the enemy of achievement.

Pumping iron to show off is not only laughable; it is the direct opposite of training for results. How many times have you seen someone at the gym, dangerously arching his back or hyper-extending his knees because he loaded his barbell with a ridiculous amount of weights?

Leave your ego at the door and come to the training floor with results in mind. On the floor, your only opponent is yourself. You are the only one you have to impress and nurture, so cut the bragging and just do your best. Success comes gradually, and results are best achieved when you train correctly and focus on your personal bests. Also, ask for a spotter if you need one—it shows respect for your training regimen, and you are likely to pick up some good tips from seasoned weight lifters if you allow positive criticism or advice.

Progressive Overload

A bodybuilder at my local gym—a former Mr. Universe finalist—once told me something I have never forgotten. In fact, every time I want to give up in the middle of an insane workout, I hear his words: "Success lies well beyond the comfort zone."

Setting realistic goals is imperative to successful gains without injury or disappointment. That brings us to the subject of "progressive overload." Progressive overload is a principle pivotal to muscle growth in that it promotes mass gains by occasionally increasing your workload and increasing the demand on your musculoskeletal system. Forcing your muscles to work harder than what they are used to will trigger more testosterone and human growth hormone to facilitate the work, and we all know that these are favorable hormones.

If you do not frequently employ more strength by increasing your weight load, your muscles will essentially grow lazy, stagnate, even atrophy. The latter will cause a decrease in size and strength, sending all your work down the drain.

Again, do not go crazy and add weights that you cannot effectively maintain with correct form, but add about 10% of your current best just to smash that plateau and give your muscles a good shock. From there, you will begin to escalate your ability until your 10% becomes your new comfort zone. This way, you will safely advance to heavier weights and obtain more mass.

Volume and Intensity

Volume and intensity are terms you will hear from many avid weight-training enthusiasts, especially those who look the part. Volume is the amount of work you do per exercise; in other words, your amount of reps and sets. These principles can be shuffled around in many ways to achieve everything from mass gain, definition, cutting fat—you name it!

Intensity is the amount of weight load you use for every set. For instance, if you increase your intensity while maintaining low reps, the chances are that you are training for bulk. Decreasing your intensity and increasing your reps will aid in fat burning rather than size, for instance.

How Many Reps Should I Do?

Your sets are entirely dependent on your endgame. As I explained in the previous paragraph, your goals define your training regimen for a particular time frame. Some people train for six weeks to bulk, using only low reps of heavy weights, whereafter they switch to high reps, lighter loads for cutting fat, or increasing endurance. It all depends on what you want to achieve and how much time you have to complete your goal.

Typically, you can measure your set goals by starting with four to six repetitions with heavier weight for hypertrophy. Usually, training specifically for strength hits at about eight to 12 reps. If you want to condition your muscles for endurance, the general rule of thumb sits at approximately 10 to 15 reps.

The number of reps for optimal growth is as varied as there are opinions. It is a controversial topic in the gym locker room. Once again, it is essential to find what works best for your individual physique. However, the best way to go is to alternate to prevent stagnation.

Most will agree that the secret is not necessarily the number of reps but the deliberate focus on employing the entire muscle group with every rep. Instead, concentrate on the range of motion and correct form to tax the muscle enough to trigger the necessary hormone releases. You will find your own number of reps that cause failure, and from there, you can determine what amount of reps you will need to achieve the best degree of muscle damage for a trigger.

Take note that "muscle damage" is not a reference to injury but the occurrence of minor tears to muscle fibers during a workout that triggers growth during recovery.

The bottom line is—stop counting reps and make each rep count.

For too long, most aspiring mass gainers have worried too much about how many reps they can crush instead of actually focusing on each. After all, your muscles are not impressed by your overdone reps, are they? No, they are impressed by what you can do to them!

The full range of motion that works the muscle, bone joint, and connective tissue are as crucial as executing the work with safe form. These two aspects are invaluable for getting the results you want. Crank out ten good, properly executed reps instead of 25 lashes of catastrophe that yield nothing.

Training to Failure

Researchers agree that training to failure incurs more strength and size than not saving energy for the next rep. That being said, if you plan to go hard, it's best to leave those sets for last. Wreaking havoc on your muscles to failure at the beginning of your workout will significantly reduce your ability to train as long as you had wished, not to mention promoting incorrect form with those fatigued muscles!

On a cellular level, the difference between light work and heavy work is that your nervous system needs those fast-twitch muscle fibers to lift the heavier load. In other words, it does not only put a strain on your muscle, but it burdens your nervous system as well. I will discuss the mind-muscle connection a little later on, but basically, the nervous system and the musculature should be prepared to work together efficiently.

Now, if you employ a lighter load/ higher rep combination to achieve failure, your muscles will quickly be depleted of glycogen—the essential energy source for heavy lifting. This is why it is essential to do your heavy load/low rep work first, while you still have adequate glycogen in your muscle tissue. It makes sense, doesn't it? After you have completed your heavy work, you will be able to cash out on the last bit of energy by training to failure.

Training for size holds primarily three factors—shorter rest intervals between sets, gradually increasing volume, and using techniques that induce failure.

The best method for intensity in training to failure is persistence. Take a short break between failure sets and continue hitting it again. You will notice that with each set your reps will decrease before failure. This is a good sign. It is also an excellent way to gauge your fatigue level so that you can alter your reps for the next time.

Concentric Versus Eccentric

Mostly, failure suggests the fatigue of the muscle during the concentric (contraction stage) portion, but you should also focus on your eccentric (negative) strength as well to fully compress the taxing of the muscle. For example, during a pull-up, this will be the lowering part. But eccentric motion relies on the strongest fibers; therefore, deliberately slowing down your eccentric contraction to almost maximum effort will significantly enhance strength results. Eccentric failure should make you feel as if you cannot control the movement anymore but force your muscle fibers to maintain the action.

In conclusion, save all failure sets for last and add eccentric failure sets to optimize strength building, and you will be amazed at what you can achieve in a short time!

Compartmentalize Your Body Parts

Compartmentalization allows you to concentrate on a particular area with each session, which is typically advantageous when chiseling or toning for good definition or aesthetics.

People choose to work specific muscle groups together to optimize the targeted area. This is especially beneficial when you have less time than most because it enhances the effects of your workout on that area, allowing those specific muscles to rest when you target the next group.

Depending on how many days per week you work out, you can separate your major muscle groups and perhaps group them together if you feel up to it, for example:

Day 1: Chest, arms
Day 2: Legs, abs
Day 3: Back, shoulders

Activating the Right Muscles

You've heard it a million times—you have to warm up before doing any physical exercise!

What you don't know is how crucial it is to stretch before taking on the weights. Most guys skip this part because they think they will not look cool enough warming up, but this is the quickest way to tear a muscle or destroy your joints. After all, your muscles are but one of several things that facilitate your range of motion. Even with the simplest bicep curl, you utilize bone, connective tissue, smaller muscle fibers, and joints.

Therefore, activating the right muscle is paramount to ensure that you prepare the joint and all the tissue around it to handle what you are about to lay on it. Not activating the muscle is almost guaranteed to cause injury and damage the ligaments. There are many activation techniques to target the muscle group you are about to work; some are combined with strength exercises unilaterally or bilaterally.

For example, if you are about to take on an overhead press, it is essential to activate the core muscles to help with stabilization. If you are going to do pull-ups, you should make sure to warm up your deltoid and scapular muscles to execute the pull-up better. Imagine not warming up your quads before going into a heavy squat—that would be the wrong kind of pain!

Mind-Muscle Connection

A lot of weight lifters neglect to remember that the most basic exercise is a practice of motor function and electrical activity between the brain and the fast-twitch fibers in the muscle.

No doubt, you may have seen those boys and girls in the gym, swinging away every rep with no care, dead eyes staring out to the mirror in front of them. This manner of training contains no focus or purpose, just repping for the sake of sets. There is no mind-muscle connection.

In order to correctly execute movements and really work the muscle, a mind-muscle connection will ensure that you focus on doing it correctly and thoroughly because it is a deliberate contraction. Focusing on the tension you create helps you to complete each rep with intention fully.

Cues: To achieve active muscle-mind connection, you can create cues in your mind that represent various actions during the exercise. For instance, you can create a cue for positioning your body before the exercise; another for the first portion of the exercise and another for the second part of the movement. These cues are conscious decisions to focus your execution on and help you do each rep consciously and feel the burn you are conjuring up!

Focus on the specific muscle you are working on and concentrate on the tension during each movement—like the contraction of your bicep when you lift the weight and the deliberate stress with which you bring the dumbbell down again.

Time under tension: One of the most effective ways to grow muscle is to hold the tension for longer, just like you do during isometric exercises. The prolonged strain on the muscle forces it to produce more strength to maintain the position, so this is another good mind-muscle coordination to employ while you rep.

No distraction: Any sort of concentration requires deliberate focus on the action, so switching off from all external distractions is an excellent way to zone in on the cues of your exercise. However, in total silence, you are likely to lose interest and may feel a bit bored. Music is always a good method to keep things exciting while shutting out distractions to apply yourself better.

Guide to Working Out without a Gym

Whatever your reason for not getting to the gym, there is never an excuse to neglect your workouts because the at-home options are just as potent as the weights and machines. There are a few points to pay attention to when you have to make do without the gym. First and foremost, as always, you have to spend time to warm up, stretch, and activate those muscles before applying any strain.

Stretching is not some quick reaches and big steps. Take your time to do them correctly—do not lock your joints, make sure to hold the stretch long enough to feel the burn and keep that back aligned. A good rule is to stretch your legs, arms, chest and back, calves, and neck.

Activate each muscle and joint by holding the stretch for about 30 seconds each, repeating three times, ideally.

Accessories are fantastic aids for keeping up strength and stabilization exercises.

- Resistance bands provide proper strain for isometric and isotonic movements. Their portability and compact nature make them a favorite for travelers or vacationers who like to keep fit. Using rubber bands, for instance, you can increase the burden on the muscle by shortening the length of the band to increase resistance considerably.
- A balance ball presents endless possibilities for strength, conditioning, cardio and isometric exercises that rely on core stabilization and balance. For example, you can use it as a static aid, like placing your feet on it for planking, or you can use exercises where the ball moves to work your stabilizing muscles along with basic contraction.
- Kettlebells are all the rage for a reason. Coming in all sizes and weights, they give you the best full-body workout in the shortest amount of time. Combining compound movements with resistance/weight training, kettlebells provide a power training option with added cardiovascular conditioning. But make sure to execute the kettlebell swing correctly to prevent injury! Once you know how to keep your posture, it is one of the best exercises to yield visible results quickly.

Apart from accessories, calisthenics will do nicely in place of irons. These tried and tested exercises will have you burning it up in no time. Even the dreaded plank with its deceptive simplicity will keep those core muscles in check.

- Push-ups are one of the oldest exercises with excellent results. Push-ups employ your core, back, shoulders, and back alignment, using smaller stabilizing muscle groups to assist the major muscles involved.
- Pull-ups are perfect for full body conditioning and strength training when you do not have the luxury of cables, machines, and free weights. Mount a bar in a doorway and change your hand grips for different muscle group targeting.
- Crunches and leg raises will hit the core and abdominals, even the quads, depending on the variation you use. Like push-ups, ab exercises take up very little space and will help you easily keep in shape without the gym.
- Walking lunges are better than static lunges if you have the space. Not only is this an excellent compound exercise that works the quadriceps, hamstrings, and glutes, but the balance and movement involved will considerably elevate the heart rate to promote cardiovascular fitness as well.

Before we move on to the next chapter, I want to reiterate that patience is key when it comes to making gains. Yes, if your time is constrained, there are things you can do to optimize each workout, but reducing your workout to once a week is not ideal. It will inevitably place too much strain on the muscles, leaving too long for recovery before the next workout.

If you are pressed for time, try to get in at least two sessions a week, keeping your exercises relatively constant and balanced. Increasing your volume per workout is far more effective to muscle mass gain than frequency, so make sure you heavy it up (safely, of course) during those elusive sessions you pack in when you find the time. Once again, it is not the time you put in but the efficiency of your training that accomplishes the best results.

Chapter 4 Supplements

In this chapter, I'll cover everything you need to know to build muscle fast—without wasting your money on fancy supplements. The fact of the matter is, a lot of supplements out there claim to have marvelous results, but when you dig into the research, very few remain standing.

But before we divide the good from the bad, let's first find out if ectomorphs even need supplements. To begin, we have to realize again that we're doing things backward. The studies and research are mostly tailored toward people who want to lose weight, whereas we're trying to achieve the opposite. This means we have to look at the criteria used to evaluate a supplement's effectiveness from a different angle.

Does it deliver more calories?
Will it cause weight gain?
Does it increase appetite?

These are only some of the questions we have to ask, and it's vastly different from what the general public wants to know.

Take branched-chain amino acids (BCAAs) as an example. They're incredibly popular, but ultimately, BCAAs are the 'light' version of protein powder. A scoop of BCAAs contains the exact same nutrients as a standard serving of protein powder, minus the amino acids and extra nutrients.

For someone who is trying to cut calories, BCAAs would be a good option. For us ectomorphs, protein powder comes out on top. It contains more calories and all the amino acids, not just BCAAs. So, as you move forward and delve deeper into the world of supplements, keep your eye on the prize: muscle growth.

Do Hardgainers Need Supplements?

In essence, the answer is no—you can meet your goals by following a hypertrophy exercise program, eating bulk-friendly foods (and enough of them), getting enough sleep, and limiting stress.

But if you know the fundamentals of bulking, supplements can help you.

- It can make your bulking experience easier. Protein powder is an excellent example of a supplement that makes it easier for us to cross one of the obstacles we face: a small stomach. Since it isn't very filling, one shake and you have a good dose of protein and calories.
- It speeds up the rate at which you build muscle. Drinking creatine may be the difference between gaining twenty pounds in twenty or fifteen weeks.
- Your gains will stay leaner. Since creatine speeds up your muscle growth, it will help you stay lean—any extra calories will go toward building muscle and won't have time to be stored as fat.
- It can improve consistency. Caffeine keeps you going for longer. It is addictive, but maybe it's a gateway drug to becoming addicted to your exercise routine!

Although none of these supplements are a must-have, they can possibly help you in some areas.

Best of the Best

Eating enough is hard—it's probably the hardest part of trying to build muscle. I'm sure some of you share my sentiment. It's this struggle that supplements can help us overcome, but it's all about a calorie surplus.

Protein powder and weight-gainer shakes (mass builders) are excellent sources of calories. They're digested easily and quickly and don't require a lot of space in your stomach. How else will you be able to consume 1,000+ calories in a matter of seconds?

This brings me to the three best supplements for skinny guys:

Creatine: You'll be able to build muscle at a faster rate.

Whey protein: Digestible source of protein.

Maltodextrin: Source of easily-digestible carbs.

Before I break down each one in more detail, another reason why these supplements made the top three is that they're affordable. In fact, they may even be cheaper than buying chicken or rice. There are fancier and more expensive supplements out there, but the jury is still out on whether they actually work. Until then, let's stick to the basics—they're going to give you the best results anyway.

Creatine

This supplement is famous for good reason—study after study proves that it increases the speed at which muscle grows and it increases strength (Buford, et al., 2007).

But is it safe?

Creatine has been studied for several decades, and the results stay the same: it's healthy and safe (Groeneveld, et al., 2005). The only time when creatine may be dangerous is if you have kidney disorders or stand a chance of developing kidney disease. In that case, have a chat with your doctor to remove any concerns you may have about kidney damage.

The only thing you need to worry about when you're talking creatine is your hydration levels—creatine draws water into your muscles. If there isn't enough fluid in your body, you will have to deal with cramps and a possible stomach ache.

How does it work?

It replenishes your muscles' ATP—a type of fuel used during weight lifting. This makes it possible for you to push yourself for one last rep, all the time stimulating more muscle growth.

It helps with protein synthesis and glycogen storage in muscles. That's using some big words to say that you'll not only build more muscle when you train, you'll also gain muscle from the food you're eating.

How much extra muscle will you build?

This is probably the most common question newbies will ask—how much weight can I gain from taking creatine? It's not an easy question to answer since it depends on the amount of creatine you already have in your body. There are people who respond eagerly and end up gaining several pounds in the first couple of weeks. Others don't see any results at all. One study looked at two groups where only one group was supplementing with creatine (Tarnopolsky, et al., 2001). The results confirmed what we've known all along: creatine can boost muscle growth by up to 50% in beginners. That translates to an extra three pounds. This effect will slow as their muscles get used to the extra creatine, but the faster rate of muscle growth won't go away; it will just temper down a bit.

What does it do to fat gains?

Creatine will fight fat when you're bulking by improving your muscles' insulin sensitivity. As we know, the more insulin sensitive your muscle cells are, the less likely it is for excess calories to be stored as fat—your muscles will be hungry! Although hardgainers don't really need any help on the insulin sensitivity front, it's not something to scoff at.

Maltodextrin

Most mass-builder supplements consist of protein powder and carbohydrate powder. Although maltodextrin is most commonly used, you can also use pea protein or ground oats. Again, it's all about the carbs and the calories you get from it.

There are two reasons why maltodextrin is popular in weight lifting circles. First, it is super easy to digest. It will break down into glucose quickly, which means your muscles will have a comfortable supply of fuel. Given how efficient it is, the chances of maltodextrin getting stored as fat is close to zero. Second, it is so cheap you may mistake it for flour (and you wouldn't be entirely wrong). The only real difference between maltodextrin and flour is that you can eat maltodextrin raw, making it easy to mix into protein shakes.

Can it make you fat?

As an ectomorph, no. If you remember, earlier in this book I explained how a high-carb diet actually helps hardgainers gain muscle and burn fat. If you were an endomorph, my answer wouldn't be so clear-cut.

It circles back to insulin sensitivity and the fact that any surplus calories consumed after exercise will most likely be stored as muscle and not fat. The secret is to take a holistic approach: stay lean, follow a healthy diet, and keep active to make sure your blood sugar levels remain normal—everything you'll be doing religiously on your bulking journey.

Whey Protein

Whey protein is probably the most easily-digested source of protein you can get your hands on. It is found in milk and is minimally processed to ensure it stays high in nutrients. Some nutritionists and dieticians will tell you that whey protein is a whole food, and they will liken it to cheese and yogurt. But whey protein packs more punch than those protein sources and is closer to a chicken breast when you compare the nutritional value.

Why use whey protein?

We know that protein is the building block of muscle tissue, and if we don't eat enough protein, we are limited in how much muscle we can build. If our bodies don't have the right ingredients to build muscle, any excess calories will be stored as fat instead. This makes whey protein a powerful and important supplement when bulking. If you see you didn't meet your day's protein macros, then shake up some whey protein to feed your muscles and make them grow big and strong.

What's the limit of whey protein per day?

If you recall, for optimal muscle growth, it is best if you consume roughly 1 gram of protein per pound of body weight. Less than that, and your muscle growth will be slow, more than that, and you're wasting your time and money—you'll be better off eating more carbohydrates than focusing on extra protein. How you eat (or drink) your protein doesn't matter. So, if you want to, you can meet your protein needs by only drinking whey protein shakes. If your diet is naturally rich in protein, you can use whey protein on the days where you fall behind on your protein consumption. It's entirely up to you.

Why whey?

Whey protein is the best because it gets digested extremely efficiently. It also contains all the amino acids necessary for building muscle, so drinking a whey protein shake will give you all the benefits of BCAAs and HMB supplement, and you'll be paying a fraction of the price. I'm not done yet. Whey protein also contains several times the calories, vitamins, and minerals than other amino acid supplements.

The amino acid leucine is excellent when it comes to promoting muscle growth, and you'll find heaps of it in whey protein. So, you can drink it before, during, or after hitting the gym and expect great results. To take things to the next level, combine whey protein with maltodextrin, and you have a powerhouse supplement that will make your muscle-building dreams a reality.

If you're still not convinced that whey protein is the best of the best, here's a recap of all its benefits.

- It's high in calories.
- It won't affect your appetite negatively.
- It's quick to prepare, consume, and digest.
- It's affordable when compared to other protein sources.

Now that we've covered the supplements worth your money, let's look at the more mediocre ones where the effects are minor, but the damage to your bank account is major.

In the Bulking Bad Bin

Citrulline Malate

I mentioned the 'pump' earlier: blood vessels dilate, making it possible for more blood to enter your muscles as you train. Citrulline malate is one of the best supplements on the market to help enhance muscle pump. But then again, if you add higher-rep sets to your exercise routine, you'll get precisely the same effect without paying a cent.

Beta-Alanine

This is creatine's younger (and smaller) brother. My argument here is: if you can get a more powerful supplement that does exactly the same and has more positive side effects, then why even consider the second-rate option?

Ashwagandha

Ashwagandha is intriguing, to say the least. According to a study, this supplement speeds up muscle growth, increases strength, boosts testosterone, manages cortisol, and reduces fat gains all in a day's work (Wankhede, et al., 2015). The study found a 15% increase in testosterone and a 44-pound surge in bench press strength compared to the control group. But I'm not getting too excited yet. When it comes to ashwagandha, the body of evidence is too scarce, and not all the findings are as positive as the study cited above. There's just not enough substantiation to make supplementing with ashwagandha scientifically-sound but anecdotal evidence does exist.

Vitamin D

Vitamin D increases your testosterone levels but only within normal ranges. This may seem like nothing, but considering that most people are deficient in vitamin D, it can have a positive impact. If you're a guy who doesn't get a lot of sun, then taking a vitamin D supplement can raise your muscle-building potential. The reason why this is in the "bad bin" is that sunlight is free and works better than any pill can.

Turmeric

Turmeric, or rather the active compound curcumin, has shot to fame overnight. The list of health benefits is as long as my arm. Although muscle growth isn't a direct advantage of taking curcumin, this powerhouse spice reduces overall inflammation, which means you'll be back in the gym sooner. It not only decreases muscle soreness but also makes it possible for us to lift heavier for longer. When it comes to digestion, hardgainers can have a difficult time taking into account the mountains of food we have to eat to gain muscle. Curcumin can help out there, too—it improves your digestion. Considering that there's a lot of evidence behind turmeric's overall health benefits, and consuming it has no real downsides, I would give it a shot. It may turn out to be a great bulking supplement for hardgainers.

In summary, your diet and the quality of your workout far outweigh the use of supplements in your bulking routine. Don't waste your money on fancy supplements that promise you gains for days if you do want some extra help. Instead, stick to the basics: creatine, whey protein, and maltodextrin are the only supplements you need.

Here's a recipe for my post-workout shake (which I sometimes drink pre-workout or during).

- 30-90 grams of protein powder
- 60-180 grams maltodextrin
- 5 grams creatine

This shake will meet all your nutrient needs post-workout. If you mix at the higher end, it turns into a mass-gainer that will help you gain weight. I usually mix 90 grams protein powder with 180 grams maltodextrin on days where I feel skinny, and the scale just won't budge. It works wonders, but you have to keep drinking for a few days to see a difference.

As a hardgainer myself, I think this formula is the secret to success for us skinny guys. You get a good bump of protein and carbs without having to force-feed yourself and put unnecessary strain on your stomach.

What About Our Vegan Friends?

It's entirely possible for vegan and vegetarians to build muscle on a plant-based bulking diet. If you've sworn off any animal products, you most likely know that you will have to supplement to make up for the nutrients you're missing out on. The same applies to bulking.

Here are the top supplements you have to consider taking for optimum muscle gains and good health in general.

Vitamin B-12: You're probably already drinking a vitamin B-12 supplement since it is widely known that most vegans run into a deficiency at one point or another. Too little B-12 in your body may lead to anemia, and it may also negatively affect your nervous system.

Creatine: Meat is naturally high in creatine, but since that is off the menu for you, you'll benefit from supplementing with creatine. You also don't have to worry; creatine supplements are 100% plant-based.

Calcium and zinc: A lot of fruits and veggies contain calcium and zinc. The problem is that the phytates and oxalates found in these same plants reduce nutrient absorption. So, although vegans and vegetarians can meet their nutritional needs, they have to eat so much more to reach efficient quantities. We all know that eating more is easier said than done when you're an ectomorph. A pill takes up much less space in your stomach than a bowl of fibrous veggies!

Vitamin D: We've already established that most people have a vitamin D deficiency. Vegans definitely don't get enough vitamin D from their diet, considering that they don't consume dairy that is fortified. It is best to supplement with vitamin D directly—look for D3; it is the most effective.

Chapter 5 Meal Prep Basics

What is Meal Prepping

Simply put, meal prep is the act of preparing and storing in advance several individual servings of one or more weekly meals and snacks. Although meal planning is involved, meal prep takes the selection and scheduling of meals a step further by actually having them fully cooked and boxed. Meal prepping can be done one or two days each week, depending on your individual needs and schedule. The same meal will be divided and boxed for several meals throughout the week and be ready to heat-and-eat, like a casserole, or eat cold, like a salad. But the benefits of meal prepping go a lot further than just convenience.

Why Meal Prep?

Meal prepping is the number one reason I am able to feed myself and my family healthy, delicious meals each day. The benefits of meal prepping include:

Saving money: If you know what you are going to cook, you can purchase accordingly. You can purchase meat and other ingredients in bulk, divide them into meal portions, and place them in resealable plastic bags in the refrigerator or freezer. This stretches your food dollar.

Saving time: Although you will spend some time in the kitchen on a set day of your choosing, during the week you won't be slaving for hours over a hot stove. Plus, you won't have much cleanup to do during those busy weeknights. That extra 30 to 60 minutes can be spent as quality time with loved ones instead!

Controlling portions: In order to make a meal last, you need to divide the food and account for portions. Each of my recipes provides exact measurements for portions to help make your life easier. By controlling portions, you not only save money, but also keep meal and snack calories in check.

Getting more done with less effort: Some nights it just feels like you are cooking nonstop while your to-do list gets longer and longer. It takes less effort to prepare a double batch of chili or burgers in advance than it does to cook a new meal every night; even on busy weeknights you'll be able to sit down, breathe, and enjoy a healthy meal.

Eating healthier: A stop at a fast-food joint or hitting up the vending machine will be a thing of the past. These unhealthy choices are where many high-calorie, high-fat, and high-sugar foods are eaten. When you're armed with prepared meals and snacks, these unhealthy eating habits start to disappear.

Improving multitasking skills: Meal prepping will hone your multitasking skills and even improve them. You'll learn to set a timer for the oven while preparing the dressing for your lunch salad. Multitasking allows you to save time and become more efficient at meal prepping.

Meal Prep Principles

Developing smart meal prepping habits is part of the learning process. Here are some meal prep dos and don'ts worth keeping in mind as you get started:

- ✔ DO flag healthy recipes you love. After trying healthy recipes, keep the ones you love in a folder or mark them in the cookbook.
- ✔ DO go at your own pace. You can successfully meal prep with three recipes or six recipes. You don't need to prepare 10 or more recipes for the week. Start slowly and build your way up.
- ✔ DO work with your schedule. Some weeks you'll be able to prepare more recipes than other weeks. Do whatever works for you and your schedule.
- ✔ DO freeze extras. Some weeks you will have a few extra meals. Freezer-friendly meals can be frozen and kept for up to a few months, as noted in the recipes.
- ✔ DO make cleanup easy. You'll have many vegetable scraps, eggshells, and empty containers to toss, so keep your recycling, compost bin, and trash nearby for easy cleanup.
- ✘ DON'T leave everything until the last minute. Plan ahead for best results. Meal prepping is about scheduling your time in advance, so you can get to the market and buy the ingredients you need, then spend the necessary time at home preparing them.
- ✘ DON'T divide meals later. The last step of meal prepping is to divide recipes into individual portions and pack them into containers. Don't skip this step or divide meals right before digging into one. Dividing meals up front helps maintain good portion control, prevents last-minute scrambling to divide meals, and ensures your meals will last through the week.
- ✘ DON'T overprep. The last thing you want to do is prep meals that will go uneaten, unless of course you can freeze them. To get into the meal prepping jive, start slow and get to know your meal prepping needs. You can meal prep one or two days a week—do whatever works with your schedule.

The Art of Storage

I hope that meal prep will become a regular routine in your home like it is in ours. In order to make that happen, it is essential that you invest in and choose the right storage containers. When I was ready to invest in a set of containers, I bought a few different options—glass, metal, and plastic (BPA-free, of course). This way I could do a trial run to figure out what I liked best before I made a big purchase. Trying a few to see what you like and what works best in your kitchen will save you time and money in the long run.

Good-quality containers are essential for keeping your food fresh as long as possible. Here are some things to look for when buying containers for meal prepping:

BPA-free. I'm sure you have read or seen BPA-free on containers or other plastic items before, and here's why it's important. BPA stands for bisphenol A, which is a chemical found in plastics like food containers, water bottles, food cans, and consumer goods. Research has shown that BPA can seep into food or beverages from plastic containers made of BPA. Possible side effects of BPA exposure include increased blood pressure, mental health issues, and negative effects on fetuses, infants, and children.

Stackable. I know we all have a cupboard or a drawer packed full of containers and lids. If you begin to make meal prep a part of your regular routine, that means a lot of containers will start to accumulate. Having containers that are stackable will keep your cupboards functional and looking organized, making life easier.

Freezer-safe. There will be times when you prep and have more than you need for the week. That's when having containers that are freezer-safe is key. I will also purposely double recipes so I can throw them in the freezer for future use.

Microwave-safe. It is totally up to you how you reheat your meals. Most likely microwaving is going to be the most convenient method. So, choosing containers that are microwave-friendly is something you will want to pay attention to.

Dishwasher-safe. This one is obvious, at least it is for me.

Glass Containers

In our house we use glass containers for many reasons. Glass is environmentally friendly. It performs safely at different temperatures, allowing me to reheat meals in the prep containers right in the microwave or oven. Although glass is a little more of an investment than plastic, with glass containers you get safety and durability. They also don't retain any of the smells of food after cleaning, which is a nice bonus. Square, rectangular, and circular glass containers are available; choose a mixture of sizes for the most versatility.

Plastic Containers

Plastic containers are very popular for meal prep—they're lightweight, stack easily, and many are now microwavable as well as freezable. But as I mentioned, my go-to is glass. Plastic containers may leach harmful substances into the food stored in them. Plastic is not biodegradable, which means it isn't possible for our earth to naturally absorb the material back into the soil; instead, plastic actually contaminates it. Unlike glass and metal, plastic absorbs odors and tastes like whatever you stored in it previously. If you have ever stored fish in a plastic container, I'm guessing it still smells like fish to this day. While it's a fact that plastic is cheaper than other options, it's also true that it will not last as long. If you do choose to go with plastic containers, always look for an indicator that they are BPA-free.

Mason Jars

Mason (canning) jars are also great for storing food. Made of glass, Mason jars are inexpensive and perfect for storing salads and salad dressings. A combination of wide-mouth quart and pint jars, as well as some smaller four-ounce jars for dressings, will go a long way when doing meal preps. I incorporate them a few times throughout the preps for quick storage.

Stainless Steel

Stainless steel containers will last a lot longer than plastic. They look nicer, maintain hot and cold temperatures well, and are super durable. They are the most expensive option, and one drawback to keep in mind is that metal can't be reheated in the microwave.

Whichever type of storage container you decide to purchase, I recommend getting at least 15 containers as well as five pint-size or quart-size Mason jars so you have enough storage for your meals through one week of prep.

Food Storage Guidelines

When buying meats and dairy from your local grocery store, look for products with the "sell by" date farthest in the future. It may take some digging, but the food products will store longer for your meal prep.

Make sure to let your prepped meals completely cool before you cover them and put them in the refrigerator or freezer. If you don't wait and put the lid on while the meal is still hot, it will create steam within your storage container. This will result in the meal continuing to cook, which can lead to overcooked vegetables or dried-out proteins.

When storing food in your refrigerator and freezer, it's really important to always label and date the containers. Of course you'll want to rotate and use the earliest dates first to minimize food spoilage. When storing food in the refrigerator, place raw foods at the bottom, wrapped to catch any juices. Ready-to-eat foods like cooked dishes and fresh food like fruits, vegetables, and yogurt should be stored above the raw food. This will help minimize the risk of cross-contamination and potential foodborne illness. It's also important to use foods when they're at their peak of freshness and nutrition. Below is a chart illustrating freezer and refrigerator storage times of popular foods.

	FRIDGE	FREEZER
Salads: egg salad, tuna salad, chicken salad, pasta salad	3 TO 5 DAYS	DOES NOT FREEZE WELL
Hamburger, meatloaf, and other dishes made with ground meat (raw)	1 TO 2 DAYS	3 TO 4 MONTHS
Steaks: beef, lamb pork, (raw)	3 TO 5 DAYS	3 TO 4 MONTHS
Chops: beef, lamb pork, (raw)	3 TO 5 DAYS	4 TO 6 MONTHS
Roasts: beef, lamb pork, (raw)	3 TO 5 DAYS	4 TO 12 MONTHS
Whole chicken turkey or (raw)	1 TO 2 DAYS	1 YEAR
Pieces: chicken turkey or (raw)	1 TO 2 DAYS	9 MONTHS
Soups and stews with vegetables and meat	3 TO 4 DAYS	2 TO 3 MONTHS
Pizza	3 TO 4 DAYS	1 TO 2 MONTHS
Beef, lamb, pork, or chicken (cooked)	3 TO 4 DAYS	2 TO 6 MONTHS

How to Thaw Safely

You can thaw raw proteins like meat, poultry, and fish in several ways. First, you can place it in the refrigerator the night before. For a whole turkey or chicken you will need 2 to 3 days in the refrigerator for proper thawing. Smaller items, like frozen shrimp, can be run under cool water for 1 to 2 hours. Make sure there are no dishes in the sink when thawing food in this manner. You can also thaw frozen raw proteins in the microwave. However, because you get an uneven distribution of heat, some of the meats or fish may start to cook. If you do use the microwave to thaw, it is recommended to cook the food right away.

For cooked meals, you can use the same methods mentioned above. Thawing in the refrigerator is best since the food is at a safe temperature the entire time. After the food is thawed completely, it can be stored in the refrigerator for 3 to 4 days. The internal temperature of any reheated food should reach 165°F and should be measured with a thermometer placed in the thickest part of the dish.

Safe Reheating Guidelines

You can safely reheat your prepped meals by following a few simple guidelines in the microwave, in the oven, or on the stovetop.

Safely Reheating Meals in The Microwave

While a microwave won't always produce the same results as an oven, using a microwave for reheating prepped meals is often much faster and more convenient. Here are a few general tips for getting the best results when reheating your prepped meals in a microwave oven.

Always Remove The Lids

Always remove the lid from prep containers prior to microwaving to ensure the expanding heat does not create an explosion inside the microwave. You can cover the uncovered container with a damp paper towel to ensure moisture is retained during the reheating process.

Be Sure to Thaw Frozen Meals Before Reheating

Many of the meals in this book include instructions for freezing. If you're reheating a frozen meal, be sure to remove the meal from the freezer at least one day prior to reheating and serving to ensure that the meal is reheated properly and evenly. If you forget to remove the meal from the freezer, most microwave ovens have a defrost mode that can be used to partially thaw the meal prior to cooking.

Three Minutes on High Usually Does The Trick

As a general rule, microwaving refrigerated prepped meals for about 3 minutes on high should be sufficient for most of the recipes in this book. If possible, larger ingredients such as proteins should be removed from containers and reheated in the microwave first to ensure other foods don't become overcooked in the process. Also, make sure the surface of the food is as even as possible to ensure even reheating.

Only Reheat Glass Containers

You should never reheat food in containers made of anything other than glass. Microwaving metal can cause a dangerous arcing effect in a microwave oven, and microwaving plastic can leach dangerous chemicals into your meals.

Safely Reheating Meals in an Oven or on The Stovetop

Reheating prepped meals in the oven is simple. And while it might take a little longer than it would in a microwave, an oven reheats food more evenly than a microwave and can result in more desirable textures for some foods. Here are a few best practices for reheating meals in the oven or on the stovetop.

Reheat to the Same Temperature the Meal Was Prepared to

When reheating your meals, the meals should be reheated to the same temperatures they were originally cooked to, and for most recipes in this book, reheating your meals on the middle oven rack for 20 minutes in a preheated oven set to 350°F (180°C) should be sufficient. Use a thermometer to check the meals every 5 minutes, after 10 minutes have passed.

Only Use Metal or Glass Containers That are Marked "Oven-Safe"

Be sure to only reheat meals in glass or metal prep containers that are marked "oven-safe," and always remove the lid from the container before placing it in the oven. Some oven-safe containers may have lids that are not actually oven-safe, and these lids can melt or become superheated inside an oven, which can be dangerous.

Use a Baking Sheet to Minimize the Mess

Whenever reheating a meal in the oven, place it on a baking tray lined with parchment paper. This will prevent any liquids that bubble over from the container from dripping onto the surface of your oven, which can create a mess.

When Time is Short, Opt for the Broiler

If you want to speed up the reheating process in the oven, you can place meals under a broiler set to 350°F (180°C). However, this method can result in some foods burning more quickly, and it may not heat the meals as evenly from top to bottom, so watch the meals carefully. Also, it's best to use a metal container under the broiler since some oven-safe glass containers may still crack at higher temperatures.

Stick to the Stovetop for Certain Recipes

While a conventional oven or microwave oven will work for reheating the majority of the recipes in this book, some recipes that were originally prepared in a frying pan or in a pot, such as soups, are best reheated in a large frying pan or pot placed over medium heat on the stovetop.

Use a Thermometer to Check the Temperature

Whichever method you follow to reheat your meals, it's best to check the internal temperature of the food to ensure it's been reheated to the proper cooking temperature. A simple oven or kitchen thermometer is all you'll need to do this.

Chapter 6 Step-By-Step Meal Plans

Bulking Meal Plan-1 (Calorie Goal: 3500-4000)

Day	Breakfast	Snack/Dessert	Lunch	Dinner	Snack/Dessert	Preworkout Meal
1	Polenta Squares with Blueberry Sauce and Banana calories: 467 | fat: 7.9g | carbs: 71.7g | protein: 27.3g	Banana-Peanut Butter Mug Muffins calories: 325 | fat: 14.7g | carbs: 35.1g | protein: 15.4g	Chickpea and Baby Spinach Salad calories: 944 | fat: 33.1g | carbs: 139.8g | protein: 34.2g	Tangy Kale Salad calories: 721 | fat: 20.2g | carbs: 123.1g | protein: 27.2g	Banana-Peanut Butter Mug Muffins calories: 325 | fat: 14.7g | carbs: 35.1g | protein: 15.4g	Baked Mango Quinoa Bowl with Tempeh calories: 733 | fat: 42.3g | carbs: 39.2g | protein: 46.4g
2	Polenta Squares with Blueberry Sauce and Banana calories: 467 | fat: 7.9g | carbs: 71.7g | protein: 27.3g	Banana-Peanut Butter Mug Muffins calories: 325 | fat: 14.7g | carbs: 35.1g | protein: 15.4g	Chickpea and Baby Spinach Salad calories: 944 | fat: 33.1g | carbs: 139.8g | protein: 34.2g	Tangy Kale Salad calories: 721 | fat: 20.2g | carbs: 123.1g | protein: 27.2g	Banana-Peanut Butter Mug Muffins calories: 325 | fat: 14.7g | carbs: 35.1g | protein: 15.4g	Baked Mango Quinoa Bowl with Tempeh calories: 733 | fat: 42.3g | carbs: 39.2g | protein: 46.4g
3	Polenta Squares with Blueberry Sauce and Banana calories: 467 | fat: 7.9g | carbs: 71.7g | protein: 27.3g	Banana-Peanut Butter Mug Muffins calories: 325 | fat: 14.7g | carbs: 35.1g | protein: 15.4g	Chickpea and Baby Spinach Salad calories: 944 | fat: 33.1g | carbs: 139.8g | protein: 34.2g	Tangy Kale Salad calories: 721 | fat: 20.2g | carbs: 123.1g | protein: 27.2g	Banana-Peanut Butter Mug Muffins calories: 325 | fat: 14.7g | carbs: 35.1g | protein: 15.4g	Baked Mango Quinoa Bowl with Tempeh calories: 733 | fat: 42.3g | carbs: 39.2g | protein: 46.4g
4	Polenta Squares with Blueberry Sauce and Banana calories: 467 | fat: 7.9g | carbs: 71.7g | protein: 27.3g	Banana-Peanut Butter Mug Muffins calories: 325 | fat: 14.7g | carbs: 35.1g | protein: 15.4g	Chickpea and Baby Spinach Salad calories: 944 | fat: 33.1g | carbs: 139.8g | protein: 34.2g	Tangy Kale Salad calories: 721 | fat: 20.2g | carbs: 123.1g | protein: 27.2g	Banana-Peanut Butter Mug Muffins calories: 325 | fat: 14.7g | carbs: 35.1g | protein: 15.4g	Baked Mango Quinoa Bowl with Tempeh calories: 733 | fat: 42.3g | carbs: 39.2g | protein: 46.4g

Day	Breakfast	Snack/ Dessert	Lunch	Dinner	Snack/ Dessert	Preworkout Meal
5	Polenta Squares with Blueberry Sauce and Banana calories: 467 | fat: 7.9g | carbs: 71.7g | protein: 27.3g	Banana-Peanut Butter Mug Muffins calories: 325 | fat: 14.7g | carbs: 35.1g | protein: 15.4g	Chickpea and Baby Spinach Salad calories: 944 | fat: 33.1g | carbs: 139.8g | protein: 34.2g	Polenta Squares with Blueberry Sauce and Banana calories: 467 | fat: 7.9g | carbs: 71.7g | protein: 27.3g	Banana-Peanut Butter Mug Muffins calories: 325 | fat: 14.7g | carbs: 35.1g | protein: 15.4g	Baked Mango Quinoa Bowl with Tempeh calories: 733 | fat: 42.3g | carbs: 39.2g | protein: 46.4g
6	Polenta Squares with Blueberry Sauce and Banana calories: 467 | fat: 7.9g | carbs: 71.7g | protein: 27.3g	Banana-Peanut Butter Mug Muffins calories: 325 | fat: 14.7g | carbs: 35.1g | protein: 15.4g	Chickpea and Baby Spinach Salad calories: 944 | fat: 33.1g | carbs: 139.8g | protein: 34.2g	Tangy Kale Salad calories: 721 | fat: 20.2g | carbs: 123.1g | protein: 27.2g	Banana-Peanut Butter Mug Muffins calories: 325 | fat: 14.7g | carbs: 35.1g | protein: 15.4g	Baked Mango Quinoa Bowl with Tempeh calories: 733 | fat: 42.3g | carbs: 39.2g | protein: 46.4g
7	Polenta Squares with Blueberry Sauce and Banana calories: 467 | fat: 7.9g | carbs: 71.7g | protein: 27.3g	Banana-Peanut Butter Mug Muffins calories: 325 | fat: 14.7g | carbs: 35.1g | protein: 15.4g	Tangy Kale Salad calories: 721 | fat: 20.2g | carbs: 123.1g | protein: 27.2g	Baked Mango Quinoa Bowl with Tempeh calories: 733 | fat: 42.3g | carbs: 39.2g | protein: 46.4g	Banana-Peanut Butter Mug Muffins calories: 325 | fat: 14.7g | carbs: 35.1g | protein: 15.4g	Baked Mango Quinoa Bowl with Tempeh calories: 733 | fat: 42.3g | carbs: 39.2g | protein: 46.4g

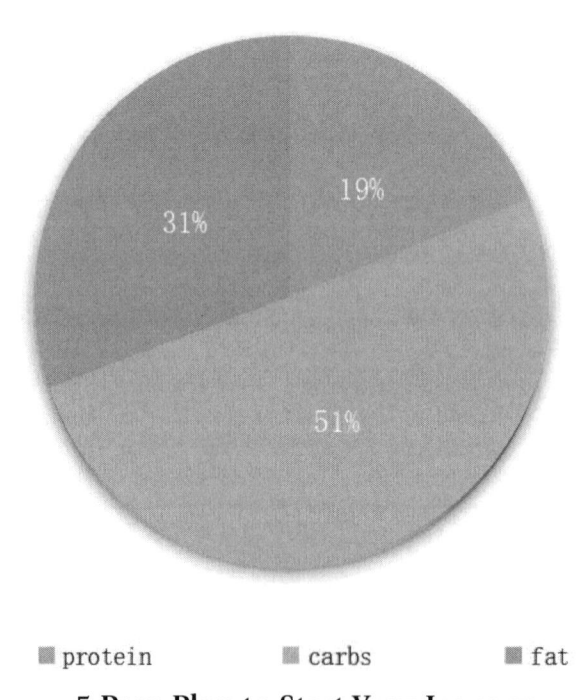

- protein 31%
- carbs 51%
- fat 19%

5 Prep Plan to Start Your Journey
Bulking Meal Plan-1 (Calorie Goal: 3500-4000)

Prep Plan #1

This is a fantastic starter plan with 1 breakfast, 1 lunch, 1 dinner, 1 preworkout meal and 2 desserts that will keep you covered up to 7 days of eating.

Recipe 1 : Polenta Squares with Blueberry Sauce and Banana | Calories: 467 | Fat: 7.9g | Carbs: 71.7g | Protein: 27.3g

Prep time: 10 minutes | Cook time: 14 minutes | Serves 4

3 cups water
3 cups 2% milk
2 teaspoons salt
1¾ cups yellow cornmeal
3 scoops vanilla protein powder
2 cups fresh or frozen blueberries
1 tablespoon honey
2 teaspoons extra-virgin olive oil
1 banana, peeled and sliced

Steps:
1. In a large, heavy-duty pot over medium-high heat, bring water and milk to a boil. Add salt and gradually whisk in cornmeal.
2. Reduce the heat to low and cook until the mixture thickens and cornmeal is tender, stirring often, about 10 to 15 minutes. Remove from the heat. Add the protein powder and stir until no lumps are visible. Pour the polenta into an 8-inch by 8-inch casserole dish and place in the fridge to set, about 30 to 45 minutes. After the mixture solidifies, cut it into 2-inch by 2-inch squares.
3. To prepare blueberry sauce, add blueberries and honey into a blender. Process until smooth, about 1 minute.
4. Warm oil in a large skillet over medium-high heat. Working in batches, brown polenta squares, cooking about 2 minutes per side. Transfer polenta squares to a dish.
5. Add blueberry sauce to the skillet. Stirring constantly, let the blueberry sauce warm over medium-high heat. Pour hot blueberry sauce over polenta and top with banana slices.

Recipe 2 : Banana-Peanut Butter Mug Muffins | Calories: 325 | Fat: 14.7g | Carbs: 35.1g | Protein: 15.4g

Prep time: 10 minutes | Cook time: 2 minutes | Serves 3

Nonstick cooking spray
1 ripe banana, mashed
¾ cup egg whites
¾ cup quick oats
3 tablespoons peanut butter
1½ teaspoons vanilla extract
1½ teaspoons ground cinnamon
3 tablespoons mini chocolate chips (optional)

Steps:
1. Spray 3 large mugs with nonstick cooking spray.
2. In a medium bowl, combine the banana, egg whites, oats, peanut butter, vanilla, and cinnamon. Mix well, then fold in the chocolate chips (if using).
3. Divide the batter equally among the 3 mugs.
4. Microwave each mug on high for 2 minutes, or until the muffin is cooked through and the top is firm to the touch.
5. Remove from the microwave. Free the sides of the muffins from the mugs with a butter knife, and turn the mugs upside down to shake onto a plate. Let cool.
6. Into each of 3 airtight storage containers, place 1 muffin and seal.
7. Store the airtight containers in the refrigerator for up to 1 week.

Recipe 3 : Chickpea And Baby Spinach Salad | Calories: 944 | Fat: 33.1g | Carbs: 139.8g | Protein: 34.2g

Prep time: 10 minutes | Cook time: 0 minutes | Serves 1

3 cups roughly chopped baby spinach
2 cups cooked chickpeas
1 cup chopped mushrooms
1 tomato, chopped
1 avocado, peeled, pitted, and chopped
⅛ teaspoon pink Himalayan salt
⅛ teaspoon freshly ground black pepper
Juice of 1 large lemon
1 tablespoon sunflower seeds, for topping (optional)
1 teaspoon hulled hemp seeds, for topping (optional)

Steps:
1. In a large bowl, combine the spinach, chickpeas, mushrooms, tomato, and avocado. Add the salt, pepper, and lemon juice. Mix thoroughly so all the flavors combine and the avocado is mixed in well.
2. Top with the seeds (if using). Enjoy immediately or store in a reusable container in the refrigerator for up to 5 days.

Recipe 4 : Tangy Kale Salad | Calories: 721 | Fat: 20.2g | Carbs: 123.1g | Protein: 27.2g

Prep time: 5 minutes | Cook time: 0 minutes | Serves 2

4 cups chopped kale
2 tablespoons freshly squeezed lemon juice
⅛ teaspoon pink Himalayan salt
1 cup cooked wild rice
1 cup cooked quinoa
1 small tomato, chopped
1 small avocado, pitted, peeled, and chopped

Steps:
1. In a large bowl, massage the kale with the lemon juice and salt for a few minutes, or until the kale softens.
2. Add the rice, quinoa, tomato, and avocado to the bowl and mix well.
3. Serve immediately or store in the refrigerator for up to 3 days.

Recipe 5 : Baked Mango Quinoa Bowl with Tempeh | Calories: 733 | Fat: 42.3g | Carbs: 39.2g | Protein: 46.4g

Prep time: 5 minutes | Cook time: 15 minutes | Serves 4

1 cup fresh mango cubes
1 (14-ounce / 397-g) pack tempeh, sliced
1 cup peanut butter
1 cup cooked black beans
2 cups cooked quinoa

Optional Toppings:

Chili flakes
Shredded coconut

Steps:
1. Blend the mango into a smooth purée using a blender or food processor, and set it aside.
2. Add the tempeh slices and the peanut butter to an airtight container. Close the lid and shake well until the tempeh slices are evenly covered with the peanut butter.
3. Preheat the oven to 375°F (190°C) and line a baking sheet with parchment paper.
4. Transfer the tempeh slices onto the baking sheet and bake for about 15 minutes or until the tempeh is browned and crispy.
5. Divide the black beans, quinoa, mango purée and tempeh slices between two bowls, serve with the optional toppings and enjoy.

Shopping Lists

Dairy

- Eggs
- Oats

Fruits, Vegetables, Spices & Herbs

- Salt
- Yellow Cornmeal
- Vanilla Protein Powder
- Blueberries
- Honey
- Extra-virgin olive oil
- Banana
- Peanut Butter
- Vanilla Extract
- Cinnamon
- Chocolate Chips
- Spinach
- Chickpeas
- Mushrooms
- Tomato
- Avocado
- Himalayan Salt
- Black Pepper
- Lemon
- Sunflower Seeds
- Hemp Seeds
- Kale
- Wild rice
- Quinoa
- Tomato
- Mango
- Pack Tempeh
- Peanut Butter
- Black Beans
- Chili Flakes
- Coconut

Meal Prep Plan

Start your breakfast with **Polenta Squares with Blueberry Sauce and Banana**. First, in a large, heavy-duty pot over medium-high heat, bring water and milk to a boil. Add salt and gradually whisk in cornmeal. Reduce the heat to low and cook until the mixture thickens and cornmeal is tender, stirring often, about 10 to 15 minutes. Remove from the heat. Add the protein powder and stir until no lumps are visible. Pour the polenta into an 8-inch by 8-inch casserole dish and place in the fridge to set, about 30 to 45 minutes. After the mixture solidifies, cut it into 2-inch by 2-inch squares. To prepare blueberry sauce, add blueberries and honey into a blender. Process until smooth, about 1 minute. Warm oil in a large skillet over medium-high heat. Working in batches, brown polenta squares, cooking about 2 minutes per side. Transfer polenta squares to a dish. Add blueberry sauce to the skillet. Stirring constantly, let the blueberry sauce warm over medium-high heat. Pour hot blueberry sauce over polenta and top with banana slices.

After preparing for your breakfast, you can now start to prepare the **Banana-Peanut Butter Mug Muffins** for your after snacks. First, Spray 3 large mugs with nonstick cooking spray. In a medium bowl, combine the banana, egg whites, oats, peanut butter, vanilla, and cinnamon. Mix well, then fold in the chocolate chips (if using). Divide the batter equally among the 3 mugs. Microwave each mug on high for 2 minutes, or until the muffin is cooked through and the top is firm to the touch. Remove from the microwave. Free the sides of the muffins from the mugs with a butter knife, and turn the mugs upside down to shake onto a plate. Let cool. Into each of 3 airtight storage containers, place 1 muffin and seal. Store the airtight containers in the refrigerator for up to 1 week.

Next is the **Chickpea And Baby Spinach Salad** for your lunch. First, In a large bowl, combine the spinach, chickpeas, mushrooms, tomato, and avocado. Add the salt, pepper, and lemon juice. Mix thoroughly so all the flavors combine and the avocado is mixed in well. Top with the seeds (if using). Enjoy immediately or store in a reusable container in the refrigerator for up to 5 days.

Next, you can now prepare for the **Tangy Kale Salad** for your dinner. In a large bowl, massage the kale with the lemon juice and salt for a few minutes, or until the kale softens. Add the rice, quinoa, tomato, and avocado to the bowl and mix well. Serve immediately or store in the refrigerator for up to 3 days. Then you can eat your snacks after the dinner.

Finally, you can now prepare on **Sushi Bowl with Vegetable** for your prework-out meal. Blend the mango into a smooth purée using a blender or food processor, and set it aside. Add the tempeh slices and the peanut butter to an airtight container. Close the lid and shake well until the tempeh slices are evenly covered with the peanut butter. Preheat the oven to 375°F (190°C) and line a baking sheet with parchment paper. Transfer the tempeh slices onto the baking sheet and bake for about 15 minutes or until the tempeh is browned and crispy. Divide the black beans, quinoa, mango purée and tempeh slices between two bowls, serve with the optional toppings and enjoy.

Bulking Meal Plan-2 (Calorie Goal: 3000-3500)

Day	Breakfast	Snack/Dessert	Lunch	Dinner	Snack/Dessert	Preworkout Meal
1	Eggs Benedict with Hollandaise-Mustard Sauce calories: 575 | fat: 24.1g | carbs: 62.2g | protein: 33.4g	Quick Lemon Drop Energy Balls calories: 265 | fat: 13.7g | carbs: 35.2g | protein: 5.4g	Chicken Breast Burrito Bowl calories: 675 | fat: 14.7g | carbs: 47.1g | protein: 90.2g	Lemony Tuna Nicoise Salad calories: 667 | fat: 35.8g | carbs: 45.8g | protein: 46.2g	Quick Lemon Drop Energy Balls calories: 265 | fat: 13.7g | carbs: 35.2g | protein: 5.4g	Banana, Raisins, and Oats Smoothie calories: 706 | fat: 21.2g | carbs: 102.8g | protein: 33.6g
2	Eggs Benedict with Hollandaise-Mustard Sauce calories: 575 | fat: 24.1g | carbs: 62.2g | protein: 33.4g	Quick Lemon Drop Energy Balls calories: 265 | fat: 13.7g | carbs: 35.2g | protein: 5.4g	Chicken Breast Burrito Bowl calories: 675 | fat: 14.7g | carbs: 47.1g | protein: 90.2g	Lemony Tuna Nicoise Salad calories: 667 | fat: 35.8g | carbs: 45.8g | protein: 46.2g	Quick Lemon Drop Energy Balls calories: 265 | fat: 13.7g | carbs: 35.2g | protein: 5.4g	Banana, Raisins, and Oats Smoothie calories: 706 | fat: 21.2g | carbs: 102.8g | protein: 33.6g
3	Eggs Benedict with Hollandaise-Mustard Sauce calories: 575 | fat: 24.1g | carbs: 62.2g | protein: 33.4g	Quick Lemon Drop Energy Balls calories: 265 | fat: 13.7g | carbs: 35.2g | protein: 5.4g	Chicken Breast Burrito Bowl calories: 675 | fat: 14.7g | carbs: 47.1g | protein: 90.2g	Lemony Tuna Nicoise Salad calories: 667 | fat: 35.8g | carbs: 45.8g | protein: 46.2g	Quick Lemon Drop Energy Balls calories: 265 | fat: 13.7g | carbs: 35.2g | protein: 5.4g	Banana, Raisins, and Oats Smoothie calories: 706 | fat: 21.2g | carbs: 102.8g | protein: 33.6g
4	Eggs Benedict with Hollandaise-Mustard Sauce calories: 575 | fat: 24.1g | carbs: 62.2g | protein: 33.4g	Quick Lemon Drop Energy Balls calories: 265 | fat: 13.7g | carbs: 35.2g | protein: 5.4g	Chicken Breast Burrito Bowl calories: 675 | fat: 14.7g | carbs: 47.1g | protein: 90.2g	Lemony Tuna Nicoise Salad calories: 667 | fat: 35.8g | carbs: 45.8g | protein: 46.2g	Quick Lemon Drop Energy Balls calories: 265 | fat: 13.7g | carbs: 35.2g | protein: 5.4g	Banana, Raisins, and Oats Smoothie calories: 706 | fat: 21.2g | carbs: 102.8g | protein: 33.6g
5	Eggs Benedict with Hollandaise-Mustard Sauce calories: 575 | fat: 24.1g | carbs: 62.2g | protein: 33.4g	Quick Lemon Drop Energy Balls calories: 265 | fat: 13.7g | carbs: 35.2g | protein: 5.4g	Chicken Breast Burrito Bowl calories: 675 | fat: 14.7g | carbs: 47.1g | protein: 90.2g	Lemony Tuna Nicoise Salad calories: 667 | fat: 35.8g | carbs: 45.8g | protein: 46.2g	Quick Lemon Drop Energy Balls calories: 265 | fat: 13.7g | carbs: 35.2g | protein: 5.4g	Banana, Raisins, and Oats Smoothie calories: 706 | fat: 21.2g | carbs: 102.8g | protein: 33.6g

Day	Breakfast	Snack/Dessert	Lunch	Dinner	Snack/Dessert	Preworkout Meal
6	Eggs Benedict with Hollandaise-Mustard Sauce calories: 575 | fat: 24.1g | carbs: 62.2g | protein: 33.4g	Quick Lemon Drop Energy Balls calories: 265 | fat: 13.7g | carbs: 35.2g | protein: 5.4g	Chicken Breast Burrito Bowl calories: 675 | fat: 14.7g | carbs: 47.1g | protein: 90.2g	Lemony Tuna Nicoise Salad calories: 667 | fat: 35.8g | carbs: 45.8g | protein: 46.2g	Quick Lemon Drop Energy Balls calories: 265 | fat: 13.7g | carbs: 35.2g | protein: 5.4g	Banana, Raisins, and Oats Smoothie calories: 706 | fat: 21.2g | carbs: 102.8g | protein: 33.6g
7	Eggs Benedict with Hollandaise-Mustard Sauce calories: 575 | fat: 24.1g | carbs: 62.2g | protein: 33.4g	Quick Lemon Drop Energy Balls calories: 265 | fat: 13.7g | carbs: 35.2g | protein: 5.4g	Lemony Tuna Nicoise Salad calories: 667 | fat: 35.8g | carbs: 45.8g | protein: 46.2g	Lemony Tuna Nicoise Salad calories: 667 | fat: 35.8g | carbs: 45.8g | protein: 46.2g	Quick Lemon Drop Energy Balls calories: 265 | fat: 13.7g | carbs: 35.2g | protein: 5.4g	Banana, Raisins, and Oats Smoothie calories: 706 | fat: 21.2g | carbs: 102.8g | protein: 33.6g

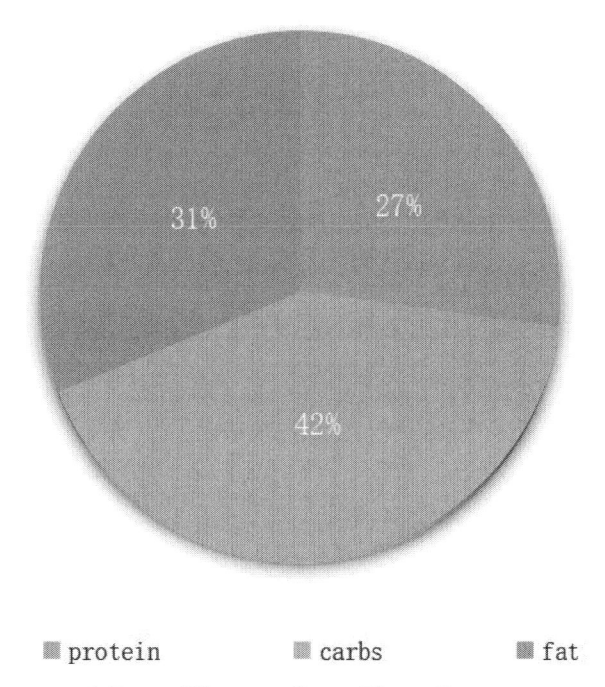

5 Prep Plan to Start Your Journey
Bulking Meal Plan-1 (Calorie Goal: 3000-3500)

Prep Plan #2

This is a fantastic starter plan with 1 breakfast, 1 lunch, 1 dinner, 1 preworkout meal, and 2 snacks that will keep you covered up to 7 days of eating.

Recipe 1 : Eggs Benedict With Hollandaise-Mustard Sauce | Calories: 575 | Fat: 24.1g | Carbs: 62.2g | Protein: 33.4g

Prep time: 15 minutes | Cook time: 10 minutes | Serves 1

For the Hollandaise-Mustard Sauce:

1 tablespoon light mayonnaise
½ tablespoon water
1 teaspoon whole-grain mustard
½ teaspoon lemon juice
Pinch of ground cayenne pepper

For the Eggs Benedict:

1 tablespoon white vinegar
½ tablespoon extra-virgin olive oil
1 ounce (28 g) Canadian bacon, diced
½ small onion, thinly sliced
4 cups chopped kale (stems removed)
Ground black pepper, to taste
1 whole-grain English muffin, split
2 tomato slices
2 large eggs

Steps:

1. To make the sauce, into a blender or food processor, add mayonnaise, water, mustard, lemon juice, and cayenne. Process until smooth. Transfer the sauce to a small bowl and reserve.
2. To prepare eggs, add about 3 inches of water into a large skillet. Pour in vinegar and bring to a low simmer over medium heat.
3. Meanwhile, warm oil in medium nonstick skillet over medium-high heat. Sauté the Canadian bacon and onion, stirring constantly, until golden brown, about 4 minutes. Remove the pan from heat and toss in kale. Stir until the greens wilt, about 2 minutes, and season with pepper.
4. Toast English muffin halves until lightly golden. Place onto a plate, layering a tomato slice and kale mixture onto each half. Place the pan in the oven to stay warm (keep the oven turned off).
5. Crack eggs into a mug one by one and slip them into the simmering water. Cook approximately 3 to 5 minutes, carefully removing the eggs with a slotted spoon once they reach desired doneness. Top poached eggs onto the prepared English muffins and drizzle with Hollandaise-style sauce. Serve.

Recipe 2 : Quick Lemon Drop Energy Balls | Calories: 265 | Fat: 13.7g | Carbs: 35.2g | Protein: 5.4g

Prep time: 5 minutes | Cook time: 0 minutes | Makes 12 to 14 energy balls

Nonstick cooking spray
1¼ cups raw cashews
10 Medjool dates, pitted
½ cup shredded, unsweetened coconut, divided
1 tablespoon coconut oil
Zest of 1 lemon
1 tablespoon freshly squeezed lemon juice

Steps:

1. In a food processor, process the cashews until roughly ground so that only tiny pieces remain. Remove from the food processor and set aside.
2. In the food processor, combine the dates, ¼ cup of coconut, and the coconut oil and lemon zest, and process until the dates are mashed.
3. Add the ground cashews and lemon juice, and process until a ball of dough starts to form.
4. Remove the dough from the food processor and, with your hands, roll into 1½-inch balls.
5. In a shallow bowl, place the remaining ¼ cup of coconut and roll the balls in the shredded coconut until well covered.
6. Into each of 6 resealable storage bags (freezer bags if freezing), place 2 energy balls, and seal.
7. Store the airtight bags in the refrigerator for up to 2 weeks.
8. Store the airtight bags in the freezer for up to 3 months.

Recipe 3 : Chicken Breast Burrito Bowl | Calories: 721 | Fat: 20.2g | Carbs: 123.1g | Protein: 27.2g

Prep time: 15 minutes | Cook time: 22 minutes | Serves 3

Nonstick cooking spray
3 (8-ounce / 227-g) boneless, skinless chicken breasts
1 tablespoon fresh chopped garlic
1 tablespoon ground cumin
1½ teaspoons chili powder
1 tablespoon paprika
Sea salt, to taste
Freshly ground black pepper, to taste
1½ cups cooked rice, divided
1½ cups cooked black beans, divided
¾ cup salsa or pico de gallo, divided
6 tablespoons guacamole, divided
6 tablespoons reduced-fat sour cream (5%) or nonfat Greek yogurt, divided
3 teaspoons minced jalapeño, divided
3 scallions, green parts only, sliced, divided
1½ tablespoons fresh chopped cilantro, divided

Steps:
1. Preheat the oven to 400°F (205°C). Spray an 8-by-10-inch baking dish with cooking spray.
2. Rub the chicken breasts with the garlic, cumin, chili powder, and paprika, and season with salt and pepper.
3. Place the seasoned chicken in the baking dish and bake for 22 to 26 minutes, or until the chicken reaches an internal temperature of 165°F (74°C) and the juices run clear. Allow it to rest briefly, then cut into half-inch-thick strips. Let cool.
4. Into each of 3 airtight storage containers, place ½ cup of rice, ½ cup of black beans, and 1 chicken breast. Top each with ¼ cup of salsa, 2 tablespoons of guacamole, 2 tablespoons of sour cream, 1 teaspoon of jalapeño, 1 scallion, and ½ tablespoon of cilantro, and seal.
5. Store the airtight containers in the refrigerator for up to 5 days. To reheat, microwave uncovered on high for 1 to 2 minutes.

Recipe 4 : Lemony Tuna Nicoise Salad | Calories: 667 | Fat: 35.8g | Carbs: 45.8g | Protein: 46.2g

Prep time: 10 minutes | Cook time: 0 minutes | Serves 3

¼ cup freshly squeezed lemon juice
¾ cup extra-virgin olive oil
6 fresh basil leaves, minced
Sea salt, to taste
Freshly ground black pepper, to taste
1½ cups cherry or grape tomatoes, halved
8 ounces (227 g) waxy potatoes, cooked and sliced
½ cup frozen shelled edamame, thawed
3 hard-boiled eggs, peeled and cut into wedges
3 canned artichoke hearts, halved
2 (6-ounce / 170-g) cans flaked or solid tuna, in water
¼ cup pitted kalamata olives

Steps:
1. In a small bowl, whisk together the lemon juice, olive oil, basil, salt, and pepper. Set aside.
2. In a medium bowl, toss the tomatoes, potatoes, edamame, eggs, artichoke hearts, tuna, and olives.
3. Divide the salad evenly among 3 airtight storage containers. Drizzle each salad with 2 tablespoons of the dressing. Store any remaining dressing in a separate airtight container in the refrigerator for up to 1 week.
4. Store the airtight containers in the refrigerator for up to 5 days.

Recipe 4 : Banana, Raisins, and Oats Smoothie | Calories: 667 | Fat: 35.8g | Carbs: 45.8g | Protein: 46.2g

Prep time: 5 minutes | Cook time: 0 minutes | Serves 1

1 frozen banana, sliced
1 cup vanilla almond milk
¼ cup old-fashioned oats
¼ cup raisins
1 tablespoon flaxseed meal
¼ teaspoon cinnamon
3 tablespoons vanilla protein powder

Steps:
1. Add all the ingredients to a blender and blend until very smooth.
2. Serve immediately.

Shopping Lists
Dairy
- Eggs
- Sour Cream / non-fat Greek Yogurt
- Almond Milk
- Oats

Meats and Seafoods
- Chicken
- Tuna

Fruits, Vegetables, Spices & Herbs
- Mayonnaise
- Mustard
- Lemon
- Cayenne Pepper
- White Vinegar
- Extra-virgin olive oil
- Onion
- Kale
- Black Pepper
- Muffin
- Tomato
- Cashews
- Medjool dates
- Coconut
- Coconut oil
- Garlic
- Cumin
- Paprika
- Salk
- Rice
- Black Beans
- Salsa/ Pico de Gallo
- Guacamole
- Jalapeño
- Scallions
- Cilantro
- Basil Leaves
- Cherry/ grape Tomatoes
- Edame
- Artichoke Hearts
- Kalamata Olives
- Banana
- Raisins
- Flaxseed
- Cinnamon
- Vanilla Protein Powder

Meal Prep Plan

Start your breakfast with **Eggs Benedict With Hollandaise-Mustard Sauce**. First, to make the sauce, into a blender or food processor, add mayonnaise, water, mustard, lemon juice, and cayenne. Process until smooth. Transfer the sauce to a small bowl and reserve. To prepare eggs, add about 3 inches of water into a large skillet. Pour in vinegar and bring to a low simmer over medium heat. Meanwhile, warm oil in medium nonstick skillet over medium-high heat. Sauté the Canadian bacon and onion, stirring constantly, until golden brown, about 4 minutes. Remove the pan from heat and toss in kale. Stir until the greens wilt, about 2 minutes, and season with pepper. Toast English muffin halves until lightly golden. Place onto a plate, layering a tomato slice and kale mixture onto each half. Place the pan in the oven to stay warm (keep the oven turned off). Crack eggs into a mug one by one and slip them into the simmering water. Cook approximately 3 to 5 minutes, carefully removing the eggs with a slotted spoon once they reach desired doneness. Top poached eggs onto the prepared English muffins and drizzle with Hollandaise-style sauce.

After preparing for your breakfast, you can now start to prepare the **Quick Lemon Drop Energy Balls** for your after snacks. First, in a food processor, process the cashews until roughly ground so that only tiny pieces remain. Remove from the food processor and set aside. In the food processor, combine the dates, ¼ cup of coconut, and the coconut oil and lemon zest, and process until the dates are mashed. Add the ground cashews and lemon juice, and process until a ball of dough starts to form. Remove the dough from the food processor and, with your hands, roll into 1½-inch balls. In a shallow bowl, place the remaining ¼ cup of coconut and roll the balls in the shredded coconut until well covered. Into each of 6 resealable storage bags (freezer bags if freezing), place 2 energy balls, and seal. Store the airtight bags in the refrigerator for up to 2 weeks. Store the airtight bags in the freezer for up to 3 months.

Next is the **Chicken Breat Burrito Bowl** for your lunch. First, Preheat the oven to 400°F (205°C). Spray an 8-by-10-inch baking dish with cooking spray. Rub the chicken breasts with the garlic, cumin, chili powder, and paprika, and season with salt and pepper. Place the seasoned chicken in the baking dish and bake for 22 to 26 minutes, or until the chicken reaches an internal temperature of 165°F (74°C) and the juices run clear. Allow it to rest briefly, then cut into half-inch-thick strips. Let cool. Into each of 3 airtight storage containers, place ½ cup of rice, ½ cup of black beans, and 1 chicken breast. Top each with ¼ cup of salsa, 2 tablespoons of guacamole, 2 tablespoons of sour cream, 1 teaspoon of jalapeño, 1 scallion, and ½ tablespoon of cilantro, and seal. Store the airtight containers in the refrigerator for up to 5 days. To reheat, microwave uncovered on high for 1 to 2 minutes.

Next, you can now prepare for the **Lemony Tuna Nicoise Salad** for your dinner. In a small bowl, whisk together the lemon juice, olive oil, basil, salt, and pepper. Set aside. In a medium bowl, toss the tomatoes, potatoes, edamame, eggs, artichoke hearts, tuna, and olives. Divide the salad evenly among 3 airtight storage containers. Drizzle each salad with 2 tablespoons of the dressing. Store any remaining dressing in a separate airtight container in the refrigerator for up to 1 week. Store the airtight containers in the refrigerator for up to 5 days. Then you can eat your snacks after the dinner.

Finally, you can now prepare on **Banana, Raisins, and Oats Smoothie** for your pre-work-out meal. Just add all the ingredients to a blender and blend until very smooth and serve immediately.

Bulking Meal Plan-3 (Calorie Goal: 2500-3000)

Day	Breakfast	Snack/Dessert	Lunch	Dinner	Snack/Dessert	Preworkout Meal
1	Cinnamon Sweet Potato Pancakes calories: 506 | fat: 11.2g | carbs: 63.1g | protein: 38.9g	Beef Cheeseburger Bites calories: 242 | fat: 12.8g | carbs: 3.1g | protein: 28.4g	Chicken Breast with Tomato-Corn Salad calories: 603 | fat: 41.9g | carbs: 32.2g | protein: 32.1g	Teriyaki Sweet Potato and Broccoli Bowl calories: 550 | fat: 24.1g | carbs: 51.2g | protein: 32.3g	Beef Cheeseburger Bites calories: 242 | fat: 12.8g | carbs: 3.1g | protein: 28.4g	Sushi Bowl with Vegetable calories: 665 | fat: 32.1g | carbs: 80.8g | protein: 21.3g
2	Cinnamon Sweet Potato Pancakes calories: 506 | fat: 11.2g | carbs: 63.1g | protein: 38.9g	Beef Cheeseburger Bites calories: 242 | fat: 12.8g | carbs: 3.1g | protein: 28.4g	Chicken Breast with Tomato-Corn Salad calories: 603 | fat: 41.9g | carbs: 32.2g | protein: 32.1g	Teriyaki Sweet Potato and Broccoli Bowl calories: 550 | fat: 24.1g | carbs: 51.2g | protein: 32.3g	Beef Cheeseburger Bites calories: 242 | fat: 12.8g | carbs: 3.1g | protein: 28.4g	Sushi Bowl with Vegetable calories: 665 | fat: 32.1g | carbs: 80.8g | protein: 21.3g
3	Cinnamon Sweet Potato Pancakes calories: 506 | fat: 11.2g | carbs: 63.1g | protein: 38.9g	Beef Cheeseburger Bites calories: 242 | fat: 12.8g | carbs: 3.1g | protein: 28.4g	Chicken Breast with Tomato-Corn Salad calories: 603 | fat: 41.9g | carbs: 32.2g | protein: 32.1g	Teriyaki Sweet Potato and Broccoli Bowl calories: 550 | fat: 24.1g | carbs: 51.2g | protein: 32.3g	Beef Cheeseburger Bites calories: 242 | fat: 12.8g | carbs: 3.1g | protein: 28.4g	Sushi Bowl with Vegetable calories: 665 | fat: 32.1g | carbs: 80.8g | protein: 21.3g
4	Cinnamon Sweet Potato Pancakes calories: 506 | fat: 11.2g | carbs: 63.1g | protein: 38.9g	Beef Cheeseburger Bites calories: 242 | fat: 12.8g | carbs: 3.1g | protein: 28.4g	Chicken Breast with Tomato-Corn Salad calories: 603 | fat: 41.9g | carbs: 32.2g | protein: 32.1g	Teriyaki Sweet Potato and Broccoli Bowl calories: 550 | fat: 24.1g | carbs: 51.2g | protein: 32.3g	Beef Cheeseburger Bites calories: 242 | fat: 12.8g | carbs: 3.1g | protein: 28.4g	Sushi Bowl with Vegetable calories: 665 | fat: 32.1g | carbs: 80.8g | protein: 21.3g
5	Cinnamon Sweet Potato Pancakes calories: 506 | fat: 11.2g | carbs: 63.1g | protein: 38.9g	Beef Cheeseburger Bites calories: 242 | fat: 12.8g | carbs: 3.1g | protein: 28.4g	Chicken Breast with Tomato-Corn Salad calories: 603 | fat: 41.9g | carbs: 32.2g | protein: 32.1g	Teriyaki Sweet Potato and Broccoli Bowl calories: 550 | fat: 24.1g | carbs: 51.2g | protein: 32.3g	Beef Cheeseburger Bites calories: 242 | fat: 12.8g | carbs: 3.1g | protein: 28.4g	Sushi Bowl with Vegetable calories: 665 | fat: 32.1g | carbs: 80.8g | protein: 21.3g
6	Cinnamon Sweet Potato Pancakes calories: 506 | fat: 11.2g | carbs: 63.1g | protein: 38.9g	Beef Cheeseburger Bites calories: 242 | fat: 12.8g | carbs: 3.1g | protein: 28.4g	Chicken Breast with Tomato-Corn Salad calories: 603 | fat: 41.9g | carbs: 32.2g | protein: 32.1g	Teriyaki Sweet Potato and Broccoli Bowl calories: 550 | fat: 24.1g | carbs: 51.2g | protein: 32.3g	Beef Cheeseburger Bites calories: 242 | fat: 12.8g | carbs: 3.1g | protein: 28.4g	Sushi Bowl with Vegetable calories: 665 | fat: 32.1g | carbs: 80.8g | protein: 21.3g
7	Cinnamon Sweet Potato Pancakes calories: 506 | fat: 11.2g | carbs: 63.1g | protein: 38.9g	Beef Cheeseburger Bites calories: 242 | fat: 12.8g | carbs: 3.1g | protein: 28.4g	Chicken Breast with Tomato-Corn Salad calories: 603 | fat: 41.9g | carbs: 32.2g | protein: 32.1g	Chicken Breast with Tomato-Corn Salad calories: 603 | fat: 41.9g | carbs: 32.2g | protein: 32.1g	Beef Cheeseburger Bites calories: 242 | fat: 12.8g | carbs: 3.1g | protein: 28.4g	Sushi Bowl with Vegetable calories: 665 | fat: 32.1g | carbs: 80.8g | protein: 21.3g

■ protein   ■ carbs   ■ fat

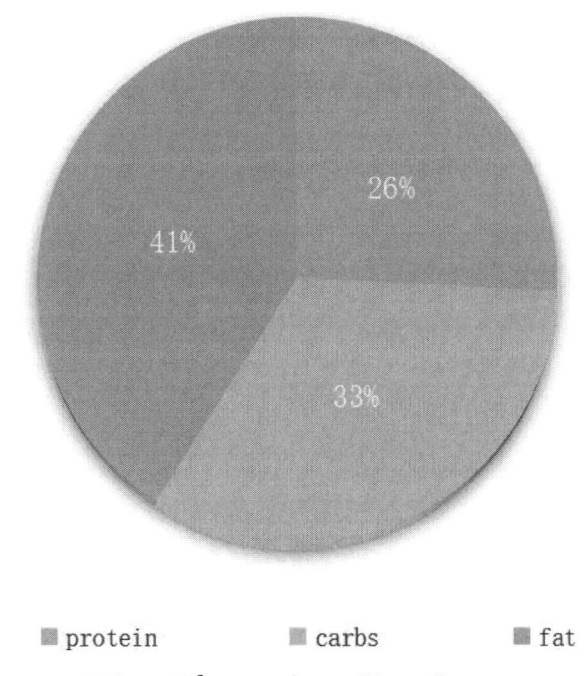

5 Prep Plan to Start Your Journey
Bulking Meal Plan-1 (Calorie Goal: 2500-3000)

Prep Plan #3

This is a fantastic starter plan with 1 breakfast, 1 lunch, 1 dinner, 1 preworkout meal, and 2 snacks that will keep you covered up to 7 days of eating.

Recipe 1 : Cinnamon Sweet Potato Pancakes | Calories: 506 | Fat: 11.2g | Carbs: 63.1g | Protein: 38.9g

Prep time: 10 minutes | Cook time: 6 minutes | Serves 1

1 (5-ounce / 142-g) medium sweet potato
½ cup old-fashioned oats
1 large egg
4 egg whites or ¾ cup liquid egg white substitute
½ teaspoon vanilla extract
½ teaspoon ground cinnamon
¼ cup 2% plain yogurt

Steps:
1. Prick sweet potato several times with a fork. Wrap potato in a wet paper towel and microwave for 5 minutes on high power. Carefully run potato under cool water and then remove its skin with a knife.
2. Add oats into a blender or a food processor and process until oats are powder-like. Transfer to a medium bowl and reserve.
3. Add the sweet potato into the blender or food processor, puréeing until smooth. Place into the bowl with oats. Stir in whole egg, egg whites, vanilla, cinnamon, and yogurt. Mix well until the batter is smooth.
4. Coat a medium nonstick pan with cooking spray and warm over medium-low heat.
5. Spoon half the batter into the pan and cook until golden brown, about 1 to 2 minutes. Use a spatula to flip the pancake and cook again until golden brown and firm, about another 30 to 60 seconds. Transfer the pancake to a plate.
6. Reapply cooking spray to the pan and repeat with remaining batter. Serve.

Recipe 2 : Beef Cheeseburger Bites | Calories: 242 | Fat: 12.8g | Carbs: 3.1g | Protein: 28.4g

Prep time: 10 minutes | Cook time: 20 minutes | Serves 4

1 pound (454 g) lean ground sirloin
2 teaspoons coconut flour
2 large eggs
2 teaspoons no-sugar-added ketchup
2 teaspoons spicy brown mustard
½ cup low-fat shredded Mozzarella cheese
¼ cup diced white onion

Steps:

1. Preheat oven to 350°F (177°C). Spray an 8-cup muffin tin with non-stick cooking spray.
2. In a large bowl, combine the ground sirloin, coconut flour, eggs, ketchup, mustard, Mozzarella cheese, and onion. Mix the ingredients until just incorporated. (Do not over mix, as the burgers can become tough.)
3. Spoon equal amounts of the mixture into the muffin cups. Bake for 20 minutes, or until the internal temperature reaches 160°F (71°C). Serve hot.

Recipe 3 : Chicken Breast with Tomato-Corn Salad | Calories: 603 | Fat: 41.9g | Carbs: 32.2g | Protein: 32.1g

Prep time: 15 minutes | Cook time: 12 minutes | Serves 4

For the Chicken Strips:

½ cup shredded, unsweetened coconut
1 cup cornflakes, crushed
1 tablespoon ranch seasoning
1 cup unsweetened coconut or almond milk
1 tablespoon apple cider vinegar
3 (8-ounce / 227-g) boneless, skinless chicken breasts, cut lengthwise into strips

For the Tomato-Corn Salad:

1½ tablespoons extra-virgin olive oil
1 tablespoon freshly squeezed lemon or lime juice
½ teaspoon dried basil
Sea salt, to taste
Freshly ground black pepper, to taste
1½ cups frozen corn kernels, thawed
¾ cup cherry or grape tomatoes, quartered
¼ cup chopped red onion

Steps:

Make the Chicken Strips

1. Preheat the oven to 450°F (235°C). Line a large baking sheet with parchment paper.
2. In a medium bowl, mix together the shredded coconut, cornflakes, and ranch seasoning.
3. In another medium bowl, whisk together the coconut milk and the apple cider vinegar and let sit for 5 to 10 minutes.
4. Dip the chicken strips first into the "buttermilk," then into the cornflake mixture, and lay out on the baking sheet, spacing out the chicken strips so that none overlap or touch.
5. Place in the oven and bake for 12 minutes, or until no longer pink inside (and the chicken reaches an internal temperature of at least 165°F / 74°C). Remove from the oven and let cool.

Make the Tomato-Corn Salad

6. Meanwhile, in a small bowl, whisk together the olive oil, lemon juice, and basil. Season with salt and pepper.
7. In a medium bowl, stir together the corn, tomatoes, and red onion. Pour in the olive oil mixture, and stir to combine
8. Into each of the 4 containers, place a quarter of the salad followed by a quarter of the chicken strips and seal.
9. Store for up to 5 days. Serve cold, or to reheat, microwave the chicken strips on high for 1 to 2 minutes.

Recipe 4 : Teriyaki Sweet Potato and Broccoli Bowl | Calories: 550 | Fat: 24.1g | Carbs: 51.2g | Protein: 32.3g

Prep time: 5 minutes | Cook time: 18 minutes | Serves 2

4 sweet potatoes, cubed
1 (7-ounce / 198-g) pack smoked tofu, cubed
2 cups broccoli florets
¼ cup teriyaki sauce
¼ cup peanut butter
½ cup water

Optional Toppings:
Chili flakes
Shredded coconut
Roasted sesame seeds

Steps:
1. Cook the sweet potato cubes, covered with water, in a medium pot over medium-high heat for about 10 minutes.
2. Add the broccoli florets, and cook for another 3 minutes.
3. Take the pot off the heat, drain the excess water from the broccoli and sweet potatoes and set aside.
4. Put a nonstick deep frying pan over medium-high heat and add the teriyaki sauce, the water and tofu cubes.
5. Keep stirring continuously until everything is cooked, then add the broccoli florets and sweet potato cubes to the frying pan.
6. Cook for about 5 minutes while stirring occasionally.
7. Turn the heat off, leave to cool down for a minute, then drain the excess water.
8. Divide between 2 plates, drizzle half of the peanut butter on top of each plate with the optional toppings and enjoy!

Recipe 5 : Sushi Bowl with Vegetable | Calories: 665 | Fat: 32.1g | Carbs: 80.8g | Protein: 21.3g

Prep time: 15 minutes | Cook time: 0 minutes | Serves 1

1 cup cooked brown rice
1 small avocado, pitted, peeled, and cut into strips
½ cup shelled edamame
½ cup thinly sliced carrots
½ cucumber, cut into thin strips
1 scallion, chopped
½ nori sheet, cut into thin strips

Optional Toppings:
Low-sodium soy sauce
Pickled ginger
Black sesame seeds
Wasabi

Steps:
1. Put the rice in a serving bowl and layer on the avocado, edamame, carrots, cucumber, scallion, and nori. Add your toppings of choice (if using).
2. Serve immediately or store in a reusable container in the refrigerator for up to 5 days.

Shopping Lists

Dairy
- Oats
- Eggs
- Plain Yogurt
- Mozzarella Cheese
- Coconut Milk
- Almond Milk

Meats and Seafoods
- Sirloin
- Tuna
- Chicken

Fruits, Vegetables, Spices & Herbs
- Sweet Potato
- Vanilla Extract
- Cinnamon
- Coconut Flour
- Ketchup
- Mustard
- White Onion
- Unsweetened Coconut
- Cornflakes
- Ranch Seasoning
- Apple Cider Vinegar
- Lemon
- Basil
- Sea Salt
- Black Pepper
- Corn Kernels
- Grape Tomatoes
- Red Onion
- Potatoes
- Tofu
- Broccoli
- Teriyaki Sauce
- Peanut Butter
- Chili Flakes
- Coconut
- Sesame Seeds
- Brown Rice
- Avocado
- Shelled Edamame
- Carrots
- Scallion
- Nori Sheet
- Black Sesame Seeds
- Low Sodium Soy Sauce

Meal Prep Plan

Start your breakfast with **Cinnamon Sweet Potato Pancakes**. First, Prick sweet potato several times with a fork. Wrap potato in a wet paper towel and microwave for 5 minutes on high power. Carefully run potato under cool water and then remove its skin with a knife. Add oats into a blender or a food processor and process until oats are powder-like. Transfer to a medium bowl and reserve. Add the sweet potato into the blender or food processor, puréeing until smooth. Place into the bowl with oats. Stir in whole egg, egg whites, vanilla, cinnamon, and yogurt. Mix well until the batter is smooth. Coat a medium nonstick pan with cooking spray and warm over medium-low heat. Spoon half the batter into the pan and cook until golden brown, about 1 to 2 minutes. Use a spatula to flip the pancake and cook again until golden brown and firm, about another 30 to 60 seconds. Transfer the pancake to a plate. Reapply cooking spray to the pan and repeat with remaining batter.

After preparing for your breakfast, you can now start to prepare the **Beef Cheeseburger Bites** for your after snacks. First, Preheat oven to 350°F (177°C). Spray an 8-cup muffin tin with non-stick cooking spray. In a large bowl, combine the ground sirloin, coconut flour, eggs, ketchup, mustard, Mozzarella cheese, and onion. Mix the ingredients until just incorporated. (Do not over mix, as the burgers can become tough.) Spoon equal amounts of the mixture into the muffin cups. Bake for 20 minutes, or until the internal temperature reaches 160°F (71°C).

Next is the **Chicken Breast with Tomato-Corn Salad** for your lunch. In Making the Chicken Strips, Preheat the oven to 450°F (235°C). Line a large baking sheet with parchment paper. In a medium bowl, mix together the shredded coconut, cornflakes, and ranch seasoning. In another medium bowl, whisk together the coconut milk and the apple cider vinegar and let sit for 5 to 10 minutes. Dip the chicken strips first into the "buttermilk," then into the cornflake mixture, and lay out on the baking sheet, spacing out the chicken strips so that none overlap or touch. Place in the oven and bake for 12 minutes, or until no longer pink inside (and the chicken reaches an internal temperature of at least 165°F / 74°C). Remove from the oven and let cool. Meanwhile, you can already make the Tomato-Corn Salad. In a small bowl, whisk together the olive oil, lemon juice, and basil. Season with salt and pepper. In a medium bowl, stir together the corn, tomatoes, and red onion. Pour in the olive oil mixture, and stir to combine into each of the 4 containers, place a quarter of the salad followed by a quarter of the chicken strips and seal. Store for up to 5 days. Serve cold, or to reheat, microwave the chicken strips on high for 1 to 2 minutes.

Next, you can now prepare for the **Teriyaki Sweet Potato and Broccoli Bowl** for your dinner. Cook the sweet potato cubes, covered with water, in a medium pot over medium-high heat for about 10 minutes. Add the broccoli florets, and cook for another 3 minutes. Take the pot off the heat, drain the excess water from the broccoli and sweet potatoes and set aside. Put a nonstick deep-frying pan over medium-high heat and add the teriyaki sauce, the water and tofu cubes. Keep stirring continuously until everything is cooked, then add the broccoli florets and sweet potato cubes to the frying pan. Cook for about 5 minutes while stirring occasionally. Turn the heat off, leave to cool down for a minute, then drain the excess water. Divide between 2 plates, drizzle half of the peanut butter on top of each plate with the optional toppingsThen you can eat your snacks after the dinner.

Finally, you can now prepare on **Sushi Bowl with Vegetable** for your prework-out meal. Put the rice in a serving bowl and layer on the avocado, edamame, carrots, cucumber, scallion, and nori. Add your toppings of choice (if using). Serve immediately or store in a reusable container in the refrigerator for up to 5 days.

Cutting Meal Plan-1 (Calorie Goal: 2000-2500)

Day	Breakfast	Snack/Dessert	Lunch	Dinner	Snack/Dessert	Preworkout Meal
1	Banana, Blueberry, and Peach Smoothie Bowl calories: 458 | fat: 19.2g | carbs: 66.1g | protein: 24.9g	Simple Dough Oats calories: 317 | fat: 11.4g | carbs: 22.8g | protein: 30.8g	Stir Fried Pork and Bok Choy Noodle calories: 413 | fat: 7.9g | carbs: 53.7g | protein: 28.1g	Coconut-Crusted Chicken Breast Salad calories: 454 | fat: 20.6g | carbs: 36.1g | protein: 31.5g	Simple Dough Oats calories: 317 | fat: 11.4g | carbs: 22.8g | protein: 30.8g	Veggie Quinoa Bowl with Basil Pesto calories: 536 | fat: 22.8g | carbs: 9.2g | protein: 20.2g
2	Banana, Blueberry, and Peach Smoothie Bowl calories: 458 | fat: 19.2g | carbs: 66.1g | protein: 24.9g	Simple Dough Oats calories: 317 | fat: 11.4g | carbs: 22.8g | protein: 30.8g	Stir Fried Pork and Bok Choy Noodle calories: 413 | fat: 7.9g | carbs: 53.7g | protein: 28.1g	Coconut-Crusted Chicken Breast Salad calories: 454 | fat: 20.6g | carbs: 36.1g | protein: 31.5g	Simple Dough Oats calories: 317 | fat: 11.4g | carbs: 22.8g | protein: 30.8g	Veggie Quinoa Bowl with Basil Pesto calories: 536 | fat: 22.8g | carbs: 9.2g | protein: 20.2g
3	Banana, Blueberry, and Peach Smoothie Bowl calories: 458 | fat: 19.2g | carbs: 66.1g | protein: 24.9g	Simple Dough Oats calories: 317 | fat: 11.4g | carbs: 22.8g | protein: 30.8g	Stir Fried Pork and Bok Choy Noodle calories: 413 | fat: 7.9g | carbs: 53.7g | protein: 28.1g	Coconut-Crusted Chicken Breast Salad calories: 454 | fat: 20.6g | carbs: 36.1g | protein: 31.5g	Simple Dough Oats calories: 317 | fat: 11.4g | carbs: 22.8g | protein: 30.8g	Veggie Quinoa Bowl with Basil Pesto calories: 536 | fat: 22.8g | carbs: 9.2g | protein: 20.2g
4	Banana, Blueberry, and Peach Smoothie Bowl calories: 458 | fat: 19.2g | carbs: 66.1g | protein: 24.9g	Simple Dough Oats calories: 317 | fat: 11.4g | carbs: 22.8g | protein: 30.8g	Stir Fried Pork and Bok Choy Noodle calories: 413 | fat: 7.9g | carbs: 53.7g | protein: 28.1g	Coconut-Crusted Chicken Breast Salad calories: 454 | fat: 20.6g | carbs: 36.1g | protein: 31.5g	Simple Dough Oats calories: 317 | fat: 11.4g | carbs: 22.8g | protein: 30.8g	Veggie Quinoa Bowl with Basil Pesto calories: 536 | fat: 22.8g | carbs: 9.2g | protein: 20.2g
5	Banana, Blueberry, and Peach Smoothie Bowl calories: 458 | fat: 19.2g | carbs: 66.1g | protein: 24.9g	Simple Dough Oats calories: 317 | fat: 11.4g | carbs: 22.8g | protein: 30.8g	Stir Fried Pork and Bok Choy Noodle calories: 413 | fat: 7.9g | carbs: 53.7g | protein: 28.1g	Coconut-Crusted Chicken Breast Salad calories: 454 | fat: 20.6g | carbs: 36.1g | protein: 31.5g	Simple Dough Oats calories: 317 | fat: 11.4g | carbs: 22.8g | protein: 30.8g	Veggie Quinoa Bowl with Basil Pesto calories: 536 | fat: 22.8g | carbs: 9.2g | protein: 20.2g

Day	Breakfast	Snack/Dessert	Lunch	Dinner	Snack/Dessert	Preworkout Meal
6	Banana, Blueberry, and Peach Smoothie Bowl calories: 458 | fat: 19.2g | carbs: 66.1g | protein: 24.9g	Simple Dough Oats calories: 317 | fat: 11.4g | carbs: 22.8g | protein: 30.8g	Stir Fried Pork and Bok Choy Noodle calories: 413 | fat: 7.9g | carbs: 53.7g | protein: 28.1g	Coconut-Crusted Chicken Breast Salad calories: 454 | fat: 20.6g | carbs: 36.1g | protein: 31.5g	Simple Dough Oats calories: 317 | fat: 11.4g | carbs: 22.8g | protein: 30.8g	Veggie Quinoa Bowl with Basil Pesto calories: 536 | fat: 22.8g | carbs: 9.2g | protein: 20.2g
7	Banana, Blueberry, and Peach Smoothie Bowl calories: 458 | fat: 19.2g | carbs: 66.1g | protein: 24.9g	Simple Dough Oats calories: 317 | fat: 11.4g | carbs: 22.8g | protein: 30.8g	Stir Fried Pork and Bok Choy Noodle calories: 413 | fat: 7.9g | carbs: 53.7g | protein: 28.1g	Stir Fried Pork and Bok Choy Noodle calories: 413 | fat: 7.9g | carbs: 53.7g | protein: 28.1g	Simple Dough Oats calories: 317 | fat: 11.4g | carbs: 22.8g | protein: 30.8g	Veggie Quinoa Bowl with Basil Pesto calories: 536 | fat: 22.8g | carbs: 9.2g | protein: 20.2g

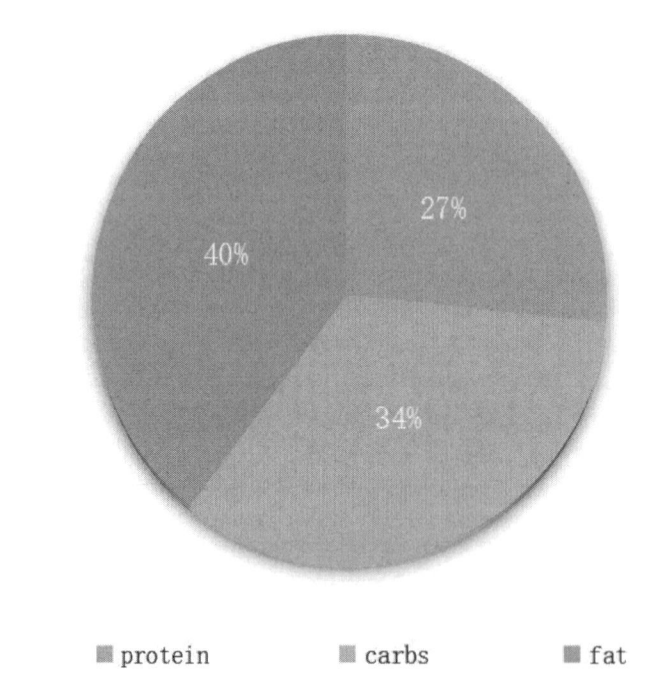

5 Prep Plan to Start Your Journey
Cutting Meal Plan Meal Plan-1 (Calorie Goal: 2000-2500)

66 • Chapter 6 Step-By-Step Meal Plans

Prep Plan #4

This is a fantastic starter plan with 1 breakfast, 1 lunch, 1 dinner, 1 preworkout meal, and 2 snacks that will keep you covered up to 7 days of eating.

Recipe 1 : Banana, Blueberry, and Peach Smoothie Bowl | Calories: 458 | Fat: 19.2g | Carbs: 66.1g | Protein: 24.9g

Prep time: 10 minutes | Cook time: 0 minutes | Serves 4

For the Smoothie Packs:

4 fresh or frozen bananas, chopped, divided
4 cups frozen blueberries, divided
2 cups frozen peaches, divided
28 ice cubes, divided
4 scoops vegan vanilla protein powder, divided
4 tablespoons almond butter, divided
4 tablespoons ground flaxseed, divided
Freshly grated ginger, for topping

For the Smoothies:

4 cups unsweetened vanilla coconut or almond milk, divided
½ lemon, cut into wedges

Steps:

Make the Smoothie Packs

1. In each of 4 resealable freezer bags, place 1 banana, 1 cup of blueberries, ½ cup of peaches, 7 ice cubes, 1 scoop of protein powder, 1 tablespoon of almond butter, 1 tablespoon of flaxseed, and a pinch of grated ginger. Lay the bags flat and remove as much air as possible before sealing. Store in the freezer until ready to use.

Make a Smoothie

2. In a blender, combine 1 cup of almond milk and a squeeze of lemon juice, followed by the contents of 1 smoothie pack, and blend until smooth.
3. Store the airtight bags in the freezer for up to 3 months.

Recipe 2 : Simple Dough Oats | Calories: 317 | Fat: 11.4g | Carbs: 22.8g | Protein: 30.8g

Prep time: 5 minutes | Cook time: 0 minutes | Serves 2

½ cup quick or rolled oats
1 tablespoon flaxseeds
2 scoops vanilla flavor vegan protein powder
1 cup unsweetened almond milk
1 tablespoon peanut butter
1 tablespoon carob chips (optional)
1 tablespoon maple syrup (optional)

Steps:

1. Take a lidded bowl or jar and add the oats, flaxseed, protein powder, and almond milk.
2. Stir until everything is thoroughly combined and the mixture looks runny; if not, add a little more almond milk.
3. Blend in the peanut butter with a spoon until everything is mixed well.
4. Place or close the lid on the bowl or jar and transfer it to the refrigerator.
5. Allow the jar to sit overnight or for at least five hours, so the flavors can set.
6. Serve the dough oats, and if desired, topped with the optional carob chips and a small cap of maple syrup.
7. Serve immediately.

Recipe 3 : Stir Fried Pork and Bok Choy Noodle | Calories: 413 | Fat: 7.9g | Carbs: 53.7g | Protein: 28.1g

Prep time: 10 minutes | Cook time: 10 minutes | Serves 4

Salt, to taste
8 ounces (227 g) rice noodles
⅓ cup water
¼ cup Shao Hsing rice wine or dry sherry
2 tablespoons less-sodium soy sauce
2 teaspoons cornstarch
1 tablespoon peanut oil or canola oil
1 onion, thinly sliced
1 pound (454 g) bok choy, cored and cut into long, thin strips
1 pound (454 g) pork tenderloin, trimmed of fat and cut into thin strips
2 cloves garlic, peeled and minced
1 tablespoon chili garlic sauce (sambal oelek)

Steps:
1. Bring a large pot of lightly salted water to a boil over high heat. Cook rice noodles according to package instructions. Drain and reserve.
2. In a small bowl, whisk together water, rice wine, soy sauce, and cornstarch.
3. Warm oil in a Dutch oven over medium heat. Once hot, add onion and cook until softened, about 2 to 3 minutes. Add bok choy and cook, stirring occasionally, until it begins to soften, about 5 minutes.
4. Add the pork, garlic, and chili garlic sauce. Stir occasionally until pork is just cooked through, about 1 minute.
5. Give the cornstarch mixture a quick whisk and pour into the Dutch oven. Bring to a boil, stirring frequently for 2 minutes until the sauce thickens. Serve pork stir-fry on top of noodles.

Recipe 4 : Coconut-Crusted Chicken Breast Salad | Calories: 454 | Fat: 20.6g | Carbs: 36.1g | Protein: 31.5g

Prep time: 15 minutes | Cook time: 25 minutes | Serves 2

For the Vinaigrette:

1 tablespoon extra-virgin olive oil
1 tablespoon honey
1 tablespoon white vinegar
2 teaspoons Dijon mustard

For the Chicken Salad

6 tablespoons shredded unsweetened coconut
¼ cup panko breadcrumbs
2 tablespoons crushed cornflakes
Salt and ground black pepper, to taste
3 egg whites, lightly beaten, or ½ cup liquid egg white substitute
1 (6-ounce / 170-g) boneless, skinless chicken breast, trimmed of fat
6 cups mixed baby greens
¾ cup shredded carrots
1 cucumber, sliced
1 tomato, sliced

Steps:
1. Preheat the oven to 375°F (190°C). Line a baking sheet with parchment paper.
2. In a small bowl, whisk together oil, honey, vinegar, and mustard. Reserve.
3. In a small, shallow dish, mix coconut, panko, cornflakes, salt, and pepper. In another bowl large enough to fit the chicken, add egg whites and lightly beat them with a fork.
4. Season chicken with salt and pepper. Dip chicken in egg whites followed by the coconut-panko mixture, using your fingers to press coconut mixture onto the chicken if needed. Place chicken onto the prepared baking sheet, lightly coat with cooking spray, and bake for 15 minutes. Flip chicken and bake until cooked through, about 10 to 15 more minutes.
5. To serve, add 3 cups baby greens to each plate. Top with carrots, cucumber, and tomato. Slice chicken diagonally and divide evenly between each salad. Drizzle with dressing.

Recipe 5 : Veggie Quinoa Bowl with Basil Pesto | Calories 548 | Fat: 22.5g | Carbs: 63.4g | Protein: 23.4g

Prep time: calories: 536 | fat: 22.8g | carbs: 9.2g | protein: 20.2g

1 teaspoon olive oil, or 1 tablespoon low-sodium vegetable broth or water
1 cup chopped onion
1 garlic clove, minced
1 cup chopped zucchini
Pinch of sea salt
1 tomato, chopped
2 tablespoons chopped sun-dried tomatoes
2 to 3 tablespoons basil pesto
1 cup chopped spinach
2 cups cooked quinoa

Steps:
1. Heat the oil in a large skillet on medium-high, then sauté the onion for about 5 minutes. Add the garlic when the onion has softened, then add the zucchini and salt.
2. Once the zucchini is somewhat soft, about 5 minutes, turn off the heat and add the fresh and sun-dried tomatoes. Mix to combine, then toss in the pesto. Toss the vegetables to coat them.
3. Layer the spinach, then quinoa, then the zucchini mixture on a plate and serve.

Shopping Lists
Dairy
- Almond Butter
- Almond Milk

Meats and Seafoods
- Pork
- Chicken

Fruits, Vegetables, Spices & Herbs
- Bananas
- Blueberries
- Peaches
- Vegan Vanilla Coconut
- Flaxseed
- Ginger
- Lemon
- Oats
- Vegan Protein Powder
- Peanut Butter
- Carob Chips
- Maple Syrup
- Salt
- Rice Noodles
- Hsing rice wine / dry sherry
- Soy Sauce
- Cornstarch
- Peanut Oil / Canola Oil
- Onion
- Bok Choy
- Garlic
- Chili Garlic Sauce
- Extra-virgin olive oil
- Honey
- White Vinegar
- Dijon Mustard
- Unsweetened coconuy
- Panko Breadcrumbs
- Cornflakes
- Black Pepper
- Mixed Baby Greens
- Carrots
- Cucumber
- Tomato
- Zucchini
- Basil
- Spinach
- Quinoa

Meal Prep Plan

Start your breakfast with **Banana, Blueberry, and Peach Smoothie Bowl.** First make the smoothie packs, In each of 4 resealable freezer bags, place 1 banana, 1 cup of blueberries, ½ cup of peaches, 7 ice cubes, 1 scoop of protein powder, 1 tablespoon of almond butter, 1 tablespoon of flaxseed, and a pinch of grated ginger. Lay the bags flat and remove as much air as possible before sealing. Store in the freezer until ready to use. Then make a smoothie, In a blender, combine 1 cup of almond milk and a squeeze of lemon juice, followed by the contents of 1 smoothie pack, and blend until smooth. Store the airtight bags in the freezer for up to 3 months.

After preparing for your breakfast, you can now start to prepare the **Simple Dough Oats** for your after snacks. First, Take a lidded bowl or jar and add the oats, flaxseed, protein powder, and almond milk. Stir until everything is thoroughly combined and the mixture looks runny; if not, add a little more almond milk. Blend in the peanut butter with a spoon until everything is mixed well. Place or close the lid on the bowl or jar and transfer it to the refrigerator. Allow the jar to sit overnight or for at least five hours, so the flavors can set. Serve the dough oats, and if desired, topped with the optional carob chips and a small cap of maple syrup. Serve immediately.

Next is the **Stir Fried Pork and Bok Choy Noodle** for your lunch. Bring a large pot of lightly salted water to a boil over high heat. Cook rice noodles according to package instructions. Drain and reserve. In a small bowl, whisk together water, rice wine, soy sauce, and cornstarch. Warm oil in a Dutch oven over medium heat. Once hot, add onion and cook until softened, about 2 to 3 minutes. Add bok choy and cook, stirring occasionally, until it begins to soften, about 5 minutes. Add the pork, garlic, and chili garlic sauce. Stir occasionally until pork is just cooked through, about 1 minute. Give the cornstarch mixture a quick whisk and pour into the Dutch oven. Bring to a boil, stirring frequently for 2 minutes until the sauce thickens. Serve pork stir-fry on top of noodles.

Next, you can now prepare for the **Coconut-Crusted Chicken Breast Salad** for your dinner. Preheat the oven to 375°F (190°C). Line a baking sheet with parchment paper. In a small bowl, whisk together oil, honey, vinegar, and mustard. Reserve. In a small, shallow dish, mix coconut, panko, cornflakes, salt, and pepper. In another bowl large enough to fit the chicken, add egg whites and lightly beat them with a fork. Season chicken with salt and pepper. Dip chicken in egg whites followed by the coconut-panko mixture, using your fingers to press coconut mixture onto the chicken if needed. Place chicken onto the prepared baking sheet, lightly coat with cooking spray, and bake for 15 minutes. Flip chicken and bake until cooked through, about 10 to 15 more minutes. To serve, add 3 cups baby greens to each plate. Top with carrots, cucumber, and tomato. Slice chicken diagonally and divide evenly between each salad. Drizzle with dressing.

Finally, you can now prepare on **Veggie Quinoa Bowl with Basil Pesto** for your pre-work-out meal. Heat the oil in a large skillet on medium-high, then sauté the onion for about 5 minutes. Add the garlic when the onion has softened, then add the zucchini and salt. Once the zucchini is somewhat soft, about 5 minutes, turn off the heat and add the fresh and sun-dried tomatoes. Mix to combine, then toss in the pesto. Toss the vegetables to coat them. Layer the spinach, then quinoa, then the zucchini mixture on a plate and serve.

Cutting Meal Plan-2 (Calorie Goal: 1500-2000)

Day	Breakfast	Snack/Dessert	Lunch	Dinner	Snack/Dessert	Preworkout Meal
1	Ham and Cheese Quiche calories: 322 | fat: 17.8g | carbs: 6.1g | protein: 33.2g	Simple Dough Oats calories: 317 | fat: 11.4g | carbs: 22.8g | protein: 30.8g	Adobo Sirloin Steak calories: 237 | fat: 6.9g | carbs: 1.7g | protein: 39.2g	Japanese Chicken Yakitori calories: 225 | fat: 1.9g | carbs: 4.1g | protein: 41.3g	Simple Dough Oats calories: 317 | fat: 11.4g | carbs: 22.8g | protein: 30.8g	Tofu and Brown Rice Bowl calories: 548 | fat: 22.5g | carbs: 63.4g | protein: 23.4g
2	Honey Greek Yogurt Parfait calories: 343 | fat: 15.9g | carbs: 53.1g | protein: 31.3g	Simple Dough Oats calories: 317 | fat: 11.4g | carbs: 22.8g | protein: 30.8g	Adobo Sirloin Steak calories: 237 | fat: 6.9g | carbs: 1.7g | protein: 39.2g	Japanese Chicken Yakitori calories: 225 | fat: 1.9g | carbs: 4.1g | protein: 41.3g	Simple Dough Oats calories: 317 | fat: 11.4g | carbs: 22.8g | protein: 30.8g	Tofu and Brown Rice Bowl calories: 548 | fat: 22.5g | carbs: 63.4g | protein: 23.4g
3	Honey Greek Yogurt Parfait calories: 343 | fat: 15.9g | carbs: 53.1g | protein: 31.3g	Simple Dough Oats calories: 317 | fat: 11.4g | carbs: 22.8g | protein: 30.8g	Adobo Sirloin Steak calories: 237 | fat: 6.9g | carbs: 1.7g | protein: 39.2g	Japanese Chicken Yakitori calories: 225 | fat: 1.9g | carbs: 4.1g | protein: 41.3g	Simple Dough Oats calories: 317 | fat: 11.4g | carbs: 22.8g | protein: 30.8g	Tofu and Brown Rice Bowl calories: 548 | fat: 22.5g | carbs: 63.4g | protein: 23.4g
4	Honey Greek Yogurt Parfait calories: 343 | fat: 15.9g | carbs: 53.1g | protein: 31.3g	Simple Dough Oats calories: 317 | fat: 11.4g | carbs: 22.8g | protein: 30.8g	Adobo Sirloin Steak calories: 237 | fat: 6.9g | carbs: 1.7g | protein: 39.2g	Japanese Chicken Yakitori calories: 225 | fat: 1.9g | carbs: 4.1g | protein: 41.3g	Simple Dough Oats calories: 317 | fat: 11.4g | carbs: 22.8g | protein: 30.8g	Tofu and Brown Rice Bowl calories: 548 | fat: 22.5g | carbs: 63.4g | protein: 23.4g
5	Honey Greek Yogurt Parfait calories: 343 | fat: 15.9g | carbs: 53.1g | protein: 31.3g	Simple Dough Oats calories: 317 | fat: 11.4g | carbs: 22.8g | protein: 30.8g	Adobo Sirloin Steak calories: 237 | fat: 6.9g | carbs: 1.7g | protein: 39.2g	Japanese Chicken Yakitori calories: 225 | fat: 1.9g | carbs: 4.1g | protein: 41.3g	Simple Dough Oats calories: 317 | fat: 11.4g | carbs: 22.8g | protein: 30.8g	Tofu and Brown Rice Bowl calories: 548 | fat: 22.5g | carbs: 63.4g | protein: 23.4g
6	Honey Greek Yogurt Parfait calories: 343 | fat: 15.9g | carbs: 53.1g | protein: 31.3g	Simple Dough Oats calories: 317 | fat: 11.4g | carbs: 22.8g | protein: 30.8g	Adobo Sirloin Steak calories: 237 | fat: 6.9g | carbs: 1.7g | protein: 39.2g	Japanese Chicken Yakitori calories: 225 | fat: 1.9g | carbs: 4.1g | protein: 41.3g	Simple Dough Oats calories: 317 | fat: 11.4g | carbs: 22.8g | protein: 30.8g	Tofu and Brown Rice Bowl calories: 548 | fat: 22.5g | carbs: 63.4g | protein: 23.4g
7	Honey Greek Yogurt Parfait calories: 343 | fat: 15.9g | carbs: 53.1g | protein: 31.3g	Simple Dough Oats calories: 317 | fat: 11.4g | carbs: 22.8g | protein: 30.8g	Adobo Sirloin Steak calories: 237 | fat: 6.9g | carbs: 1.7g | protein: 39.2g	Japanese Chicken Yakitori calories: 225 | fat: 1.9g | carbs: 4.1g | protein: 41.3g	Simple Dough Oats calories: 317 | fat: 11.4g | carbs: 22.8g | protein: 30.8g	Tofu and Brown Rice Bowl calories: 548 | fat: 22.5g | carbs: 63.4g | protein: 23.4g

protein *carbs* *fat*

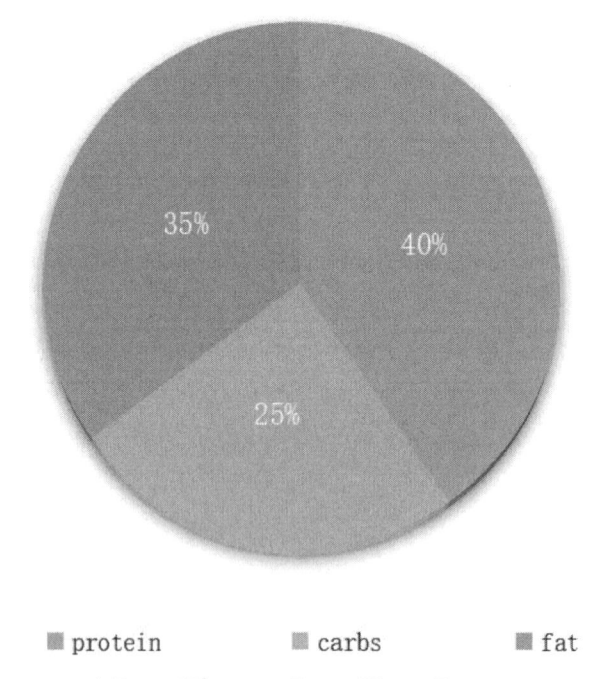

5 Prep Plan to Start Your Journey
Cutting Meal Plan Meal Plan-2 (Calorie Goal: 1500-2000)

Prep Plan #5

This is a fantastic starter plan with 1 breakfast, 1 lunch, 1 dinner, 1 preworkout meal, and 2 snacks that will keep you covered up to 7 days of eating.

Recipe 1 : Ham and Cheese Quiche | Calories: 322 | Fat: 17.8g | Carbs: 6.1g | Protein: 33.2g

Prep time: 10 minutes | Cook time: 45 minutes | Serves 4

Nonstick cooking spray
4 large eggs
1½ cups egg whites
1 cup reduced-fat cottage cheese (1%)
5 bacon slices, cooked and crumbled
½ cup finely chopped extra-lean ham
¼ cup crumbled feta cheese
½ onion, finely chopped
1 green bell pepper, finely chopped
½ teaspoon sea salt
¼ teaspoon freshly ground black pepper

Steps:
1. Preheat the oven to 350°F (180°C). Coat the bottom and sides of an 8-by-8-inch square glass baking dish with nonstick cooking spray.
2. In a large bowl, combine the eggs, egg whites, cottage cheese, bacon, ham, feta, onion, bell pepper, salt, and pepper. Pour the mixture into the prepared baking dish.
3. Bake for 45 minutes, or until the center is set.
4. Remove from the oven and let cool.
5. Cut into 8 equal pieces. Into each of 4 airtight storage containers, place 2 pieces of quiche and seal.
6. Store the airtight containers in the refrigerator for up to 4 days. To reheat, microwave uncovered on high for 1 to 2 minutes.

Recipe 2 : Simple Dough Oats | Calories: 317 | Fat: 11.4g | Carbs: 22.8g | Protein: 30.8g

Prep time: 5 minutes | Cook time: 0 minutes | Serves 2

½ cup quick or rolled oats
1 tablespoon flaxseeds
2 scoops vanilla flavor vegan protein powder
1 cup unsweetened almond milk
1 tablespoon peanut butter
1 tablespoon carob chips (optional)
1 tablespoon maple syrup (optional)

Steps:
8. Take a lidded bowl or jar and add the oats, flaxseed, protein powder, and almond milk.
9. Stir until everything is thoroughly combined and the mixture looks runny; if not, add a little more almond milk.
10. Blend in the peanut butter with a spoon until everything is mixed well.
11. Place or close the lid on the bowl or jar and transfer it to the refrigerator.
12. Allow the jar to sit overnight or for at least five hours, so the flavors can set.
13. Serve the dough oats, and if desired, topped with the optional carob chips and a small cap of maple syrup.
14. Serve immediately.

Recipe 3 : Adobo Sirloin Steak | Calories: 237 | Fat: 6.9g | Carbs: 1.7g | Protein: 39.2g

Prep time: 10 minutes | Cook time: 8 minutes | Serves 4

Juice of 1 lime
1 tablespoon minced garlic
1 teaspoon dried oregano
1 teaspoon ground cumin
2 tablespoons finely chopped canned chipotle chiles in adobo sauce plus 2 tablespoons sauce
4 (6-ounce / 170-g) sirloin steaks, trimmed of fat
Salt and ground black pepper, to taste

Steps:
1. In a small bowl, combine lime juice, garlic, oregano, cumin, chiles, and adobo sauce. Mix well to combine.
2. Season meat with salt and pepper. Place steaks into a large Ziploc bag with adobo marinade. Seal tightly and shake to coat. Refrigerate for at least 2 hours, shaking occasionally.
3. Prepare a grill to high heat. Lightly coat the grill grates with cooking spray. Once the grill is hot, cook steaks until desired doneness, about 4 to 5 minutes on each side. Let the steaks rest for 10 minutes and serve

Recipe 4 : Japanese Chicken Yakitori | Calories: 225 | Fat: 1.9g | Carbs: 4.1g | Protein: 41.3g

Prep time: 10 minutes | Cook time: 3 minutes | Serves

½ cup less-sodium soy sauce
½ cup sherry or white cooking wine
½ cup low-sodium chicken broth
½ teaspoon ground ginger
Pinch of garlic powder
½ cup chopped scallions
4 (6-ounce / 170-g) boneless, skinless chicken breasts, trimmed of fat and cut into 2-inch cubes

Steps:
1. If using bamboo skewers versus metal skewers, soak in water for 30 minutes to prevent the wood from burning.
2. Into a small pot, add soy sauce, sherry, chicken broth, ginger, garlic powder, and scallions. Bring ingredients to a boil over medium-high heat and immediately remove from heat. Reserve.
3. Preheat the oven's broiler. Start threading chicken onto skewers.
4. Coat a broiler pan with cooking spray and place chicken skewers on the pan. Brush each skewer with sherry sauce.
5. Place the pan under the broiler until chicken is browned, about 3 minutes. Remove the pan from the oven to turn each chicken skewer over, brushing sauce onto chicken again.
6. Return the pan to the broiler until chicken is cooked through and nicely browned. Serve.

Recipe 5 : Tofu and Brown Rice Bowl | Calories 548 | Fat: 22.5g | Carbs: 63.4g | Protein: 23.4g

Prep time: 15 minutes | Cook time: 5 minutes | Serves 2

1 cup firm tofu, cubed
2 tablespoons coconut oil
6 cups cooked brown rice
1 cup shelled edamame, steamed
1 large carrot, peeled
½ cucumber, sliced
1 radish, sliced
¼ cup pickled red cabbage (optional)
Roasted sesame seeds (optional)
Soy Hoisin Sauce:
3 tablespoons hoisin sauce
1 teaspoon sriracha
¼ cup soy sauce
1 lime, squeezed

Steps:
1. Put all the ingredients for soy hoisin sauce into a small bowl and stir well. Set the sauce aside.
2. Take a large skillet, put it on medium heat and add the coconut oil.
3. Stir fry the tofu for about 5 minutes until brown before stirring in the hoisin sauce.
4. Serve the cooked rice with the tofu and sauce in a bowl.
5. Top the dish with the steamed edamame, carrot, cucumber and raw radish.
6. Add the optional roasted sesame seeds and pickled red cabbage.
7. Serve and enjoy or store the fresh and cooked ingredients in multiple-compartment containers.

Shopping Lists

Dairy

- Eggs
- Cottage Cheese
- Feta Cheese
- Almond Milk

Meats and Seafoods

- Bacon
- Ham
- Chicken

Fruits, Vegetables, Spices & Herbs

- Onion
- Bell Pepper
- Sea Salt
- Black Pepper
- Oats
- Flaxseed
- Vegan Protein Powder
- Peanut Butter
- Carob Chips
- Maple Syrup
- Soy Sauce
- Sherry / White Cooking Wine
- Ground Ginger
- Garlic Powder
- Scallions
- Tofu
- Coconut Oil
- Brown Rice
- Edamame
- Carrot
- Cucumber
- Radish
- Red Cabbage
- Sesame Seeds
- Hoisin Sauce
- Sriracha
- Lime

Meal Prep Plan

Start your breakfast with **Ham and Cheese Quiche.** First, Preheat the oven to 350°F (180°C). Coat the bottom and sides of an 8-by-8-inch square glass baking dish with nonstick cooking spray. In a large bowl, combine the eggs, egg whites, cottage cheese, bacon, ham, feta, onion, bell pepper, salt, and pepper. Pour the mixture into the prepared baking dish. Bake for 45 minutes, or until the center is set. Remove from the oven and let cool. Cut into 8 equal pieces. Into each of 4 airtight storage containers, place 2 pieces of quiche and seal. Store the airtight containers in the refrigerator for up to 4 days. To reheat, microwave uncovered on high for 1 to 2 minutes.

After preparing for your breakfast, you can now start to prepare the **Simple Dough Oats** for your after snacks. First, Take a lidded bowl or jar and add the oats, flaxseed, protein powder, and almond milk. Stir until everything is thoroughly combined and the mixture looks runny; if not, add a little more almond milk. Blend in the peanut butter with a spoon until everything is mixed well. Place or close the lid on the bowl or jar and transfer it to the refrigerator. Allow the jar to sit overnight or for at least five hours, so the flavors can set. Serve the dough oats, and if desired, topped with the optional carob chips and a small cap of maple syrup. Serve immediately.

Next is the **Adobo Sirloin Steak** for your lunch. In a small bowl, combine lime juice, garlic, oregano, cumin, chiles, and adobo sauce. Mix well to combine. Season meat with salt and pepper. Place steaks into a large Ziploc bag with adobo marinade. Seal tightly and shake to coat. Refrigerate for at least 2 hours, shaking occasionally. Prepare a grill to high heat. Lightly coat the grill grates with cooking spray. Once the grill is hot, cook steaks until desired doneness, about 4 to 5 minutes on each side. Let the steaks rest for 10 minutes and serve.

Next, you can now prepare for the **Japanese Chicken Yakitori** for your dinner. If using bamboo skewers versus metal skewers, soak in water for 30 minutes to prevent the wood from burning. Into a small pot, add soy sauce, sherry, chicken broth, ginger, garlic powder, and scallions. Bring ingredients to a boil over medium-high heat and immediately remove from heat. Reserve. Preheat the oven's broiler. Start threading chicken onto skewers. Coat a broiler pan with cooking spray and place chicken skewers on the pan. Brush each skewer with sherry sauce. Place the pan under the broiler until chicken is browned, about 3 minutes. Remove the pan from the oven to turn each chicken skewer over, brushing sauce onto chicken again. Return the pan to the broiler until chicken is cooked through and nicely browned.

Finally, you can now prepare on **Tofu and Brown Rice Bowl** for your prework-out meal. Put all the ingredients for soy hoisin sauce into a small bowl and stir well. Set the sauce aside. Take a large skillet, put it on medium heat and add the coconut oil. Stir fry the tofu for about 5 minutes until brown before stirring in the hoisin sauce. Serve the cooked rice with the tofu and sauce in a bowl. Top the dish with the steamed edamame, carrot, cucumber and raw radish. Add the optional roasted sesame seeds and pickled red cabbage. Serve and enjoy or store the fresh and cooked ingredients in multiple-compartment containers.

Chapter 7 Fast Carb Pre-Workout Meals

Perfect Fluffy Basmati Rice

Prep time: 5 minutes | Cook time: 15 minutes | Serves 8

2 cups Basmati rice, rinsed and drained
4 cups water
1 teaspoon avocado oil
1 teaspoon salt

1. In a large pot, combine the rice, water, avocado oil, and salt. Bring to a boil over high heat, stirring once, then cover, reduce the heat to low, and cook for 15 minutes.
2. Remove the pot from the heat and allow the rice to rest for 15 minutes. Fluff the cooked rice with a fork. Serve hot.

Per Serving
calories: 170 | fat: 2.1g | carbs: 33.4g | protein: 3.2g

Black Beans and White Quinoa

Prep time: 10 minutes | Cook time: 20 minutes | Serves 8

1 jalapeño pepper, seeds and stem removed, finely diced
2 teaspoons minced garlic
2 cups low fat chicken broth
1½ cups uncooked white quinoa, rinsed 3 to 4 times
1 (15-ounce / 425-g) can diced fire-roasted tomatoes, not drained
½ teaspoon chipotle powder
1 teaspoon ground cumin
1 teaspoon onion powder
1 teaspoon paprika
1 (15-ounce / 425-g) can black beans, drained and rinsed
1 cup frozen corn kernels

1. Spray a large skillet with non-stick cooking spray and place over medium heat. Add the jalapeño and garlic to the pan and cook for 1 minute, or until the garlic starts to soften and becomes fragrant. Stir frequently.
2. Add the chicken broth, quinoa, tomatoes, chipotle powder, cumin, onion powder, and paprika to the pan. Increase the heat to high and bring to a boil, stirring constantly. As soon as the mixture reaches a boil, reduce the heat to low, cover, and cook for 15 minutes.
3. Add the black beans and corn. Stir, cover, and continue to cook for an additional 4 to 5 minutes, or until the quinoa is tender. Serve hot.

Per Serving
calories: 154 | fat: 2.4g | carbs: 28.5g | protein: 5.6g

Fluffy Brown Rice Pilaf

Prep time: 10 minutes | Cook time: 41 minutes | Serves 4

1 tablespoon unsalted butter
1 shallot, peeled and finely chopped
1 cup long-grain brown rice, rinsed
Salt and ground black pepper, to taste
2 cups low-sodium chicken broth
1 clove garlic, peeled and smashed
2 sprigs fresh thyme
3 tablespoons chopped fresh flat-leaf parsley
3 scallions, thinly sliced

1. Melt butter in a medium heavy-duty pot over medium heat. Add shallot and cook until tender, about 1 to 2 minutes.
2. Add rice, stirring well to coat with the butter and shallots. Cook for a few minutes until rice is glossy. Season with salt and pepper.
3. Stir in chicken broth, garlic, and thyme. Cover with a tight-fitting lid, reduce heat to low, and cook for 40 minutes. Remove from heat and let sit for 10 minutes.
4. Use a fork to fluff rice and stir in parsley and scallions. Serve.

Per Serving
calories: 218 | fat: 4.2g | carbs: 38.7g | protein: 5.1g

Tangy Kale Salad

Prep time: 5 minutes | Cook time: 0 minutes | Serves 2

4 cups chopped kale
2 tablespoons freshly squeezed lemon juice
⅛ teaspoon pink Himalayan salt
1 cup cooked wild rice
1 cup cooked quinoa
1 small tomato, chopped
1 small avocado, pitted, peeled, and chopped

1. In a large bowl, massage the kale with the lemon juice and salt for a few minutes, or until the kale softens.
2. Add the rice, quinoa, tomato, and avocado to the bowl and mix well.
3. Serve immediately or store in the refrigerator for up to 3 days.

Per Serving
calories: 721 | fat: 20.2g | carbs: 123.1g | protein: 27.2g

Sushi Bowl with Vegetable

Prep time: 15 minutes | Cook time: 0 minutes | Serves 1

1 cup cooked brown rice
1 small avocado, pitted, peeled, and cut into strips
½ cup shelled edamame
½ cup thinly sliced carrots
½ cucumber, cut into thin strips
1 scallion, chopped
½ nori sheet, cut into thin strips

Optional Toppings:

Low-sodium soy sauce
Pickled ginger
Black sesame seeds
Wasabi

1. Put the rice in a serving bowl and layer on the avocado, edamame, carrots, cucumber, scallion, and nori. Add your toppings of choice (if using).
2. Serve immediately or store in a reusable container in the refrigerator for up to 5 days.

Per Serving
calories: 665 | fat: 32.1g | carbs: 80.8g | protein: 21.3g

Tofu and Brown Rice Bowl

Prep time: 15 minutes | Cook time: 5 minutes | Serves 2

1 cup firm tofu, cubed
2 tablespoons coconut oil
6 cups cooked brown rice
1 cup shelled edamame, steamed
1 large carrot, peeled
½ cucumber, sliced
1 radish, sliced
¼ cup pickled red cabbage (optional)
Roasted sesame seeds (optional)

Soy Hoisin Sauce:

3 tablespoons hoisin sauce
1 teaspoon sriracha
¼ cup soy sauce
1 lime, squeezed

8. Put all the ingredients for soy hoisin sauce into a small bowl and stir well. Set the sauce aside.
9. Take a large skillet, put it on medium heat and add the coconut oil.
10. Stir fry the tofu for about 5 minutes until brown before stirring in the hoisin sauce.
11. Serve the cooked rice with the tofu and sauce in a bowl.
12. Top the dish with the steamed edamame, carrot, cucumber and raw radish.
13. Add the optional roasted sesame seeds and pickled red cabbage.
14. Serve and enjoy or store the fresh and cooked ingredients in multiple-compartment containers.

Per Serving
calories: 548 | fat: 22.5g | carbs: 63.4g | protein: 23.4g

Beans and Spinach Rice Bowl

Prep time: 20 minutes | Cook time: 0 minutes | Makes 1 bowl

½ cup shelled edamame beans. steamed
¾ cup cooked brown rice, or quinoa, millet, or other whole grain
½ cup chopped spinach
¼ cup sliced avocado
¼ cup sliced bell pepper
¼ cup chopped fresh cilantro
1 scallion, chopped
¼ nori sheet
1 to 2 tablespoons tamari, or soy sauce
1 tablespoon sesame seeds

1. Combine the edamame, rice, spinach, avocado, bell pepper, cilantro, and scallions in a bowl.
2. Cut the nori with scissors into small ribbons and sprinkle on top.
3. Drizzle the bowl with tamari and top with sesame seeds. Serve immediately.

Per Serving
calories: 466 | fat: 20.1g | carbs: 6.3g | protein: 22.1g

Soya Mince Brown Rice Noodle Bowl

Prep time: 10 minutes | Cook time: 13 minutes | Serves 2

2 packs brown rice noodles
1½ cups water, divided
¼ cup low-sodium soy sauce
2 yellow onions, minced
4 cloves garlic, minced
1 (7-ounce / 198-g) pack textured soya mince

Optional Toppings:

Sauerkraut
Chili flakes
Roasted sesame seeds

1. In a large pot of boiling water, cook the noodles for 8 minutes. Drain the excess water with a strainer and set aside.
2. Put a medium pot over medium heat and add ½ cup of the water, soy sauce, minced onion and garlic.
3. Add the soya mince and cook for about 5 minutes, stirring occasionally to prevent the soya mince from sticking to the pan, until the mince has cooked, and half of the water has evaporated.
4. Add the remaining 1 cup of the water and bring to a boil while stirring occasionally.
5. Turn off the heat, add the noodles and stir well until everything is evenly mixed.
6. Divide the noodles and mince between 2 bowls, serve with the optional toppings and enjoy.

Per Serving

calories: 227 | fat: 0.8g | carbs: 26.4g | protein: 25.4g

Classic Scotcheroos

Prep time: 5 minutes | Cook time: 4 minutes | Makes 6 scotcheroos

1 tablespoon coconut oil
2 tablespoons smooth peanut butter
2 tablespoons almond flour
1 cup gluten-free crispy brown rice cereal
½ cup dairy-free dark chocolate chips

Per Serving

calories: 184 | fat: 12.1g | carbs: 15.2g | protein: 3.3g

1. Line a standard size 6-cup muffin pan with paper baking cups. Set aside.
2. In a small saucepan, melt the coconut oil and peanut butter over medium heat for 1 minute. Add the almond flour and stir until fully incorporated, about 2 minutes. Turn off the heat and add the rice cereal, stirring until fully coated.
3. Divide the rice mixture evenly among the 6 baking cups. Using the bottom of a drinking glass, press the rice mixture firmly into each baking cup to create a dense, even layer.
4. In a small saucepan or double boiler, melt the chocolate over medium-low heat. Stir continuously until fully melted, about 1 minute. Pour the chocolate evenly over the rice mixture, adding an equal amount to each of the 6 cups. Shake and tilt the pan gently from side to side to make sure the chocolate spreads evenly over the rice mixture.
5. Place the tray in the freezer until candies are set, about 30 minutes.
6. Serve chilled.

Veggie Quinoa Bowl with Basil Pesto

Prep time: 10 minutes | Cook time: 10 minutes | Serves 1

1 teaspoon olive oil, or 1 tablespoon low-sodium vegetable broth or water
1 cup chopped onion
1 garlic clove, minced
1 cup chopped zucchini
Pinch of sea salt
1 tomato, chopped
2 tablespoons chopped sun-dried tomatoes
2 to 3 tablespoons basil pesto
1 cup chopped spinach
2 cups cooked quinoa

4. Heat the oil in a large skillet on medium-high, then sauté the onion for about 5 minutes. Add the garlic when the onion has softened, then add the zucchini and salt.
5. Once the zucchini is somewhat soft, about 5 minutes, turn off the heat and add the fresh and sun-dried tomatoes. Mix to combine, then toss in the pesto. Toss the vegetables to coat them.
6. Layer the spinach, then quinoa, then the zucchini mixture on a plate and serve.

Per Serving

calories: 536 | fat: 22.8g | carbs: 9.2g | protein: 20.2g

Baked Mango Quinoa Bowl with Tempeh

Prep time: 5 minutes | Cook time: 15 minutes | Serves 4

1 cup fresh mango cubes
1 (14-ounce / 397-g) pack tempeh, sliced
1 cup peanut butter
1 cup cooked black beans
2 cups cooked quinoa

Optional Toppings:

Chili flakes
Shredded coconut

6. Blend the mango into a smooth purée using a blender or food processor, and set it aside.
7. Add the tempeh slices and the peanut butter to an airtight container. Close the lid and shake well until the tempeh slices are evenly covered with the peanut butter.
8. Preheat the oven to 375°F (190°C) and line a baking sheet with parchment paper.
9. Transfer the tempeh slices onto the baking sheet and bake for about 15 minutes or until the tempeh is browned and crispy.
10. Divide the black beans, quinoa, mango purée and tempeh slices between two bowls, serve with the optional toppings and enjoy.

Per Serving

calories: 733 | fat: 42.3g | carbs: 39.2g | protein: 46.4g

Quinoa with Peas and Red Cabbage

Prep time: 5 minutes | Cook time: 15 minutes | Serves 8

2 cups quinoa, rinsed
3 cups water or vegetable broth
1 cup frozen peas
1 cup diced red cabbage
Salt, to taste

1. Add all the ingredients to a medium-sized pot over medium heat and bring to a boil.
2. Turn heat to low, let simmer for 15 minutes, or until the liquid is absorbed and the quinoa is cooked through.
3. Serve warm

Per Serving
calories: 101 | fat: 1.2g | carbs: 18.2g | protein: 4.3g

Chapter 8 Preworkout Smoothies

Vanilla Fruity Spinach Smoothie

Prep time: 10 minutes | Cook time: 0 minutes | Serves 4

For the Smoothie Packs:

3 cups sliced fresh or frozen bananas, divided
3 cups fresh or frozen blueberries, divided
2 cups spinach, divided
2 scoops vanilla vegan protein powder, divided

For the Smoothies:

2 cups unsweetened vanilla cashew milk or almond milk, divided
2 cups ice-cold water, divided
1 cup orange juice, divided

Make the Smoothie Packs

1. Into each of 4 resealable freezer bags, place ¾ cup of sliced banana, ¾ cup of blueberries, ½ cup of spinach, and ½ scoop of protein powder. Lay the bags flat, and remove as much air as possible before sealing. Store in the freezer until ready to use.

Make a Smoothie

2. In a blender, combine ½ cup of cashew milk, ½ cup of ice water, and ¼ cup of orange juice, followed by the smoothie pack contents, and blend until smooth.
3. Store the airtight bags in the freezer for up to 3 months.

Per Serving (1 smoothie)
calories: 240 | fat: 3.9g | carbs: 51.2g | protein: 11.3g

Tropical Fruits Smoothie

Prep time: 10 minutes | Cook time: 0 minutes | Serves 4

For the Smoothie Packs:

2 fresh or frozen bananas, chopped, divided
2 cups frozen pineapple pieces, divided
2 cups frozen mango pieces, divided
2 scoops vegan vanilla protein powder, divided
4 tablespoons hemp hearts, divided
4 cups spinach, divided

For the Smoothies:

4 cups coconut water or filtered water, divided

Make the Smoothie Packs

1. In each of 4 resealable freezer bags, place half a banana, ½ cup of pineapple, ½ cup of mango, ½ scoop of protein powder, 1 tablespoon of hemp hearts, and 1 cup of spinach. Lay the bags flat, and remove as much air as possible before sealing. Store in the freezer until ready to use.

Make a Smoothie

2. In a blender, combine 1 cup of coconut water with the contents of 1 smoothie pack, and blend until smooth.
3. Store the airtight bags in the freezer for up to 3 months.

Per Serving (1 smoothie)
calories: 227 | fat: 6.9g | carbs: 36.1g | protein: 17.2g

Citrus Julius Smoothie

Prep time: 10 minutes | Cook time: 0 minutes | Serves 2

For the Smoothie Packs:

1 cup frozen mango chunks, divided
1 cup chopped baby carrots, divided
1 fresh or frozen banana, chopped, divided
1 scoop vanilla vegan protein powder, divided
2 tablespoons hemp hearts, divided
8 to 12 ice cubes, divided

For the Smoothies:

½ cup orange juice, divided
½ cup unsweetened almond milk, divided

Make the Smoothie Packs

1. In each of 2 resealable freezer bags, combine ½ cup of mango, ¼ cup of carrots, half a banana, ½ scoop of protein powder, 1 tablespoon of hemp hearts, and 4 to 6 ice cubes. Lay the bags flat and remove as much air as possible before sealing. Store in the freezer until ready to use.

Make a Smoothie

2. In a blender, combine 1 smoothie pack with ¼ cup of orange juice and ¼ cup of almond milk. Blend well.
3. Store the airtight bags in the freezer for up to 3 months.

Per Serving (1 smoothie)
calories: 352 | fat: 14.9g | carbs: 44.1g | protein: 21.3g

Sunny Orange Smoothie

Prep time: 10 minutes | Cook time: 0 minutes | Serves 5

For the Smoothie Packs:

1¼ cups frozen pineapple chunks, divided
1¼ cups frozen papaya chunks, divided
1¼ cups frozen mango chunks, divided
2½ fresh or frozen bananas, chopped, divided
2½ tablespoons ground flaxseed, divided

For the Smoothies:

2½ cups nonfat vanilla Greek yogurt, divided
2½ cups orange juice, divided

Make the Smoothie Packs

1. Into each of 5 resealable freezer bags, place ¼ cup of pineapple, ¼ cup of papaya, ¼ cup of mango, half a banana, and ½ tablespoon of flaxseed. Flatten, pressing any air out of the bag, and seal. Store in the freezer until ready to use.

Make a Smoothie

2. In a blender, combine ½ cup of yogurt, ½ cup of orange juice, and the contents of 1 smoothie pack, and blend until smooth.
3. Store the airtight bags in the freezer for up to 3 months.

Per Serving (1 smoothie)
calories: 273 | fat: 1.8g | carbs: 63.1g | protein: 13.2g

Banana-Almond Milk Smoothie

Prep time: 5 minutes | Cook time: 0 minutes | Serves 1

1 banana, preferably frozen, peeled and sliced
2 tablespoons almond butter
1 cup unsweetened almond milk
1 teaspoon honey
1 tablespoon ground or whole flaxseed
1 scoop vanilla protein powder

1. In a blender, add banana, almond butter, almond milk, honey, flaxseed, and protein powder. Process until smooth, about 1 minute. Pour into a glass and serve.

Per Serving
calories: 505 | fat: 24.8g | carbs: 46.2g | protein: 33.1g

Creamy Banana and Blueberry Smoothie

Prep time: 5 minutes | Cook time: 0 minutes | Serves 2

1 banana, preferably frozen, peeled and sliced
½ cup frozen blueberries
1 teaspoon honey
½ cup 2% Greek yogurt
1 tablespoon whole flaxseed
1 cup 2% milk

1. Into a blender, add banana, blueberries, honey, yogurt, flaxseed, and milk. Process until smooth, about 1 minute. Pour into 2 glasses and serve

Per Serving
calories: 228 | fat: 7.1g | carbs: 30.9g | protein: 11.8g

Apple and Coconut Milk Smoothie

Prep time: 5 minutes | Cook time: 0 minutes | Serves 1

1 green apple, peeled, cored, and chopped
1 cup unsweetened unsweetened coconut milk
½ teaspoon cinnamon powder, plus more for topping
2 scoops vanilla flavor vegan protein powder
3 ice cubes (optional)
1 to 2 teaspoons matcha powder (optional)

1. Add all the ingredients to a blender.
2. Blend for 2 minutes.
3. Transfer the shake to a large cup or shaker.
4. Top with some additional cinnamon powder.
5. Serve immediately.

Per Serving
calories: 374 | fat: 10.2g | carbs: 21.8g | protein: 48.6g

Citrus Strawberry-Banana Smoothie

Prep time: 5 minutes | Cook time: 0 minutes | Serves 2

2 cups unsweetened unsweetened coconut milk
10 fresh strawberries
1 orange, peeled and parted
1 banana
3 scoops vanilla flavor vegan protein powder
2 ice cubes (optional)

1. Add all the ingredients to a blender.
2. Blend for 2 minutes.
3. Transfer the shake to a large cup.
4. Stir and enjoy.

Per Serving
calories: 288 | fat: 7.6g | carbs: 29.2g | protein: 25.7g

Mango and Blueberry Smoothie

Prep time: 5 minutes | Cook time: 0 minutes | Serves 2

1 orange, peeled and parted
1 cup fresh mango chunks
1 banana
½ cup blueberries
2 scoops chocolate or vanilla flavor vegan protein powder
1 tablespoon hemp seeds
1 teaspoon guarana (optional)
6 ice cubes

1. Add all the ingredients to a blender.
2. Blend for 2 minutes.
3. Transfer the shake to a large cup or shaker.
4. Serve immediately.

Per Serving
calories: 351 | fat: 6.8g | carbs: 44.5g | protein: 28.1g

Banana, Raisins, and Oats Smoothie

Prep time: 5 minutes | Cook time: 0 minutes | Serves 1

1 frozen banana, sliced
1 cup vanilla almond milk
¼ cup old-fashioned oats
¼ cup raisins
1 tablespoon flaxseed meal
¼ teaspoon cinnamon
3 tablespoons vanilla protein powder

3. Add all the ingredients to a blender and blend until very smooth.
4. Serve immediately.

Per Serving
calories: 706 | fat: 21.2g | carbs: 102.8g | protein: 33.6g

Chapter 9 Post-Workout Meals

Avocado, Veggie, and Eggs on Toast

Prep time: 10 minutes | Cook time: 4 minutes | Serves 2

Nonstick cooking spray
2 large eggs
½ cup spinach, kale, or Swiss chard (if using kale or Swiss chard, stem and chop)
2 light rye or whole-wheat bread slices
½ avocado halved, pitted, and peeled
½ tablespoon hemp hearts
⅛ teaspoon hot sauce
8 cherry tomatoes, quartered
Sea salt, to taste
Freshly ground black pepper, to taste

1. Heat a sauté pan over medium heat. Spray with cooking spray. Add 2 eggs and cook, stirring, until almost scrambled, 2 to 3 minutes. Add the spinach and cook for another 2 to 3 minutes, until wilted and well combined with the egg.
2. Meanwhile, toast the bread in the toaster.
3. In a small bowl, use a fork or potato masher to mash the avocado with the hemp hearts and hot sauce. Stir in the cherry tomatoes, and season with salt and pepper.
4. Assemble by spreading the avocado mixture on both pieces of toast, then topping with the spinach-egg mixture.
5. Into each of 2 airtight storage containers, place 1 piece of assembled toast and seal.
6. Store the airtight containers in the refrigerator for up to 3 days.

Per Serving
calories: 296 | fat: 18.9g | carbs: 35.1g | protein: 15.2g

Cantaloupe and Cottage Cheese Bowl

Prep time: 5 minutes | Cook time: 0 minutes | Serves 2

1 small cantaloupe
2 cups 1% cottage cheese
2 teaspoons slivered almonds
⅛ teaspoon ground cinnamon

1. To create the bowls, slice the cantaloupe in half crosswise, and use a spoon to scoop out the seeds of each half.
2. Add 1 cup cottage cheese to each cantaloupe bowl and top each with 1 tablespoon slivered almonds and a pinch of cinnamon. Serve immediately.

Per Serving
calories: 314 | fat: 6.7g | carbs: 32.2g | protein: 31.9g

Macadamia and Coconut French Toast

Prep time: 10 minutes | Cook time: 6 minutes | Serves 2

For the French Toast:

½ cup 2% milk
2 large eggs
2 egg whites or 6 tablespoons liquid egg white substitute
2 scoops vanilla protein powder
½ teaspoon ground cinnamon
4 slices whole-grain bread

1. In a shallow dish, add milk, eggs, and egg whites, whisking together with a fork. Add protein powder and cinnamon, whisking again until completely mixed.
2. Soak a slice of bread in the mixture until soggy — letting it sit at least 30 seconds or so is ideal.
3. Coat a medium nonstick pan with cooking spray and warm on medium-high heat. Add 1 or 2 bread slices into the pan (no crowding the pan!) and cook until golden brown, about 2 minutes. Use a spatula to flip the slices, cooking again until firm, another 1 to 2 minutes. Transfer to a plate and repeat with remaining bread.
4. Meanwhile, in a small bowl, mix banana, nuts, and coconut flakes. Garnish each French toast piece with the topping. Serve.

For the Topping:
1 banana, peeled and sliced
2 tablespoons chopped macadamia nuts
2 tablespoons unsweetened coconut flakes

Per Serving
calories: 10 | fat: 17.9g | carbs: 46.1g | protein:43.2 g

Egg Rice Skillet

Prep time: 10 minutes | Cook time: 10 minutes | Serves 2

2 cups liquid egg whites
½ teaspoon ground ginger
⅛ teaspoon red pepper flakes
1 teaspoon liquid aminos
1 cup frozen peas
2 teaspoons finely chopped scallions (green parts only)
1 teaspoon minced garlic
1 cup cooked basmati rice

1. Preheat the broiler to low. In a large bowl, make the egg mixture by whisking together the egg whites, ginger, red pepper flakes, and liquid aminos. Add the peas to the bowl, and stir well to combine. Set aside.
2. Spray a medium cast iron skillet with non-stick cooking spray and preheat over medium heat. Add the scallions and garlic, and cook for 2 to 3 minutes until soft and fragrant.
3. Increase the heat to medium-high, add the rice to the skillet, and use a wooden spoon to spread it into a thin, even layer. Toast for 1 to 2 minutes. Use the wooden spoon to press the rice into the skillet and toast for an additional 1 to 2 minutes, or until the rice is brown and crispy.
4. Reduce the heat to low. Pour the egg mixture evenly over the toasted rice. Cook for 4 to 5 minutes, then transfer the skillet to the oven. Broil for 2 to 3 minutes, or until the egg whites are set. Serve hot.

Per Serving
calories: 278 | fat: 0.5g | carbs: 32.1g | protein: 33.9g

Cuban Swiss Sandwich Quesadilla

Prep time: 5 minutes | Cook time: 0 minutes | Serves 1

1 (6-inch) whole-wheat tortilla
1 slice reduced-fat Swiss cheese
2 ounces (57 g) deli ham
1 dill pickle, thinly sliced
Dijon mustard, to taste

1. Coat a medium nonstick pan with cooking spray and warm over low heat. Add tortilla to the pan.
2. Layer ingredients on half of the tortilla in the following order: cheese, ham, pickle, and mustard. When cheese has melted, use a spatula to fold quesadilla in half and flip it to warm the other side.
3. Transfer quesadilla to a plate, slice into quarters, and serve.

Per Serving
calories: 280 | fat: 11.9g | carbs: 23.8g | protein: 24.5g

Speedy Chocolate Protein Snack Mug

Prep time: 5 minutes | Cook time: 1 minute | Serves 1

1 tablespoon unsweetened cocoa powder
1 tablespoon coconut flour
¼ cup vanilla whey protein powder
½ teaspoon baking powder
¼ cup liquid egg whites
¼ cup unsweetened almond milk

1. In a microwave-safe, medium-sized mug, combine the cocoa powder, coconut flour, protein powder, and baking powder. Stir well.
2. Add the egg whites and almond milk. Mix all ingredients well.
3. Microwave on high for 1 to 2 minutes, checking every 15 seconds for doneness. The cake is done when the center is set and no longer appears shiny. (Make sure not to overcook the cake, as it can quickly become rubbery and dry.) Serve warm.

Per Serving
calories: 190 | fat: 2.1g | carbs: 9.2g | protein: 34.3g

Balsamic Melon and Cottage Cheese

Prep time: 5 minutes | Cook time: 2 minutes | Serves 1

4 slices watermelon, rind on, sliced into 1-inch-thick (2.5cm) triangles
1 cup 1% cottage cheese
1 tablespoon roughly chopped fresh basil
1 tablespoon balsamic vinegar
Coconut oil cooking spray
Pinch of salt

1. Preheat a grill to high. Lightly spray each watermelon slice with coconut oil cooking spray, and evenly drizzle the balsamic vinegar over each watermelon slice.
2. Grill the watermelon slices for 1 to 2 minutes per side, or until they are lightly seared and develop grill marks on each side.
3. Transfer the watermelon slices to a plate. Lightly season the slices with the salt, and top with the basil. Add the cottage cheese to the plate. Serve chilled.

Per Serving

calories: 260 | fat: 3.7g | carbs: 28.1g | protein: 30.3g

Matcha Green Tea Fudge Bars

Prep time: 5 minutes | Cook time: 3 minutes | Serves 10

½ cup oat flour
⅓ cup almond butter
1 cup plus 2 tablespoons unsweetened almond milk
1 teaspoon granulated sugar
Zest of 1 lemon
2 ounces (57 g) dark chocolate, finely chopped

1. Prepare an 8-inch by 8-inch baking pan by lining it with parchment paper, using 2 sheets placed in opposite.
2. In a small bowl, add protein powder, matcha, and oat flour. Use a fork to thoroughly combine; reserve.
3. In the bowl of a stand mixer, add almond butter, almond milk, Stevia, and lemon zest. Mix on low to combine (or alternatively mix by hand with a spatula). Slowly add the protein powder mixture, stirring to combine.
4. Transfer matcha fudge to the prepared pan, using a spatula to evenly spread the mixture. Cover with plastic wrap and place in the fridge overnight.
5. Lift the parchment paper from the pan and place onto a cutting board. Slice fudge into 10 pieces.
6. Using either a microwave or double boiler on the stove, gently stir the chocolate until melted. Drizzle melted chocolate over the bars.
7. Store bars in an airtight container.

Per Serving

calories: 194 | fat: 6.8g | carbs: 12.1g | protein: 21.4g

Protein Salad with Buttermilk Dressing

Prep time: 10 minutes | Cook time: 0 minutes | Serves 1

2 cups baby spring mix
2 scallions, chopped
1 small cucumber, halved and sliced
4 white button mushrooms, halved and sliced
¼ medium avocado, peeled and chopped
½ cup 2% cottage cheese
1 hard-boiled egg, peeled and chopped
3 tablespoons low-fat buttermilk
Juice of 1 lemon
1 clove garlic, minced
Salt and ground black pepper, to taste

1. Into a medium bowl, add spring mix, scallions, cucumber, mushrooms, avocado, cottage cheese, and egg.
2. In a small bowl, add buttermilk, lemon juice, garlic, salt, and pepper. Use a fork to combine.
3. Drizzle the dressing over the salad, toss, and serve.

Per Serving

calories: 349 | fat: 14.7g | carbs: 29.2g | protein: 30.3g

Chicken Breast Salad

Prep time: 10 minutes | Cook time: 0 minutes | Serves 2

1 small head iceberg lettuce, cored and chopped
8 ounces (227 g) boneless, skinless chicken breast, cooked and cut into ¼-inch cubes
2 hard-boiled eggs, peeled, and chopped
2 tomatoes, chopped
1 avocado, peeled, pitted, and sliced
1 cup grated carrots
¼ cup shredded low-fat mild Cheddar cheese
Salad dressing, like red wine vinaigrette or cucumber ranch dressing

1. Combine everything in a large bowl and toss. Divide into separate bowls and serve with a dressing of your choice.

Per Serving
calories: 446 | fat: 22.5g | carbs: 23.1g | protein: 40.3g

Chapter 10 Breakfast

Honey Greek Yogurt Parfait

Prep time: 5 minutes | Cook time: 0 minutes | Serves 2

2 cups nonfat plain Greek yogurt
2 tablespoons creamy unsweetened peanut butter
1 tablespoon honey
1 teaspoon vanilla extract
1 large banana, sliced
¼ cup granola

1. In a medium bowl, combine the yogurt, peanut butter, honey, and vanilla. Stir until completely combined and smooth.
2. Into each of 2 airtight storage containers, place a heaping cup of yogurt, topped with half a banana and 2 tablespoons of granola, and seal.
3. Store the airtight containers in the refrigerator for up to 1 week.

Per Serving (1 parfait)
calories: 343 | fat: 15.9g | carbs: 53.1g | protein: 31.3g

French Toast with Cottage Cheese

Prep time: 15 minutes | Cook time: 1 minute | Serves 4

For the Maple-Basil Cottage Cheese:
1 cup reduced-fat cottage cheese (2%)
2 teaspoons chopped fresh basil
1 teaspoon pure maple syrup

For the French Toast:
⅔ cup egg whites
2 large eggs
2 tablespoons unsweetened vanilla almond milk
2½ tablespoons pure maple syrup
2 teaspoons vanilla extract
2 teaspoons ground cinnamon
Pinch sea salt
⅛ cup vanilla vegan protein powder
8 gluten-free French bread slices
Coconut oil or coconut oil spray, for frying
8 large strawberries, sliced
Pure maple syrup, for serving (optional)

Make the Maple-Basil Cottage Cheese
1. In a small bowl, mix together the cottage cheese with the fresh basil and maple syrup. Set aside.

Make the French Toast
2. In a large bowl, whisk together the egg whites, eggs, almond milk, maple syrup, vanilla, cinnamon, and salt. Whisk in the protein powder.
3. Soak 2 pieces of bread in the egg mixture, making sure both pieces are submerged.
4. Meanwhile, heat a large cast-iron pan over medium heat and melt just enough coconut oil to moisten the pan.
5. Add the 2 soaked slices of bread and toast just until browned on one side, then flip and cook the other side just until browned. Meanwhile, start soaking the next 2 pieces of bread, leaving them in the mixture for at least 2 minutes.
6. Repeat step 4 with the remaining bread. Note that as the pan warms up, you may need to turn down the heat slightly.
7. Into each of 4 airtight storage containers, place 2 slices of French toast, ¼ cup of the maple cottage cheese, and half of the strawberry slices and seal. Drizzle with a bit of maple syrup (if using) right before eating.
8. Store the airtight containers in the refrigerator for up to 1 week. This recipe can be enjoyed cold, but to reheat, remove the toast and microwave it uncovered on high for 30 seconds to 1 minute. Serve with the strawberries and cottage cheese.

Per Serving (2 slices)
calories: 328 | fat: 13.8g | carbs: 31.2g | protein: 28.6g

Baked Sweet Potatoes with Cottage Cheese

Prep time: 5 minutes | Cook time: 45 minutes | Serves 4

4 sweet potatoes
2 cups low-fat cottage cheese (1%)
1 tablespoon chopped fresh basil
2 teaspoons pure maple syrup
½ teaspoon ground cinnamon

1. Preheat the oven to 425°F (220°C).
2. Prick the sweet potatoes all over with a fork, and place onto a baking sheet.
3. Place the baking sheet in the oven and bake for about 45 to 50 minutes, or until the sweet potatoes can be easily pierced with a fork.
4. Meanwhile, in a medium bowl, mix together the cottage cheese, basil, and maple syrup.
5. Once tender, let the sweet potatoes cool, then cut each in half and sprinkle with the cinnamon.
6. Into each of 4 airtight storage containers, place 1 sweet potato and seal. Into each of 4 small airtight storage containers, place ½ cup of cottage cheese and seal. Add the cottage cheese to the baked potato right before eating.
7. Store the airtight containers in the refrigerator for up to 5 days. To reheat, microwave the sweet potato uncovered on high for 2 to 3 minutes.

Per Serving

calories: 169 | fat: 1.9g | carbs: 20.1g | protein: 16.3g

Cinnamon Apple Flapjacks

Prep time: 10 minutes | Cook time: 4 minutes | Makes 10 flapjacks

2 scoops vanilla vegan protein powder
1½ cups egg whites
1 apple, peeled and chopped
2 cups rolled oats
¼ cup ground flaxseed
1 tablespoon ground cinnamon
2 tablespoons pure maple syrup
2 teaspoons vanilla extract
⅓ cup raisins

1. In a high-powered blender, combine the protein powder, egg whites, apple, oats, flaxseed, cinnamon, maple syrup, and vanilla, and blend until smooth.
2. Heat a large nonstick skillet over medium heat. Add about ¼ cup of batter to the pan, then drop 7 to 8 raisins onto the pancake.
3. Cook until bubbles start to form on the surface and the edges start to look dry, about 3 minutes, then flip over and cook for another minute or so, or until both sides are golden brown.
4. Remove from the heat and let cool on a wire rack so the flapjack doesn't get soggy.
5. Repeat with the remaining batter.
6. Into each of 5 airtight containers, place 2 flapjacks and seal.
7. Store the airtight containers in the refrigerator for up to 5 days. To reheat, microwave uncovered on high for 30 seconds to 1 minute.

Per Serving (2 flapjacks)

calories: 299 | fat: 5.8g | carbs: 47.1g | protein: 20.2g

Banana, Blueberry, and Peach Smoothie Bowl

Prep time: 10 minutes | Cook time: 0 minutes | Serves 4

For the Smoothie Packs:

4 fresh or frozen bananas, chopped, divided
4 cups frozen blueberries, divided
2 cups frozen peaches, divided
28 ice cubes, divided
4 scoops vegan vanilla protein powder, divided
4 tablespoons almond butter, divided
4 tablespoons ground flaxseed, divided
Freshly grated ginger, for topping

For the Smoothies:

4 cups unsweetened vanilla coconut or almond milk, divided
½ lemon, cut into wedges

Make the Smoothie Packs

4. In each of 4 resealable freezer bags, place 1 banana, 1 cup of blueberries, ½ cup of peaches, 7 ice cubes, 1 scoop of protein powder, 1 tablespoon of almond butter, 1 tablespoon of flaxseed, and a pinch of grated ginger. Lay the bags flat and remove as much air as possible before sealing. Store in the freezer until ready to use.

Make a Smoothie

5. In a blender, combine 1 cup of almond milk and a squeeze of lemon juice, followed by the contents of 1 smoothie pack, and blend until smooth.
6. Store the airtight bags in the freezer for up to 3 months.

Per Serving (1 smoothie)

calories: 458 | fat: 19.2g | carbs: 66.1g | protein: 24.9g

Breakfast in A Jar

Prep time: 10 minutes | Cook time: 0 minutes | Serves 4

2 cups nonfat vanilla Greek yogurt
2 cups unsweetened vanilla almond milk
¼ cup rolled oats
¼ cup chia seeds
4 teaspoons creamy peanut butter
4 teaspoons honey
2 teaspoons vanilla extract
2 bananas, sliced

1. In a medium bowl, mix together the yogurt, almond milk, oats, chia seeds, peanut butter, honey, and vanilla.
2. In each of 4 airtight storage containers, place about 1 cup of the oatmeal mixture and half of a banana and seal.
3. Store the airtight containers in the refrigerator for up to 4 days. This breakfast is meant to be eaten cold.

Per Serving (1 container)
calories: 223 | fat: 4.7g | carbs: 30.1g | protein: 17.3g

Ham and Cheese Quiche

Prep time: 10 minutes | Cook time: 45 minutes | Serves 4

Nonstick cooking spray
4 large eggs
1½ cups egg whites
1 cup reduced-fat cottage cheese (1%)
5 bacon slices, cooked and crumbled
½ cup finely chopped extra-lean ham
¼ cup crumbled feta cheese
½ onion, finely chopped
1 green bell pepper, finely chopped
½ teaspoon sea salt
¼ teaspoon freshly ground black pepper

7. Preheat the oven to 350°F (180°C). Coat the bottom and sides of an 8-by-8-inch square glass baking dish with nonstick cooking spray.
8. In a large bowl, combine the eggs, egg whites, cottage cheese, bacon, ham, feta, onion, bell pepper, salt, and pepper. Pour the mixture into the prepared baking dish.
9. Bake for 45 minutes, or until the center is set.
10. Remove from the oven and let cool.
11. Cut into 8 equal pieces. Into each of 4 airtight storage containers, place 2 pieces of quiche and seal.
12. Store the airtight containers in the refrigerator for up to 4 days. To reheat, microwave uncovered on high for 1 to 2 minutes.

Per Serving
calories: 322 | fat: 17.8g | carbs: 6.1g | protein: 33.2g

Turkey Sausage-Egg Scramble

Prep time: 10 minutes | Cook time: 7 minutes | Serves 2

2 large eggs
4 large egg whites
2 tablespoons reduced-fat cream (5%)
Pinch ground cayenne pepper
Sea salt, to taste
Freshly ground black pepper, to taste
½ tablespoon coconut oil or butter
2 precooked turkey sausages, diced
2 tablespoons finely chopped scallions, white and green parts
¼ cup grated Cheddar cheese

1. In a medium bowl, combine the eggs, egg whites, cream, and cayenne. Whisk until well blended, and season with salt and pepper. Set aside.
2. In a medium skillet over medium-high heat, melt the coconut oil. Add the sausages and cook for 3 to 4 minutes, until browned. Add the scallions and sauté until translucent, about 3 minutes.
3. Pour the egg mixture into the pan and cook, stirring frequently, for about 1 minute.
4. Just before the eggs are fully cooked, sprinkle on the cheese. Continue cooking just until the cheese has melted.
5. Into each of 2 airtight storage containers, place equal amounts of sausage and eggs and seal.
6. Store the airtight containers in the refrigerator for up 5 days. To reheat, microwave uncovered on high for 1 to 2 minutes.

Per Serving
calories: 477 | fat: 35.7g | carbs: 2.9g | protein: 35.1g

Baby Spinach and Tomato Frittata

Prep time: 15 minutes | Cook time: 18 minutes | Serves 3

1 tablespoon unsalted butter or extra-virgin olive oil
3 cups sliced mushrooms
1 red bell pepper, finely chopped
1 garlic clove, minced
3 scallions, white and green parts, thinly sliced
2 teaspoons dried parsley
Sea salt and black pepper, to taste
2 large eggs
8 large egg whites
2 cups chopped, loosely packed baby spinach
1 cup chopped Roma, vine, or cherry tomatoes
¼ cup crumbled feta cheese
¼ cup grated Parmesan cheese (or aged Cheddar cheese)

1. In a large, well-seasoned, oven-safe sauté pan or skillet over medium-high heat, melt the butter. Add the mushrooms and sauté until tender, about 5 minutes. Add the bell pepper, garlic, scallions, and parsley, and sauté for another 2 to 3 minutes, until the garlic is fragrant. Season with salt and pepper.
2. Meanwhile, in a medium bowl, combine the eggs and egg whites and beat well. Stir in the spinach and tomatoes, season with salt and pepper, then pour the egg mixture into the pan over the other vegetables.
3. As the eggs begin to set around the edge of the pan, use a spatula to allow uncooked egg to flow underneath. Cook until the bottom is set and the top is almost done, 8 to 10 minutes.
4. Meanwhile, preheat the broiler to high.
5. Sprinkle the cheeses over the eggs, transfer the pan to the oven, and broil for 2 to 3 minutes, until the cheese is melted and the eggs have finished cooking. Remove from the oven and let cool. Slice into 6 equal wedges.
6. Into each container, place 2 wedges and seal.
7. Store for up to 5 days. To reheat, microwave uncovered on high for 1 to 2 minutes.

Per Serving (1 container)
calories: 290 | fat: 14.9g | carbs: 11.2g | protein: 26.5g

Banana and Oat Protein Bars

Prep time: 10 minutes | Cook time: 28 minutes | Serves 4

2 medium ripe bananas, mashed
1 cup liquid egg whites
¼ cup unsweetened vanilla almond milk
1 teaspoon vanilla extract
1½ cups old-fashioned rolled oats
½ cup vanilla whey protein powder
1 teaspoon baking powder

1. Preheat the oven to 350°F (177°C). Spray an 8 x 8in (20 x 20cm) baking dish with non-stick cooking spray.
2. In a medium bowl, combine the bananas, egg whites, almond milk, and vanilla extract. Mix well. In a separate large bowl, combine the oats, protein powder, and baking powder. Mix well.
3. To make the batter, add the wet ingredients to the dry ingredients. Stir well to combine.
4. Pour the batter into the baking dish and bake for 28 to 30 minutes, or until the top is golden brown. Cut into four equal-sized bars.

Per Serving
calories: 281 | fat: 2.7g | carbs: 34.6g | protein: 30.1g

Blueberry-Oat Muffins

Prep time: 15 minutes | Cook time: 20 minutes | Serves 12

1 cup old-fashioned rolled oats
⅔ cup gluten-free or all purpose flour
½ cup vanilla whey protein powder
1 teaspoon ground cinnamon
1 teaspoon baking powder
1 teaspoon baking soda
¼ cup powdered stevia
⅓ cup liquid egg whites
1 cup unsweetened applesauce (preferably cinnamon flavored)
¼ cup butter, softened
¾ cup unsweetened almond milk
1 teaspoon vanilla extract
1 cup fresh blueberries

1. Preheat the oven to 400°F (204°C). Spray a large muffin tin with non-stick cooking spray.
2. In a large bowl, combine the oats, flour, protein powder, cinnamon, baking powder, baking soda, and stevia. Mix well.
3. In a separate medium bowl, combine the egg whites, applesauce, butter, almond milk, and vanilla extract. Mix well.
4. Make the batter by adding the wet ingredients to the dry ingredients, and mixing until the ingredients are just incorporated. Gently fold in the blueberries, being careful not to crush them. Fill each muffin tin cup to two-thirds full with the batter.
5. Bake for 20 to 25 minutes, or until a toothpick inserted into the middle comes out clean. Serve warm.

Per Serving
calories: 135 | fat: 5.2g | carbs: 14.1g | protein: 8.7g

Breakfast Turkey Hash

Prep time: 10 minutes | Cook time: 21 minutes | Serves 4

1 medium white onion, diced
1 pound (454 g) ground turkey breast
1 teaspoon ground cumin
1 teaspoon red pepper flakes
1 teaspoon paprika
1 teaspoon salt
2 medium sweet potatoes, peeled and cut into ½-inch (1.25cm) cubes
2 cups fresh baby spinach
4 medium eggs

1. Preheat the broiler to low. Spray a medium cast iron skillet with coconut oil cooking spray and place over medium heat.
2. Add the onion to the skillet. Cook until soft and translucent, stirring frequently. Add the turkey breast, cumin, red pepper flakes, paprika, and salt. Stir well to combine, using a wooden spoon to break up the ground turkey. Cook for 6 to 8 minutes, stirring frequently, until the turkey is browned. Transfer to a large bowl and set aside.
3. Add the sweet potatoes to the skillet and cook for 8 to 10 minutes, or until soft. Add the spinach and cook for an additional 1 to 2 minutes, or until wilted. Add the turkey and onions back to the skillet. Mix well.
4. Make 4 divots in the hash and carefully crack an egg into each divot. Place the skillet in the oven and broil for 5 to 7 minutes, or until the eggs are set and the hash is lightly browned. Serve hot.

Per Serving

calories: 292 | fat: 6.6g | carbs: 23.1g | protein: 35.4g

Breakfast Skillet

Prep time: 10 minutes | Cook time: 28 minutes | Serves 4

3 cups liquid egg whites
2 teaspoons plain unsweetened almond milk
1 (20-ounce / 567-g) package frozen shredded hash brown potatoes, thawed
½ cup diced onion
1 teaspoon salt
1 teaspoon garlic powder
1 teaspoon dehydrated bell pepper flakes
1 large tomato, cut crosswise into ¼-inch (.5cm) slices

1. Preheat oven to 350°F (177°C). In a medium bowl, combine the egg whites and almond milk, and stir well to combine. Set aside.
2. Spray a large cast iron skillet with coconut oil spray and place over medium heat. Add the potatoes, onion, salt, garlic powder, and bell pepper flakes. Cook for 8 to 10 minutes, stirring frequently, until the potatoes begin to brown and the onions become soft and translucent.
3. Pour the egg white and almond milk mixture over top of the potatoes and onions. Stir gently. Place the tomato slices over top.
4. Bake for 20 to 25 minutes, or until the middle is set and firm. Cut into four equal-size slices. Serve warm.

Per Serving

calories: 225 | fat: 0.3g | carbs: 30.6g | protein: 23.1g

Egg and Canadian Bacon Cups

Prep time: 5 minutes | Cook time: 18 minutes | Serves 6

6 large eggs
12 slices nitrate-free Canadian bacon
Pinch of salt
Pinch of ground black pepper

1. Preheat the oven to 350°F (177°C). Spray a large muffin tin with non-stick cooking spray. Place 2 slices of Canadian bacon into each tin and shape them into cups.
2. Crack one egg into each cup, and season with equal amounts of salt and black pepper.
3. Bake for 18 to 20 minutes, or until the centers of the eggs are set and firm. (For creamier yolks, bake just until the centers of the yolks are set.) Serve warm.

Per Serving

calories: 264 | fat: 12.6g | carbs: 2.8g | protein: 34.6g

Chicken Breast and Polenta Pizza

Prep time: 10 minutes | Cook time: 42 minutes | Serves 4

1 cup dried polenta
3 cups low-sodium chicken broth
1 teaspoon salt
1 pound (454 g) ground chicken breast
1 teaspoon garlic powder
1 teaspoon dried oregano
2 cups fresh baby spinach
1 cup button mushrooms, thinly sliced

1. Preheat the oven to 425°F (218°C). In a large saucepan over high heat, bring the chicken broth to a boil. Reduce the heat to medium and gradually add the polenta to the pan, whisking constantly. Add ½ teaspoon salt and continue to whisk until the polenta starts to thicken.
2. Spray an 8 x 8in (20 x 20cm) baking dish with non-stick cooking spray. Spread the polenta mixture evenly across the prepared baking dish. Bake for 28 to 30 minutes.
3. While the crust is baking, spray a large skillet with non-stick cooking spray and place over medium heat. Add the ground chicken, and season with the garlic powder, oregano, and the remaining ½ teaspoon of salt. Cook for 8 to 10 minutes, stirring occasionally, and using a wooden spoon to break up the chicken.
4. Add the spinach and mushrooms to the pan. Cook for an additional 2 to 3 minutes, stirring constantly, until the spinach is wilted, the mushrooms are soft, and all of the liquid has cooked off.
5. Top the baked crust with the chicken, mushroom, and spinach mixture, making sure the mixture is evenly distributed across the crust. Place the pizza in the oven and bake for 4 to 5 minutes, or until the toppings are lightly browned. Cut into four equal-sized slices. Serve hot.

Per Serving
calories: 295 | fat: 3.2g | carbs: 33.1g | protein: 30.1g

Thyme Crustless Quiche

Prep time: 10 minutes | Cook time: 35 minutes | Serves 2

1 cup yellow squash, thinly sliced
1 cup zucchini, thinly sliced
1 large bell pepper, seeded and thinly sliced
2 teaspoons minced garlic
1 tablespoon dried thyme
1½ cups liquid egg whites
¾ cup 1% milk
¾ teaspoon salt
½ teaspoon ground black pepper
¼ cup grated Parmesan cheese

1. Preheat the oven to 350°F (177°C). Spray a large skillet with non-stick cooking spray and place over medium heat. In a large bowl, combine the egg whites, milk, salt, black pepper, and Parmesan cheese. Mix until well incorporated. Set aside.
2. Add the squash, zucchini, bell pepper, garlic, and thyme to the pan, and cook until the vegetables are slightly softened, about 5 to 6 minutes. Set aside.
3. Spray an 8-inch pie dish with non-stick cooking spray. Spoon the vegetables into the pie dish, and carefully pour the egg and milk mixture over top of the vegetables.
4. Place the pie dish on a baking sheet and bake for 30 to 35 minutes, or until the center is set. Slice into two equal-sized portions. Serve warm.

Per Serving
calories: 196 | fat: 4.1g | carbs: 11.2g | protein: 29.1g

Eggs Benedict with Hollandaise-Mustard Sauce

Prep time: 15 minutes | Cook time: 10 minutes | Serves 1

For the Hollandaise-Mustard Sauce:
1 tablespoon light mayonnaise
½ tablespoon water
1 teaspoon whole-grain mustard
½ teaspoon lemon juice
Pinch of ground cayenne pepper

For the Eggs Benedict:
1 tablespoon white vinegar
½ tablespoon extra-virgin olive oil
1 ounce (28 g) Canadian bacon, diced
½ small onion, thinly sliced
4 cups chopped kale (stems removed)
Ground black pepper, to taste
1 whole-grain English muffin, split

1. To make the sauce, into a blender or food processor, add mayonnaise, water, mustard, lemon juice, and cayenne. Process until smooth. Transfer the sauce to a small bowl and reserve.
2. To prepare eggs, add about 3 inches of water into a large skillet. Pour in vinegar and bring to a low simmer over medium heat.
3. Meanwhile, warm oil in medium nonstick skillet over medium-high heat. Sauté the Canadian bacon and onion, stirring constantly, until golden brown, about 4 minutes. Remove the pan from heat and toss in kale. Stir until the greens wilt, about 2 minutes, and season with pepper.
4. Toast English muffin halves until lightly golden. Place onto a plate, layering a tomato slice and kale mixture onto each half. Place the pan in the oven to stay warm (keep the oven turned off).
5. Crack eggs into a mug one by one and slip them into the simmering water. Cook approximately 3 to 5 minutes, carefully removing the eggs with a slotted spoon once they reach desired doneness. Top poached eggs onto the prepared English muffins and drizzle with Hollandaise-style sauce. Serve.

2 tomato slices
2 large eggs

Per Serving

calories: 575 | fat: 24.1g | carbs: 62.2g | protein: 33.4g

Cinnamon Sweet Potato Pancakes

Prep time: 10 minutes | Cook time: 6 minutes | Serves 1

1 (5-ounce / 142-g) medium sweet potato
½ cup old-fashioned oats
1 large egg
4 egg whites or ¾ cup liquid egg white substitute
½ teaspoon vanilla extract
½ teaspoon ground cinnamon
¼ cup 2% plain yogurt

Per Serving

calories: 506 | fat: 11.2g | carbs: 63.1g | protein: 38.9g

1. Prick sweet potato several times with a fork. Wrap potato in a wet paper towel and microwave for 5 minutes on high power. Carefully run potato under cool water and then remove its skin with a knife.
2. Add oats into a blender or a food processor and process until oats are powder-like. Transfer to a medium bowl and reserve.
3. Add the sweet potato into the blender or food processor, puréeing until smooth. Place into the bowl with oats. Stir in whole egg, egg whites, vanilla, cinnamon, and yogurt. Mix well until the batter is smooth.
4. Coat a medium nonstick pan with cooking spray and warm over medium-low heat.
5. Spoon half the batter into the pan and cook until golden brown, about 1 to 2 minutes. Use a spatula to flip the pancake and cook again until golden brown and firm, about another 30 to 60 seconds. Transfer the pancake to a plate.
6. Reapply cooking spray to the pan and repeat with remaining batter. Serve.

Polenta Squares with Blueberry Sauce and Banana

Prep time: 10 minutes | Cook time: 14 minutes | Serves 4

3 cups water
3 cups 2% milk
2 teaspoons salt
1¾ cups yellow cornmeal
3 scoops vanilla protein powder
2 cups fresh or frozen blueberries
1 tablespoon honey
2 teaspoons extra-virgin olive oil
1 banana, peeled and sliced

Per Serving

calories: 467 | fat: 7.9g | carbs: 71.7g | protein: 27.3g

1. In a large, heavy-duty pot over medium-high heat, bring water and milk to a boil. Add salt and gradually whisk in cornmeal.
2. Reduce the heat to low and cook until the mixture thickens and cornmeal is tender, stirring often, about 10 to 15 minutes. Remove from the heat. Add the protein powder and stir until no lumps are visible. Pour the polenta into an 8-inch by 8-inch casserole dish and place in the fridge to set, about 30 to 45 minutes. After the mixture solidifies, cut it into 2-inch by 2-inch squares.
3. To prepare blueberry sauce, add blueberries and honey into a blender. Process until smooth, about 1 minute.
4. Warm oil in a large skillet over medium-high heat. Working in batches, brown polenta squares, cooking about 2 minutes per side. Transfer polenta squares to a dish.
5. Add blueberry sauce to the skillet. Stirring constantly, let the blueberry sauce warm over medium-high heat. Pour hot blueberry sauce over polenta and top with banana slices.

Eggs and Cheery Tomato Breakfast Melts

Prep time: 10 minutes | Cook time: 3 minutes | Serves 1

1 whole-grain English muffin, split
½ teaspoon extra-virgin olive oil
2 scallions, finely chopped and divided
4 egg whites, whisked, or ¾ cup liquid egg white substitute
Salt and ground black pepper, to taste
¼ cup halved cherry tomatoes
¼ cup shredded Mexican cheese blend

Per Serving

calories: 335 | fat: 12.8g | carbs: 31.2g | protein: 27.4g

1. Preheat the broiler.
2. Add English muffin halves into a toaster and toast until golden brown. Place onto a baking sheet.
3. Warm oil in a small nonstick skillet over medium heat. Add half the scallions and sauté for about 2 to 3 minutes. Add egg whites into the pan, along with salt and pepper. Stir with a spatula until eggs are fully cooked; remove from heat.
4. Layer the muffin halves with scrambled egg whites, tomatoes, and cheese. Broil until cheese melts, about 1 to 1½ minutes. Use a spatula to transfer breakfast melts to a plate, garnish with remaining scallions, and serve.

Chapter 11 Meats

Vietnamese Beef and Rice Noodle Bowl

Prep time: 15 minutes | Cook time: 11 minutes | Serves 4

4 garlic cloves, minced, divided
3½ tablespoons fish sauce, divided
2½ tablespoons coconut sugar, divided
1 tablespoon tamari or soy sauce, divided (tamari if gluten-free)
2 scallions, green parts only, chopped, divided
¾ pound (340.2 g) beef stir-fry strips
8 ounces (227 g) rice noodles
1 tablespoon freshly squeezed lime juice
1 tablespoon rice vinegar
½ teaspoon peeled and minced fresh ginger
2 tablespoons coconut oil, divided
Salt, to taste
Freshly ground black pepper, to taste
3 to 4 shallots, chopped
3 carrots, peeled and shaved, divided
½ English cucumber, julienned, cucumber, divided
¼ cup peanut pieces, divided
¼ cup finely chopped fresh cilantro, divided

1. In a large bowl, mix together 3 minced garlic cloves, 2 tablespoons of fish sauce, 1 tablespoon of coconut sugar, the tamari, and half of the scallions. Add the beef to the bowl, stir to coat evenly, cover with a lid or plastic wrap, and place in the refrigerator to marinate for 30 to 60 minutes.
2. Bring a large pot of water to a boil. Remove from the heat, add the rice noodles, stir, and let sit for 5 to 7 minutes. Drain and rinse with cold water.
3. In a small bowl, mix together the remaining 1½ tablespoons of coconut sugar, 1½ tablespoons of fish sauce, and 1 garlic clove, as well as the lime juice, rice vinegar, and ginger, and set aside.
4. In a large skillet over high heat, melt 1 tablespoon of coconut oil. Add the beef and the marinade. Cook for 2 to 3 minutes, or until the marinade evaporates. Turn down the heat to medium-high and cook until only slightly pink inside, 1 to 2 more minutes. Season with salt and pepper and set aside.
5. In a small saucepan over medium heat, melt the remaining 1 tablespoon of coconut oil. Add the shallots and fry for 8 to 10 minutes, until golden brown and crispy. Remove from the heat.
6. Divide the noodles evenly among 4 airtight containers, then top with the carrots, cucumber, the remaining scallions, shallots, and the beef. Top each bowl with 1 tablespoon of peanut pieces and 1 tablespoon of cilantro, and seal.
7. Store the airtight containers in the refrigerator for up to 5 days. Reheat in the microwave for 30-second intervals.

Per Serving (1 container)
calories: 486 | fat: 15.8g | carbs: 58.7g | protein: 26.1g

Beef Burgers

Prep time: 10 minutes | Cook time: 18 minutes | Serves 4

1 pound (454g) extra-lean ground beef
1 large egg
3 tablespoons chopped cooked spinach, squeezed dry
1 tablespoon grated onion
½ teaspoon sea salt
Freshly ground black pepper, to taste
3 tablespoons grated medium Cheddar cheese
4 portobello mushrooms, stemmed
Extra-virgin olive oil, for brushing

1. In a medium bowl, combine the beef, egg, spinach, onion, salt, and pepper. Divide into 4 large, patty-size portions and 4 small portions.
2. Form the large portions into patties. Make an indentation in the center of each patty, and fill each with about 2 teaspoons of Cheddar cheese.
3. Flatten the small portions of the beef mixture and seal over top of the cheese.
4. In a broiler pan under a broiler on high heat or on a hot grill, broil or grill the patties for 10 minutes, flipping once, until cooked through.
5. Brush the mushrooms with olive oil. Season with salt and pepper.
6. In the broiler pan under high heat or on a grill, cook the mushroom caps for 6 to 8 minutes, until browned and slightly tender. Let cool.
7. In each container, place 1 mushroom and top with one burger patty. Store the lettuce and tomato in separate containers. Top the burgers when ready to serve.
8. Store for up to 5 days. To reheat, microwave uncovered on high for 1 to 2 minutes.

4 romaine lettuce leaves
4 ripe tomato slices

Per Serving

calories: 254 | fat: 10.9g | carbs: 5.8g | protein: 32.3g

Flank Steak with Brussels Sprouts

Prep time: 10 minutes | Cook time: 16 minutes | Serves 4

6 tablespoons extra-virgin olive oil
1½ tablespoons red wine vinegar
2 garlic cloves, minced
1½ tablespoons honey
¾ teaspoon sea salt
¼ teaspoon freshly ground black pepper
1 pound (454 g) flank steak, sliced into strips
Nonstick cooking spray
1 pound (454 g) Brussels sprouts, halved

1. In a medium bowl, whisk together the olive oil, vinegar, garlic, honey, salt, and pepper.
2. Place the steak strips in a baking dish or bowl and top with two-thirds of marinade. Cover and chill for an hour.
3. Spray a large sauté pan or skillet with cooking spray and heat over medium-high heat. Add the Brussels sprouts and sauté 8 to 10 minutes, stirring frequently, until lightly brown. Pour the remaining marinade in the pan and cook just until the Brussels sprouts are coated and the sauce has reduced.
4. Divide the Brussels sprouts evenly among 4 containers.
5. Remove the steak from the marinade and place it in the pan (still on medium-high heat). Discard any extra marinade.
6. Pan fry for about 4 minutes per side, or until the steak is only slightly pink inside. Let cool.
7. In each container, place 4 ounces of steak strips on top of the Brussels sprouts.
8. Store for up to 5 days. To reheat, microwave uncovered on high for 1 or 2 minutes.

Per Serving

calories: 477 | fat: 31.1g | carbs: 16.9g | protein: 36.3g

Bison and Portobello Buns

Prep time: 10 minutes | Cook time: 15 minutes | Serves 2

1 pound (454 g) lean ground bison, preferably 92/8 lean-to-fat ratio
¼ cup liquid egg whites
2 teaspoons dried onion flakes
1 teaspoon garlic powder
½ teaspoon salt
½ teaspoon ground black pepper
4 tablespoons no-sugar-added ketchup (optional)

For the Portobello Buns:

8 large portobello mushrooms
½ teaspoon salt
½ teaspoon ground black pepper
½ teaspoon garlic powder

1. Preheat the grill to medium. In a large bowl, combine the ground bison, egg whites, onion flakes, garlic powder, salt, and black pepper. Mix until the ingredients are well incorporated. With wet hands, shape the mixture into 8 even-sized patties. Set aside.
2. Rinse the mushrooms and pat dry with a paper towel. Remove the stems and place on a flat surface, gill-sides up. Season with the salt, black pepper, and garlic powder.
3. Place the mushrooms on the grill, gill-sides up, and grill for 3 minutes. Flip and grill for an additional 2 to 3 minutes. Transfer to a paper towel to drain, gill-sides down.
4. Place the bison patties on the grill, and cook for 4 to 5 minutes per side. Transfer to a plate and allow to rest for 5 minutes. Assemble the sliders by placing a bison patty between two portobello buns. Top each slider with 1 tablespoon ketchup (if using). Serve warm.

Per Serving

calories: 212 | fat: 8.7g | carbs: 9.1g | protein: 27.4g

Steak with Coffee-Rub

Prep time: 10 minutes | Cook time: 8 minutes | Serves 4

1 pound (454 g) sirloin or eye of round steak, trimmed of excess fat
1 tablespoon instant espresso powder
1 teaspoon garlic powder
½ teaspoon salt
¼ teaspoon ground cumin
¼ teaspoon dried oregano
¼ teaspoon chili powder
¼ teaspoon ground black pepper

1. Preheat the broiler to high. Line an 8 x 8in (20 x 20cm) baking pan with aluminum foil. Allow the steak to rest at room temperature for 30 minutes before patting dry with a paper towel.
2. In a medium bowl, combine the espresso powder, garlic powder, salt, cumin, oregano, chili powder, and black pepper. Mix well.
3. Generously season the steak with the rub, using your fingertips to gently press the rub into both sides of the steak.
4. Place the steak in the oven and broil for 2 to 3 minutes per side for medium rare, 3 to 4 minutes per side for medium, and 4 to 5 minutes per side for medium well.
5. Allow the steak to rest for 5 minutes before slicing against the grain, and into four equal-sized servings. Serve warm.

Per Serving

calories: 150 | fat: 4.4g | carbs: 0g | protein: 25.8g

Ginger Beef Sirloin and Bok Choy

Prep time: 10 minutes | Cook time: 10 minutes | Serves 4

1 tablespoon fresh ginger, minced
1 teaspoon garlic, minced
½ cup white onion, diced
1 pound (454 g) beef sirloin, sliced against the grain into ¼-inch strips
½ teaspoon red pepper flakes
½ teaspoon ground cumin
½ teaspoon ground coriander
1 tablespoon low sodium soy sauce (or liquid aminos)
1 large bok choy stalk, washed and sliced into ½-inch strips

1. Generously spray a medium skillet with non-stick cooking spray and place over medium heat. Add the ginger, garlic, and onion to the skillet, and cook until the onions are soft and translucent, stirring frequently.
2. Increase the heat to medium-high and add the sirloin strips, red pepper flakes, cumin, and coriander. Cook for 2 to 3 minutes, or until the meat is browned. Add the soy sauce, and continue to cook for an additional 1 to 2 minutes, stirring frequently.
3. Reduce the heat to low. Add the bok choy, cover, and steam for 5 minutes. Remove the lid, and continue to cook on low for an additional 2 to 3 minutes, or until the liquid is reduced. Serve hot.

Per Serving

calories: 242 | fat: 9.1g | carbs: 2.8g | protein: 35.7g

Southern Pork Medallions

Prep time: 5 minutes | Cook time: 8 minutes | Serves 4

1 pound (454 g) pork tenderloin, trimmed, silver skin removed, and sliced into 2-inch-thick medallions
1 teaspoon chili powder
1 teaspoon paprika
1 teaspoon garlic powder
1 teaspoon cumin
½ teaspoon dried oregano
½ teaspoon salt

1. Prior to starting the grill, spray the grill grate with non-stick cooking spray. Preheat grill to medium.
2. In a small bowl, combine the chili powder, paprika, garlic powder, cumin, oregano, and salt. Mix well.
3. Sprinkle the seasoning over the medallions. Use your fingertips to gently press the seasonings into both sides of the medallions.
4. Grill for 4 to 5 minutes per side. The medallions are done when the internal temperature reaches 145°F (63°C). Serve warm.

Per Serving

calories: 186 | fat: 5.5g | carbs: 0g | protein: 31.9g

Muscle-Building Beef Meatloaf

Prep time: 10 minutes | Cook time: 30 minutes | Serves 4

1 pound (454 g) lean ground beef (preferably 92/8 lean-to-fat ratio)
1 medium egg
½ cup chopped fresh mushrooms
⅓ cup finely chopped onion
¼ cup finely chopped sun-dried tomatoes
¼ cup chopped fresh parsley
½ teaspoon salt
½ teaspoon ground black pepper
⅓ cup almond flour

1. Preheat the oven to 375°F (191°C). Line a 9 x 13in (23 x 33cm) baking sheet with parchment paper.
2. In a large bowl, combine the ground beef, egg, mushrooms, onion, sun-dried tomatoes, parsley, salt, and black pepper. Mash the ingredients together with a fork until just incorporated. Sprinkle the almond flour over top, and continue to mash until all ingredients are well incorporated.
3. Form the mixture into 4 equal-sized, oval-shaped loaves. Place the loaves on the baking sheet, allowing at least ½-inch (1.25cm) between each loaf.
4. Bake for 30 to 35 minutes, or until the internal temperature reaches 165°F (74°C). Serve hot.

Per Serving

calories: 232 | fat: 13.7g | carbs: 5.2g | protein: 24.6g

Sirloin Steak

Prep time: 5 minutes | Cook time: 47 minutes | Serves 4

1 pound (454 g) sirloin steak
1 teaspoon salt
1 teaspoon ground black pepper

Per Serving

calories: 229 | fat: 9.1g | carbs: 0g | protein: 34.4g

1. Preheat the oven to 275°F (135°C). Place an oven-safe cooling rack atop a large, foil-lined baking sheet.
2. Season both sides of the steak with salt and pepper, and allow to rest at room temperature for 30 minutes.
3. Place the steak on the cooling rack and place in the oven. Bake for 30 minutes if the steak is 1 to 2 inches thick (2.5 to 5cm), or 45 minutes if the steak is 3 to 4 inches thick (7.5 to 10cm).
4. Remove the steak from the oven and allow to rest for 15 minutes.
5. Spray a large cast iron skillet with coconut oil cooking spray and preheat over high heat. Place the steak in the skillet and sear for approximately 1 minute per side. The steak is done when it's pink in the middle and the internal temperature reaches 145°F (63°C). Serve hot.

Adobo Sirloin Steak

Prep time: 10 minutes | Cook time: 8 minutes | Serves 4

Juice of 1 lime
1 tablespoon minced garlic
1 teaspoon dried oregano
1 teaspoon ground cumin
2 tablespoons finely chopped canned chipotle chiles in adobo sauce plus 2 tablespoons sauce
4 (6-ounce / 170-g) sirloin steaks, trimmed of fat
Salt and ground black pepper, to taste

4. In a small bowl, combine lime juice, garlic, oregano, cumin, chiles, and adobo sauce. Mix well to combine.
5. Season meat with salt and pepper. Place steaks into a large Ziploc bag with adobo marinade. Seal tightly and shake to coat. Refrigerate for at least 2 hours, shaking occasionally.
6. Prepare a grill to high heat. Lightly coat the grill grates with cooking spray. Once the grill is hot, cook steaks until desired doneness, about 4 to 5 minutes on each side. Let the steaks rest for 10 minutes and serve

Per Serving

calories: 237 | fat: 6.9g | carbs: 1.7g | protein: 39.2g

Cheesy Beef Stroganoff

Prep time: 15 minutes | Cook time: 10 minutes | Serves 4

Salt and ground black pepper, to taste
8 ounces (227 g) egg noodles
1 pound (454 g) beef tenderloin, trimmed of fat and sliced
2 tablespoons extra-virgin olive oil
½ medium onion, sliced
4 ounces (113 g) white mushrooms, sliced
1 tablespoon cornstarch
1 (10½-ounce / 297.7-g) can condensed beef broth, divided
1 teaspoon Dijon mustard
1 clove garlic, peeled and minced
3 tablespoons white wine
½ tablespoon Worcestershire sauce
2 tablespoons low-fat sour cream
2 tablespoons reduced-fat cream cheese

1. Bring a large pot of lightly salted water to a boil over high heat. Cook noodles according to package instructions. Drain and reserve.
2. Meanwhile, season meat with salt and pepper. Warm oil in a large skillet over medium heat. Add beef; brown on all sides and then push to one side of the pan.
3. Add onion and mushrooms, cooking until tender, about 3 to 5 minutes. Push to the side with beef. In a small bowl, combine cornstarch with 2 tablespoons cold beef broth. Add to the skillet and mix with juices in the pan to deglaze.
4. Pour in remaining beef broth. Bring to a boil, stirring frequently. Reduce the heat to low and stir in mustard, garlic, wine, and Worcestershire sauce. Cover with a tight-fitting lid and simmer for 10 minutes.
5. Two minutes before beef is done, stir in sour cream and cream cheese. Stir well and allow beef to finish cooking in the sauce. Let meat rest 5 minutes and serve.

Per Serving
calories: 301 | fat: 15.9g | carbs: 5.8g | protein: 29.1g

Beef and Chicken Sausage Stuffed Peppers

Prep time: 10 minutes | Cook time: 30 minutes | Serves 4

1 tablespoon extra-virgin olive oil
1 cup chopped onion
¼ pound 92% lean ground beef
¼ pound chicken sausage, casing removed
½ cup cooked medium-grain rice
¼ cup chopped scallions
1 teaspoon sweet paprika
½ teaspoon ground cayenne pepper
1 teaspoon dried oregano
Salt and ground black pepper, to taste
24 mini bell peppers, tops and seeds removed

1. Preheat the oven to 400°F (205°C).
2. Warm oil in a large skillet over medium heat. Add onion, stirring occasionally, and cook until translucent and lightly brown.
3. Remove from heat and transfer onion to a medium bowl. Into the bowl, add beef, sausage, rice, scallions, paprika, cayenne, oregano, salt, and pepper. Mix well.
4. Use a spoon to stuff the mixture into the cavity of each pepper. Add peppers to a shallow pan and cover with aluminum foil.
5. Bake peppers for 30 minutes or until their tops are crusty and brown. Serve hot.

Per Serving
calories: 279 | fat: 9.7g | carbs: 34.9g | protein: 16.2g

Chinese Plum Sauce-Glazed Pork Chops

Prep time: 5 minutes | Cook time: 6 minutes | Serves 4

4 (6-ounce / 170-g) boneless pork chops, trimmed of fat
¼ teaspoon salt
¼ teaspoon ground black pepper
¼ cup Chinese plum sauce
4 teaspoons yellow mustard

1. Season pork chops with salt and pepper. Coat a large nonstick skillet with cooking spray and warm over medium-high heat.
2. Add pork chops into the skillet, cooking until no longer pink in the center, about 3 minutes per side.
3. In a small bowl, combine plum sauce and mustard. Brush the mixture on top of each pork chop and serve.

Per Serving
calories: 229 | fat: 3.8g | carbs: 7.6g | protein: 39.1g

Mustard Sage-Coated Pork Tenderloin

Prep time: 5 minutes | Cook time: 24 minutes | Serves 4

1 pound (454 g) pork tenderloin, trimmed of fat
1 tablespoon extra-virgin olive oil
Salt and ground black pepper, to taste
2 tablespoons Dijon mustard
2 cloves garlic, peeled and minced
1 tablespoon finely chopped fresh sage

1. Preheat the oven to 375°F (190°C). Coat a shallow baking pan with cooking spray and set aside.
2. Use paper towels to pat the pork dry and season it with salt and pepper.
3. Warm oil in a large nonstick skillet over high heat. Once the pan is hot but not yet smoking, add pork, turning occasionally until browned on all sides, about 4 minutes. Transfer to the prepared baking pan.
4. Spread mustard, garlic, and sage over pork. Roast in the middle rack of the oven until an instant-read thermometer diagonally inserted 2 inches into the meat registers 145°F (63°C), about 20 minutes
5. Transfer pork to a cutting board and cover with aluminum foil. Let pork rest for 10 minutes before slicing and serving.

Per Serving
calories: 172 | fat: 5.8g | carbs: 0.9g | protein: 26.1g

Cajun Pork Chops with Tomatoes

Prep time: 5 minutes | Cook time: 11 minutes | Serves 4

4 (5-ounce / 142-g) boneless pork chops, ½-inch thick and trimmed of fat
2 teaspoons salt-free extra-spicy seasoning blend
½ medium yellow onion, sliced
1 jalapeño pepper, seeded and finely chopped
1 (14½-ounce / 411.1-g) can diced tomatoes, undrained

1. Rub both sides of pork chops with spicy seasoning blend.
2. Coat a large nonstick skillet with cooking spray and warm the pan over medium-high heat. Add onion and jalapeño, sautéing until slightly tender, about 2 minutes. Push the mixture to one side of the skillet.
3. On the other side of the skillet, add pork chops. Cook pork chops for 3 minutes, turning once so both sides are evenly browned.
4. Add tomatoes into the pan. When liquid begins to boil, reduce the heat to low, and cover with a lid. Cook until pork chops are no longer pink in the center, about 6 to 8 minutes. Serve chops, spooning sauce over them.

Per Serving
calories: 190 | fat: 2.9g | carbs: 5.6g | protein: 32.1g

Parmesan Breaded Pork Chops

Prep time: 10 minutes | Cook time: 18 minutes | Serves 4

¼ cup 2% milk
¼ cup grated Parmesan cheese
¼ cup seasoned breadcrumbs
¼ teaspoon salt
¼ teaspoon pepper
¼ teaspoon garlic powder
4 (6-ounce / 170-g) boneless pork chops, ½-inch thick and trimmed of fat

1. Preheat the oven to 375°F (190°C). Coat a baking sheet with cooking spray.
2. Place milk into a shallow dish. Into another shallow dish, add cheese, breadcrumbs, salt, pepper, and garlic powder; mix to combine.
3. Dip each pork chop into milk and then coat in the breadcrumb mixture. Place breaded chops onto the prepared baking sheet.
4. Bake chops in the oven until done, about 9 to 11 minutes on each side.

Per Serving
calories: 256 | fat: 5.7g | carbs: 5.9g | protein: 42.1g

Stir Fried Pork and Bok Choy Noodle

Prep time: 10 minutes | Cook time: 10 minutes | Serves 4

Salt, to taste
8 ounces (227 g) rice noodles
⅓ cup water
¼ cup Shao Hsing rice wine or dry sherry
2 tablespoons less-sodium soy sauce
2 teaspoons cornstarch
1 tablespoon peanut oil or canola oil
1 onion, thinly sliced
1 pound (454 g) bok choy, cored and cut into long, thin strips
1 pound (454 g) pork tenderloin, trimmed of fat and cut into thin strips
2 cloves garlic, peeled and minced
1 tablespoon chili garlic sauce (sambal oelek)

6. Bring a large pot of lightly salted water to a boil over high heat. Cook rice noodles according to package instructions. Drain and reserve.
7. In a small bowl, whisk together water, rice wine, soy sauce, and cornstarch.
8. Warm oil in a Dutch oven over medium heat. Once hot, add onion and cook until softened, about 2 to 3 minutes. Add bok choy and cook, stirring occasionally, until it begins to soften, about 5 minutes.
9. Add the pork, garlic, and chili garlic sauce. Stir occasionally until pork is just cooked through, about 1 minute.
10. Give the cornstarch mixture a quick whisk and pour into the Dutch oven. Bring to a boil, stirring frequently for 2 minutes until the sauce thickens. Serve pork stir-fry on top of noodles.

Per Serving
calories: 413 | fat: 7.9g | carbs: 53.7g | protein: 28.1g

Easy Eye Round Steak

Prep time: 5 minutes | Cook time: 20 minutes | Serves 2

1 (8-ounce / 227-g) boneless eye of round steak
2 pinches salt (optional)
1 teaspoon coconut oil
Freshly ground black pepper, to taste

1. Preheat the oven to 300°F (150°C).
2. Line a baking sheet with nonstick aluminum foil.
3. Pat the steak surfaces dry, and sprinkle each side with a pinch of salt (if using).
4. In a large skillet over high heat, heat the coconut oil until you see gentle smoke lifting off of the surface.
5. Using tongs, place the steak in the skillet, and sear for 1 minute on each side.
6. Place the steaks in the prepared baking sheet, and bake for 20 to 30 minutes, checking often to make sure the steak does not overcook. This steak is best served rare to medium rare.
7. Remove from the oven and let rest for 5 minutes.
8. Carve against the grain in thin slices and serve.

Per Serving
calories: 150 | fat: 5.8g | carbs: 0g | protein: 24.1g

Roasted Coffee-Rubbed Pork Tenderloin

Prep time: 5 minutes | Cook time: 20 minutes | Serves 6

2 tablespoons ground coffee
1½ teaspoons ground cayenne pepper
1½ teaspoons salt
1 (1½-pound / 680-g) pork tenderloin, trimmed of excess fat
¼ cup balsamic vinegar

1. Preheat the oven to 425°F (220°C).
2. In a small bowl, mix the coffee, cayenne, and salt together to make a rub.
3. Line a rimmed baking sheet with aluminum foil or a silicone baking mat.
4. Pat the tenderloin dry with paper towels. Sprinkle the tenderloin with the rub, and massage well to coat. Place the tenderloin on the prepared baking sheet.
5. Roast for 20 to 25 minutes, turning once halfway through, until cooked through.
6. Transfer to a cutting board and let rest for 10 minutes.
7. Using a sharp knife, slice the tenderloin against the grain into six equal portions, and transfer to a platter.
8. Drizzle the balsamic vinegar over the length of the sliced tenderloin, and serve immediately.

Per Serving
calories: 129 | fat: 2.5g | carbs: 1.8g | protein: 23.1g

Chapter 12 Vegetables and Sides

Vegan Buddha Bowl

Prep time: 15 minutes | Cook time: 25 minutes | Serves 4

2 large sweet potatoes, peeled and cubed
1 large sweet onion, sliced into large wedges
1 garlic clove, minced
Nonstick cooking spray
Sea salt and black pepper, to taste
2 tablespoons extra-virgin olive oil
2 tablespoons freshly squeezed lemon juice
2 to 2½ teaspoons honey
2 cups steamed broccoli florets, divided
1 (15½-ounce / 439.4-g) can chickpeas, rinsed and drained, divided
2 cups shredded kale, divided
1 medium avocado, sliced, divided
1 cup shredded carrots, divided
2 tablespoons hemp hearts, divided

1. Preheat the oven to 400°F (205°C).
2. In a large bowl, combine the sweet potatoes, onion, and garlic. Spray well with cooking spray, and stir to combine, then season with salt and pepper. Spread out onto a baking sheet and bake for 25 to 30 minutes, or until the potatoes are tender.
3. Meanwhile, in a small bowl, whisk together the olive oil, lemon juice, and honey, and set aside.
4. Into each of 4 airtight storage containers, place half of the roasted sweet potatoes, then top each with ½ cup of steamed broccoli, ½ cup of chickpeas, ½ cup of kale, ¼ of the avocado, and ¼ cup of shredded carrots. Drizzle each Buddha bowl with 1 tablespoon of dressing, and season with salt and pepper. Sprinkle each bowl with ½ tablespoon of hemp hearts and seal.
5. Store the airtight containers in the refrigerator for 3 to 4 days. Serve cold or microwave uncovered on high for 1 to 2 minutes.

Per Serving
calories: 414 | fat: 20.6g | carbs: 46.7g | protein: 11.9g

Maple Butternut Squash

Prep time: 10 minutes | Cook time: 50 minutes | Serves 4

1 pound (454 g) butternut squash, chopped
Sea salt, to taste
Freshly ground black pepper, to taste
¼ teaspoon ground cinnamon
⅛ teaspoon chili powder
2 tablespoons pure maple syrup
2 tablespoons freshly squeezed lime juice
1 tablespoon coconut oil

1. Preheat the oven to 350°F (180°C).
2. In a large bowl, mix the squash, salt, pepper, cinnamon, and chili powder.
3. Place the squash on a baking sheet or roasting pan, and drizzle with the maple syrup, lime juice, and coconut oil.
4. Bake, uncovered, for about 50 minutes, or until tender, stirring once halfway through baking. Remove from the oven and let cool.
5. Divide the squash evenly among 4 airtight storage containers and seal.
6. Store the airtight containers in the refrigerator for up to 5 days. To reheat, microwave uncovered on high for 1 to 2 minutes.

Per Serving
calories: 105 | fat: 3.9g | carbs: 20.1g | protein: 1.4g

Asparagus with Shiitake Mushrooms Stir-Fry

Prep time: 5 minutes | Cook time: 4 minutes | Serves 3

8 ounces (227 g) asparagus
6 ounces (170g) fresh shiitake mushrooms
1 tablespoon sesame oil
2 teaspoons minced fresh garlic
1 teaspoon peeled and minced fresh ginger
Crushed red chilies

1. Trim and discard the ends of the asparagus, and slice on the bias into 2-inch pieces. Wash and stem the mushrooms, and slice the caps into ½-inch slices.
2. In a large sauté pan or skillet over medium-high heat, heat the sesame oil.
3. Add the garlic and ginger, and stir-fry for a few seconds.
4. Add the mushrooms and asparagus, and stir-fry for 1 minute.
5. Add the crushed chilies and continue to stir-fry until the asparagus is nearly tender, about 3 minutes. Let cool.
6. Divide the vegetables evenly among 3 storage containers and seal.
7. Store the airtight containers in the refrigerator for 3 to 4 days. To reheat, microwave uncovered on high for 1 to 2 minutes.

Per Serving
calories: 106 | fat: 4.9g | carbs: 14.7g | protein: 4.3g

Maple Syrup-Glazed Carrots

Prep time: 5 minutes | Cook time: 10 minutes | Serves 4

Sea salt, to taste
2½ pounds (1.1kg) carrots
4 tablespoons butter
Freshly ground black pepper, to taste
¼ cup pure maple syrup
1 tablespoon chopped fresh parsley

1. Fill a large saucepan halfway with water and bring it to a boil over high heat. Salt the water.
2. Peel the carrots, and cut into 1-inch pieces.
3. Parboil the carrots in the salted water for about 2 minutes.
4. Drain the carrots. Wipe out the saucepan, melt the butter over medium heat, and sauté the carrots until nearly tender, 10 to 15 minutes.
5. Season with salt and pepper, and add the maple syrup. Garnish with the parsley.
6. Divide the carrots evenly among 4 airtight storage containers and seal.
7. Store the airtight containers in the refrigerator for up to 5 days. To reheat, microwave uncovered on high for 1 to 2 minutes.

Per Serving
calories: 266 | fat: 11.9g | carbs: 39.6g | protein: 2.3g

Cauliflower Purée with Fresh Thyme

Prep time: 10 minutes | Cook time: 10 minutes | Serves 6

3 cups vegetable broth
2 medium cauliflower heads, chopped into florets
3 garlic cloves, minced
2 tablespoons extra-virgin olive oil
2 tablespoons coconut oil
1 tablespoon chopped fresh thyme
1 teaspoon sea salt, plus more for seasoning
¼ teaspoon freshly ground black pepper, plus more for seasoning

1. In a large stockpot, bring the broth to a boil and add the cauliflower.
2. Reduce the heat and simmer for 10 minutes.
3. Remove the cauliflower from the heat. Using a slotted spoon and reserving the broth, remove the cauliflower from the broth and transfer to a food processor.
4. Add the garlic, olive oil, coconut oil, thyme, salt, and pepper, and process until puréed. If you want the mixture even, smoother, add a few tablespoons of the hot broth and purée until smooth.
5. Season with additional salt and pepper. Let cool.
6. Divide the purée evenly among 6 airtight storage containers, and add a protein of your choice to make a complete meal.
7. Store the airtight containers in the refrigerator for up to 1 week. To reheat, microwave uncovered on high in 30-second intervals until hot.

Per Serving (1 container)
calories: 150 | fat: 9.7g | carbs: 11.8g | protein: 7.3g

Parmesan Zucchini Fries

Prep time: 5 minutes | Cook time: 18 minutes | Serves 2

2 large zucchini, ends trimmed and sliced lengthwise into 8 wedges
¼ cup liquid egg whites
½ cup grated Parmesan cheese
½ teaspoon garlic powder
½ teaspoon ground black pepper

1. Preheat the oven to 425°F (218°C). Line a 9 x 13-inch (23 x 33cm) baking sheet with aluminum foil. Place an oven-safe cooling rack on top of the foil, and spray with non-stick cooking spray.
2. Pour the egg whites into a small bowl. In a separate small bowl, combine the Parmesan cheese, garlic powder, and black pepper. Mix well to combine.
3. Dip the zucchini wedges in the egg whites, then dredge them in the Parmesan mixture. Place the fries on the cooling rack.
4. Bake for 18 to 20 minutes, or until the fries turn golden brown. Serve hot.

Per Serving

calories: 74 | fat: 3.3g | carbs: 5.1g | protein: 7.7g

Twice-Baked Potatoes with Cheddar

Prep time: 10 minutes | Cook time: 35 minutes | Serves 4

2 medium russet potatoes
1 cup broccoli florets, chopped
2 cups cauliflower florets
½ cup unflavored coconut milk
½ tablespoon white vinegar
1 tablespoon dried chives
1 teaspoon salt
½ teaspoon ground black pepper
8 tablespoons low fat shredded Cheddar cheese

1. Preheat the oven to 400°F (204°C). Pierce the potatoes with a fork, individually wrap in aluminum foil, and place on the middle oven rack. Bake for 1 hour.
2. While the potatoes bake, fill a large pot with 1 inch (2.5cm) water, and place a steamer tray in the bottom of the pot. Place the broccoli and cauliflower in the pot, cover, and steam for 10 minutes. Use a slotted spoon to remove only the broccoli to a small bowl. Steam the cauliflower for an additional 10 minutes.
3. Remove the potatoes from the oven and allow to cool for 15 minutes. Once cooled, unwrap the potatoes and remove the foil, slice lengthwise, and use a small spoon to scoop the flesh out into a large bowl. Reserve the skins and set the bowl aside.
4. Add the cooked cauliflower to the potato, and use a fork or immersion blender to thoroughly mash the ingredients together. Add the coconut milk, vinegar, chives, salt, and black pepper, and continue to mash until all ingredients are well incorporated and smooth texture is achieved.
5. Scoop the cauliflower and potato mixture into the reserved skins. Top each with the broccoli and 2 teaspoons Cheddar cheese. Place back in the oven and bake for an additional 15 minutes. Serve hot.

Per Serving

calories: 118 | fat: 1.2g | carbs: 24.5g | protein: 4.4g

Cauliflower Rice

Prep time: 10 minutes | Cook time: 6 minutes | Serves 4

1 medium cauliflower head, rinsed and cut into small florets
½ white onion, finely diced
4 large green onions, sliced and separated into green and white pieces
½ teaspoon garlic powder
½ teaspoon ground ginger
½ teaspoon ground black pepper
1 cup frozen peas and carrots
2 teaspoons light soy sauce
¼ cup liquid egg whites

1. In small batches, add the cauliflower florets to a food processor or blender and pulse until it resembles the size and consistency of rice, stirring often. Place the riced cauliflower in a medium bowl and set aside.
2. Spray a large skillet with non-stick cooking spray and place over medium heat. Add the onion, green onion (white ends), garlic powder, ginger, and black pepper, and cook until the onions are soft and translucent.
3. Add the peas and carrots, and cook for an additional 3 to 5 minutes, stirring frequently. Move the mixture to one side of the skillet and add the egg whites. Scramble the egg whites, then gently incorporate into the vegetables.
4. Add the riced cauliflower and soy sauce, and continue to cook for an additional 3 to 5 minutes, or until the cauliflower just begins to soften. (Be careful not to overcook the cauliflower, as it can become soggy.)
5. Transfer the rice to a serving platter and garnish with the remaining green onions. Serve hot.

Per Serving

calories: 71 | fat: 0.4g | carbs: 13.1g | protein: 5.9g

Coconut Milk-Smashed Sweet Potatoes

Prep time: 5 minutes | Cook time: 1 hour | Serves 6

2 pounds (907 g) sweet potatoes, washed and ends trimmed
½ cup light coconut milk
2 teaspoons ground cinnamon
½ teaspoon ground cayenne pepper

Per Serving
calories: 139 | fat: 0.7g | carbs: 31.7g | protein: 2.1g

1. Preheat the oven to 400°F (204°C). Pierce the sweet potatoes with a fork and individually wrap in aluminum foil. Place directly on the oven rack and bake for 1 hour, turning the potatoes halfway through the baking time.
2. Remove the potatoes from the oven and allow to cool for 20 minutes. Once cooled, remove the foil and peel the skin from the potatoes.
3. In a large bowl, combine the peeled sweet potatoes, coconut milk, cinnamon, and cayenne pepper.
4. Using a fork or immersion blender, thoroughly smash the ingredients together until a smooth consistency is achieved, and no lumps remain. Serve warm.

Fresh Vegetable Stir Fry

Prep time: 10 minutes | Cook time: 5 minutes | Serves 4

2 teaspoons grated fresh ginger root
2 teaspoons minced garlic
2 cups roughly chopped bok choy
1 cup broccoli florets, fresh or frozen
3 cups shredded green cabbage
2 teaspoons light soy sauce
½ cup sliced fresh button mushrooms
¼ cup low-sodium chicken broth

Per Serving
calories: 34 | fat: 0.2g | carbs: 6.1g | protein: 3.4g

1. Spray a large frying pan with non-stick cooking spray and place over medium-high heat. Add the ginger and garlic to the pan and cook for 1 to 2 minutes, or until the garlic softens and becomes fragrant.
2. Add the bok choy, broccoli, cabbage, and soy sauce. Cook for 2 to 3 minutes, stirring frequently.
3. Add the sliced mushrooms and cook for an additional 2 minutes, stirring frequently.
4. Add the chicken broth, cover, and reduce the heat to low. Steam for 4 to 5 minutes, or until the broccoli is tender and can be pierced with a knife. Serve hot.

Hasselback Sweet Potato

Prep time: 10 minutes | Cook time: 1 hour | Serves 5

2 pounds (907 g) sweet potatoes (look for round shapes, rather than oblong)
Coconut oil cooking spray
½ teaspoon salt

For the Crema:

⅓ cup nonfat Greek yogurt
3 tablespoons jarred red enchilada sauce
½ teaspoon fresh-squeezed lime juice
¼ teaspoon powdered stevia

Per Serving
calories: 151 | fat: 0.4g | carbs: 33.8g | protein: 3.3g

1. Preheat the oven to 400°F (204°C). Spray a medium baking dish with coconut oil cooking spray.
2. Slice the sweet potatoes crosswise, about three fourths of the way through. The slices should be approximately ¼-inch (.5cm) thick. Place the sliced sweet potatoes in the baking dish and lightly spray with the coconut oil cooking spray, and season with the salt.
3. Tightly cover the dish with aluminum foil and bake for 45 minutes. Uncover and bake for an additional 15 minutes. Remove from the oven and allow to cool for 10 minutes.
4. While the sweet potatoes cool, prepare the crema by combining the Greek yogurt, enchilada sauce, lime juice, and stevia in a medium bowl. Mix well to combine.
5. Drizzle the crema over top of the potatoes. Serve warm.

Roasted Vegetables with Herb

Prep time: 10 minutes | Cook time: 30 minutes | Serves 4

2 large zucchini squash, sliced crosswise into ½-inch slices
2 large yellow squash, sliced crosswise into ½-inch slices
1 cup baby carrots
1 medium red onion, sliced into 1-inch wedges
Non-stick cooking spray
1 teaspoon garlic powder
1 teaspoon dried thyme
1 teaspoon dried parsley
1 teaspoon dried rosemary
1 teaspoon salt

1. Preheat the oven to 400°F (204°C). Line a large baking sheet with parchment paper.
2. In a large bowl, combine the zucchini, squash, carrots, and onion wedges. Lightly spray the vegetables with non-stick cooking spray.
3. Make the seasoning by combining the garlic powder, thyme, parsley, rosemary, and salt in a small bowl. Mix well. Sprinkle the seasoning mix over the vegetables and toss thoroughly to coat.
4. Spread the vegetables in an even layer on the baking sheet. Roast for 15 minutes.
5. Using tongs, flip the vegetables and roast for an additional 15 minutes, or until the vegetables are soft and slightly caramelized. Serve hot.

Per Serving
calories: 45 | fat: 0.2g | carbs: 9.4g | protein: 1.8g

Black Bean and Corn Quesadilla

Prep time: 10 minutes | Cook time: 8 minutes | Serves 4

2 teaspoons extra-virgin olive oil
½ cup finely chopped onion
1 (15-ounce / 425-g) can black beans, drained and rinsed
1½ cups frozen corn
¼ cup tomato sauce
¼ teaspoon red pepper flakes
8 (6-inch) corn tortillas
1 cup shredded low-fat Monterey Jack cheese

1. Warm oil in a large skillet over medium heat. Stir in onion and cook until softened, about 2 minutes.
2. Stir in beans, corn, tomato sauce, and pepper flakes. Mix well and cook until heated through, about 3 minutes. Transfer to a dish and reserve.
3. Use a paper towel to wipe the skillet clean and lay a tortilla in it. Sprinkle cheese evenly over the tortilla, top with about ¼ of the bean mixture, and place another tortilla on top.
4. Cook quesadilla until golden, flip it with a spatula, and cook the other side until golden too. Transfer quesadilla to a plate.
5. Repeat with remaining tortillas and filling. Serve.

Per Serving
calories: 347 | fat: 9.7g | carbs: 51.9g | protein: 19.2g

Stir-Fried Butternut Squash and Broccoli

Prep time: 10 minutes | Cook time: 6 minutes | Serves 6

1 pound (454 g) butternut squash, peeled, seeded, and cut into ¼-inch slices
1 clove garlic, peeled and minced
¼ teaspoon ground ginger
1 cup broccoli florets
½ cup thinly sliced celery
½ cup thinly sliced onion
2 teaspoons honey
1 tablespoon lemon juice
2 tablespoons sunflower seed kernels

1. Coat a large skillet with cooking spray and warm over medium-high heat. Add squash, garlic, and ginger; stir-fry for 3 minutes.
2. Add broccoli, celery, and onion and continue to stir-fry until vegetables are tender, about 3 to 4 minutes.
3. Meanwhile, in a small bowl, combine honey and lemon juice. Mix well.
4. Transfer vegetables to a large serving dish and pour the honey mixture over top. Using tongs, toss to coat. Garnish with sunflower kernels and serve.

Per Serving
calories: 71 | fat: 1.9g | carbs: 13.6g | protein: 2.3g

Mozzarella Butternut Squash

Prep time: 10 minutes | Cook time: 30 minutes | Serves 4

1 (4-pound / 1.8-kg) butternut squash, peeled, seeded, and cubed
½ yellow onion, chopped
1 tablespoon extra-virgin olive oil
1 tablespoon chopped fresh thyme leaves
Salt and ground black pepper, to taste
8 ounces (227 g) fresh Mozzarella, diced
¼ cup whole flaxseed

1. Preheat the oven to 425°F (220°C). Prepare a large baking dish by coating it with cooking spray.
2. In a large bowl, toss squash, onion, olive oil, thyme, and cheese together. Season the mixture with salt and pepper; toss again to combine.
3. Transfer mixture to the baking dish and top with flaxseed.
4. Bake until the casserole is lightly browned on top, about 30 minutes. Remove from oven and serve.

Per Serving
calories: 433 | fat: 17.8g | carbs: 58.5g | protein: 20.2g

Yummy Chile Relleno Casserole

Prep time: 5 minutes | Cook time: 40 minutes | Serves 4

2 (7-ounce / 198-g) cans whole green chile peppers, drained
2 cups shredded reduced-fat Monterey Jack cheese, divided
2 egg whites or 6 tablespoons liquid egg white substitute
1 cup 2% milk
1 (8-ounce / 227-g) can tomato sauce

1. Preheat the oven to 350°F (180°C).
2. Layer half the chiles evenly into the bottom of a medium baking dish and top with 1 cup cheese.
3. In a bowl, beat egg whites and mix with milk. Pour the mixture over chiles.
4. Top the mixture with remaining chiles, pour tomato sauce evenly over the top, and sprinkle with remaining 1 cup cheese.
5. Bake until golden brown, about 40 minutes. Remove from oven and serve.

Per Serving
calories: 226 | fat: 12.7g | carbs: 9.6g | protein: 18.4g

Breaded Squash Fries

Prep time: 10 minutes | Cook time: 15 minutes | Serves 4

1 teaspoon extra-virgin olive oil
2 egg whites or 6 tablespoons liquid egg white substitute
½ cup skim milk
⅓ cup breadcrumbs
1 tablespoon grated Parmesan cheese
½ teaspoon onion powder
½ teaspoon sweet paprika
½ teaspoon dried parsley
½ teaspoon garlic powder
¼ teaspoon ground black pepper
2 large yellow squash, quartered lengthwise and then cut in half widthwise

1. Preheat the oven to 450°F (235°C). Prepare a large baking dish by greasing with oil.
2. In a medium bowl, add egg whites and milk. Lightly whisk together.
3. In a separate medium bowl, combine breadcrumbs, cheese, onion powder, paprika, parsley, garlic powder, and pepper.
4. Place breaded squash cut-side-up into the prepared baking pan. Continue until all the squash has been breaded.
5. Bake squash in the oven until browned, about 15 minutes. Serve.

Per Serving
calories: 143 | fat: 2.8g | carbs: 20.9g | protein: 8.1g

Curried Cauliflower and Potatoes

Prep time: 10 minutes | Cook time: 22 minutes | Serves 4

Salt, to taste
1 (2- to 3-pound / 0.9- to 1.4-g) head cauliflower, cut into florets
1 pound (454 g) potatoes, peeled and cut into 1-inch cubes
1 medium onion, chopped
2 cloves garlic, peeled and minced
2 tablespoons garam masala or curry powder
1 cup low-sodium vegetable broth
2 cups frozen peas

1. Bring a pot of lightly salted water to a boil over high heat. Add the cauliflower and potatoes; cook for 4 to 5 minutes and drain.
2. Meanwhile, coat a Dutch oven with cooking spray and warm over medium heat. Add chopped onion and garlic and cook until onion softens, about 2 to 3 minutes. Add garam masala and stir for 1 minute.
3. Transfer cooked potatoes and cauliflower to the Dutch oven. Stir well, coating in the onion mixture. Add broth and deglaze the pan.
4. Cover with a lid and let mixture simmer for 10 minutes. Stir in peas, cover, and cook for another 5 to 7 minutes. Serve immediately.

Per Serving
calories: 230 | fat: 0.8g | carbs: 46.6g | protein: 12.3g

Zucchini and Baby Spinach Sauté

Prep time: 10 minutes | Cook time: 8 minutes | Serves 6

1 tablespoon extra-virgin olive oil
2 cloves garlic, peeled and minced
2 zucchini, cut into matchsticks
2 cups grape tomatoes
3 cups baby spinach
1 tablespoon lemon juice
Pinch of ground black pepper

1. Warm oil in a large pan over medium-low heat. Add garlic and cook until fragrant, about 1 minute. Add zucchini and increase the heat to medium. Cook for 3 to 4 minutes, stirring constantly.
2. Stir in tomatoes, cooking for 1 minute. Add spinach, stirring and sautéing for another 3 to 4 minutes until wilted. Add lemon juice and black pepper before removing from heat to serve.

Per Serving
calories: 46 | fat: 1.9g | carbs: 4.6g | protein: 2.3g

Teriyaki Sweet Potato and Broccoli Bowl

Prep time: 5 minutes | Cook time: 18 minutes | Serves 2

4 sweet potatoes, cubed
1 (7-ounce / 198-g) pack smoked tofu, cubed
2 cups broccoli florets
¼ cup teriyaki sauce
¼ cup peanut butter
½ cup water

Optional Toppings:
Chili flakes
Shredded coconut
Roasted sesame seeds

1. Cook the sweet potato cubes, covered with water, in a medium pot over medium-high heat for about 10 minutes.
2. Add the broccoli florets, and cook for another 3 minutes.
3. Take the pot off the heat, drain the excess water from the broccoli and sweet potatoes and set aside.
4. Put a nonstick deep frying pan over medium-high heat and add the teriyaki sauce, the water and tofu cubes.
5. Keep stirring continuously until everything is cooked, then add the broccoli florets and sweet potato cubes to the frying pan.
6. Cook for about 5 minutes while stirring occasionally.
7. Turn the heat off, leave to cool down for a minute, then drain the excess water.
8. Divide between 2 plates, drizzle half of the peanut butter on top of each plate with the optional toppings and enjoy!

Per Serving
calories: 550 | fat: 24.1g | carbs: 51.2g | protein: 32.3g

Chapter 13 Fish and Seafood

Red Snapper En Papillote

Prep time: 10 minutes | Cook time: 8 minutes | Serves 6

Nonstick cooking spray
⅓ cup thinly sliced leeks
⅓ cup thinly sliced fennel
⅓ cup shredded carrots
⅓ cup thinly sliced celery
⅓ cup thinly sliced red bell pepper
Sea salt, to taste
Freshly ground black pepper, to taste
2¼ pounds (1 kg) red snapper fillets, skin-on, cut into 6 pieces
3 tablespoons butter, melted
6 thin lemon slices

1. Preheat the oven to 450°F (235°C).
2. Cut 6 heart-shaped pieces of parchment paper large enough to contain the fish and vegetables when folded in half. Spray each piece of parchment with cooking spray and set aside.
3. In a medium bowl, toss the leeks, fennel, carrots, celery, and bell pepper. Season with salt and pepper. Divide the vegetables evenly among the pieces of prepared parchment.
4. Place one portion of red snapper on each portion of vegetables, skin-side up; brush with the melted butter, and season with salt and pepper. Place a lemon slice on top of each fillet.
5. Fold each piece of paper over the fish and vegetables, and crimp the edges to seal.
6. Place the sealed fish packets on sheet pans and bake for 8 to 10 minutes.
7. When done, the parchment paper should puff up and brown. Remove from the oven, transfer the paper packets to 6 airtight glass storage containers, open the parchment paper packets, and let cool before sealing.
8. Store the airtight containers in the refrigerator for up to 3 days. To reheat, microwave on high for 1 to 2 minutes.

Per Serving
calories: 310 | fat: 8.7g | carbs: 9.9g | protein: 46.2g

Tamari Salmon Fillet and Zucchini

Prep time: 5 minutes | Cook time: 15 minutes | Serves 4

4 (6-ounce / 170-g) salmon fillets
2 zucchini, halved lengthwise and sliced into ½-inch matchsticks
¼ cup tamari sauce
2 tablespoons extra-virgin olive oil
Sea salt, to taste
Freshly ground black pepper, to taste

1. Preheat the oven to 415°F (213°C).
2. Place the salmon fillets and zucchini slices on a baking sheet.
3. In a small bowl, mix together the tamari sauce and oil, and brush it over the salmon and zucchini. Sprinkle with salt and pepper.
4. Bake for 15 to 18 minutes, or until the salmon flakes apart when pierced with a fork. Remove from the oven and let cool.
5. Divide the zucchini among 4 airtight storage containers, place 1 salmon fillet in each, and seal.
6. Store the airtight containers in the refrigerator for up to 4 days. To reheat, microwave uncovered on high for 1 to 2 minutes.

Per Serving (1 container)
calories: 366 | fat: 19.8g | carbs: 3.9g | protein: 42.1g

Parmesan Tilapia Fillet with Asparagus

Prep time: 15 minutes | Cook time: 14 minutes | Serves 4

For the Asparagus:

1 bunch asparagus, cleaned and ends removed
1 tablespoon extra-virgin olive oil
2 tablespoons grated Parmesan cheese
Sea salt, to taste
Freshly ground black pepper, to taste

For the Tilapia:

4 tablespoons mayonnaise
2 tablespoons freshly squeezed lime juice
Nonstick cooking spray
4 (6-ounce / 170-g) large tilapia fillets
1 teaspoon dried parsley
Sea salt, to taste
Freshly ground black pepper, to taste
¼ cup gluten-free bread crumbs

Make the Asparagus

1. Preheat the oven to 425°F (220°C).
2. In a large bowl, toss the asparagus with olive oil, Parmesan, salt, and pepper.
3. Spread the asparagus out evenly onto a baking sheet while you prepare the tilapia.

Make the Tilapia

4. In a small bowl, mix the mayonnaise and lime. Place the tilapia fillets on a baking sheet sprayed with cooking spray.
5. Season the tilapia fillets with the parsley, salt, and pepper.
6. Brush the mayo mixture on the tilapia, then sprinkle with half of the bread crumbs. Flip the fillets and repeat.
7. Place the asparagus and tilapia trays in the oven.
8. After 12 to 15 minutes, check the asparagus and, if tender enough to your liking, remove from the oven. Then, check on the tilapia, which may need another 5 to 7 minutes of cooking time. The tilapia should no longer be translucent inside and will flake easily when pierced with a fork.
9. In each airtight storage container, place 6 or 7 asparagus spears and 1 fillet of tilapia and seal.
10. Store the airtight containers for up to 4 days. To reheat, microwave uncovered on high for 1 to 2 minutes.

Per Serving (1 container)
calories: 306 | fat: 11.5g | carbs: 11.9g | protein: 38.4g

Blackened Baked Tilapia Fillet

Prep time: 10 minutes | Cook time: 10 minutes | Serves 5

1 tablespoon paprika
2 teaspoons dried thyme
1 teaspoon cumin
1 teaspoon dried oregano
1 teaspoon garlic powder
1 teaspoon onion powder
1 teaspoon salt
½ teaspoon ground black pepper
½ teaspoon red pepper flakes
2 pounds (907 g) tilapia fillets (fresh or frozen)

1. Preheat the oven to 400°F (204°C). Make the rub by combining the paprika, thyme, cumin, oregano, garlic powder, onion powder, salt, black pepper, and red pepper flakes in a small bowl. Mix well.
2. Rinse the tilapia fillets and pat dry with a paper towel. Season both sides of the fillets with the rub, using your fingers to gently press the seasonings into both sides of the fillets. Allow the fillets to sit at room temperature for 15 minutes to allow the flavors to develop.
3. Spray a 9 x 13in (22 x 33cm) baking pan with non-stick cooking spray. Place the fillets in the pan and lightly spray the tops with the non-stick cooking spray.
4. Bake for 10 to 12 minutes, or until the fish is firm and flaky, and the flesh is opaque. Serve hot.

Per Serving
calories: 146 | fat: 2.7g | carbs: 0g | protein: 32.3g

Cod Fillet with Charred Tomatillo Salsa

Prep time: 10 minutes | Cook time: 12 minutes | Serves 2

5 large tomatillos, stems and husks removed
2 serrano chiles, stems and seeds removed, chopped
2 teaspoons diced white onion
¼ cup roughly chopped fresh cilantro
½ teaspoon lime juice
½ teaspoon salt
½ pound (227g) cod fillets (fresh or frozen)

1. Preheat the broiler to low. Line a small baking pan with aluminum foil and place the tomatillos and serrano chiles in the pan. Place the pan on the top oven rack and roast for 6 to 8 minutes, flipping the tomatillos and chiles halfway through the cooking process. Roast until nicely charred.
2. Add the tomatillos, chiles, onion, cilantro, lime juice, and salt to a blender. Pulse in 10 second intervals until a smooth consistency is achieved. Set aside.
3. Spray a small baking pan with non-stick cooking spray. Place the cod in the pan and season with the garlic powder, salt, and black pepper. Broil for 3 to 4 minutes per side, until the fish is lightly browned and can be flaked with a fork.
4. Transfer the baked cod to a serving platter and spoon the tomatillo salsa over top. Serve hot.

½ teaspoon garlic powder
½ teaspoon salt
½ teaspoon ground black pepper

Per Serving
calories: 137 | fat: 1.3g | carbs: 3.6g | protein: 25.9g

Fresh Snapper with Broccoli

Prep time: 5 minutes | Cook time: 10 minutes | Serves 4

1 cup low-sodium chicken broth
½ white onion, sliced crosswise
1 lemon, sliced crosswise
1 pound (454 g) fresh snapper fillets, skin on
1 (12-ounce / 340-g) package frozen broccoli florets, thawed
Pinch of salt

1. In a large stock pot, combine the chicken broth, onion slices, and lemon slices. Carefully place the snapper fillets in the pot, skin-side down, making sure the fillets are partially submerged in the broth.
2. Cover, and bring to a simmer over medium-low heat. Cook for 5 to 6 minutes, or until the fish is firm and flaky and the flesh is opaque. Using a spatula, carefully transfer the cooked fillets to a plate.
3. Keeping the pot at a simmer, add the broccoli florets, cover, and cook for 5 minutes, or until the florets develop a bright green color and become slightly soft.
4. Use a slotted spoon to remove the broccoli, onion slices, and lemon slices from the pot. Discard the lemon slices, and spoon the broccoli and onions over the fillets. Season with a pinch of salt. Serve hot.

Per Serving
calories: 194 | fat: 2.5g | carbs: 9.3g | protein: 34.4g

Creamy Fettucine with Sea Scallops

Prep time: 10 minutes | Cook time: 5 minutes | Serves 5

Salt and ground black pepper, to taste
8 ounces (227 g) whole-grain fettuccine
1 pound (454 g) large sea scallops
1 (8-ounce / 227-g) bottle clam juice (the lowest sodium available)
1 cup 2% milk
3 tablespoons cornstarch
3 cups frozen peas
¼ cup chopped chives
½ teaspoon lemon zest
1 teaspoon lemon juice
½ cup grated Parmesan cheese

1. Bring a large pot of lightly salted water to a boil over high heat. Cook fettuccine according to package instructions. Drain the pasta and reserve.
2. Meanwhile, dry scallops with a paper towel and sprinkle with salt. Coat a large nonstick skillet with cooking spray and warm over medium-high heat. Add scallops and cook until golden brown, about 2 to 3 minutes per side. Remove from pan and reserve.
3. Add clam juice to the pan. In a medium bowl, add milk, cornstarch, salt, and pepper; whisk until smooth. Pour milk mixture into the pan and whisk with clam juice. Once the mixture is simmering, stir constantly until sauce thickens, about 1 to 2 minutes.
4. Add reserved scallops and peas to clam sauce and bring to a simmer. Stir in reserved fettuccine, chives, lemon zest, lemon juice, and most of the cheese; mix well. Remove pan from the heat and top pasta with remaining cheese. Serve.

Per Serving
calories: 402 | fat: 4.6g | carbs: 55.8g | protein: 31.4g

Marinated Halibut Fillet with Leeks

Prep time: 10 minutes | Cook time: 8 minutes | Serves 4

2 tablespoons extra-virgin olive oil
2 tablespoons less-sodium soy sauce
2 tablespoons lemon juice
2 tablespoons white wine
2 cloves garlic, peeled and minced
2 fresh ginger pieces, peeled and minced
Salt and ground black pepper, to taste
4 (6-ounce / 170-g) halibut fillets

1. In a large Ziploc bag, add olive oil, soy sauce, lemon juice, white wine, garlic, ginger, salt, and pepper. Add fillets into the Ziploc bag. Seal tightly and shake to coat. Refrigerate fillets for at least 1 hour, shaking them occasionally.
2. Preheat the oven's broiler to high. Remove fillets from marinade and place in a baking dish.
3. Add marinade to a large skillet and warm over medium heat. Add leeks and red bell pepper. Cook for 15 minutes or until tender.
4. Meanwhile, place fillets under the broiler, 4 to 6 inches from the heat. Broil 4 to 5 minutes; flip with a spatula and cook until fish easily flakes with a fork, about another 4 minutes. Top fillets with vegetables and sauce; serve.

3 medium leeks (white part only), thinly sliced
2 red bell peppers, seeded and thinly sliced

Per Serving
calories: 283 | fat: 10.6g | carbs: 9.1g | protein: 37.2g

Graham Cracker-Crusted Tilapia Fillet

Prep time: 10 minutes | Cook time: 10 minutes | Serves 4

4 (4-ounce / 113-g) tilapia fillets, about ¾-inch thick
½ cup plain graham cracker crumbs
1 teaspoon lemon zest
¼ teaspoon salt
¼ teaspoon ground black pepper
¼ cup 2% milk
1 tablespoon canola oil
2 tablespoons chopped pecans, toasted

1. Position the oven rack to slightly above the middle and preheat the oven to 500°F (260°C). Coat a 13-inch by 9-inch baking dish with cooking spray.
2. Cut fillets crosswise into 2-inch wide pieces.
3. In a small bowl, add graham cracker crumbs, lemon zest, salt, and pepper. Stir to combine. Pour milk into a separate small bowl.
4. Add each fish piece into the milk mixture and then coat in graham crackers. Place fish into the prepared baking dish, continuing until each piece is breaded.
5. Drizzle oil and pecans over fillets. Bake until fish easily flakes with a fork, about 10 minutes. Remove from oven and serve.

Per Serving
calories: 222 | fat: 9.5g | carbs: 10.2g | protein: 23.8g

Mahi-Mahi Fillet with Fruity Salsa

Prep time: 10 minutes | Cook time: 10 minutes | Serves 4

4 (6-ounce / 170-g) mahi-mahi fillets
3 tablespoons avocado oil, divided
Salt and ground black pepper, to taste
1 medium avocado, peeled, pitted, and diced
1 medium mango, peeled, pitted, and diced
4 sprigs fresh cilantro, leaves thinly sliced
3 tablespoons lime juice, divided
1 teaspoon Sriracha hot sauce
4 lime wedges

1. Prepare a grill to medium-high heat. Lightly coat the grill grates with cooking spray.
2. Add fish fillets into a 13-inch by 9-inch glass baking dish. Drizzle with 2 tablespoons oil and season with salt and pepper. Let fillets marinate at room temperature for 10 minutes, turning occasionally.
3. Meanwhile, in a medium bowl, prepare salsa by gently combining avocado, mango, cilantro, remaining 1 tablespoon avocado oil, and lime juice. Season with salt, pepper, and Sriracha. Reserve.
4. Grill fillets until they are just opaque in the center, about 5 minutes per side. Transfer fillets to plates.
5. Garnish fillets with mango-avocado salsa. Serve with lime wedges.

Per Serving
calories: 358 | fat: 18.9g | carbs: 15.2g | protein: 33.4g

Almond-Crusted Baked Cod Fillet

Prep time: 10 minutes | Cook time: 15 minutes | Makes 4 (6-ounce / 170-g) fillets

1 large egg
2 egg whites
½ cup blanched almond flour
½ teaspoon mustard powder
¼ teaspoon ground cayenne pepper
¼ teaspoon garlic powder
4 (6-ounce / 170-g) cod fillets
Extra-virgin olive oil spray

1. Preheat the oven to 350°F (180°C).
2. Line a baking sheet with nonstick aluminum foil or a silicone baking mat.
3. In a medium bowl, whisk the egg and egg whites. Set aside.
4. In a large bowl, mix together the almond flour, mustard, cayenne pepper, and garlic powder.
5. On a work surface, pat the cod dry with paper towels. Dip a cod fillet into the egg, coating both sides. Shake off any excess. Dredge in the almond flour mixture, coating both sides, and place the seasoned cod on the prepared baking sheet. Repeat with the remaining cod.
6. Lightly spray each breaded fillet with olive oil spray. Bake for 15 minutes.
7. Plate the fish and serve fresh from the oven.

Per Serving
calories: 245 | fat: 9.5g | carbs: 3.1g | protein: 36.5g

Tuna Melt Stuffed Tomatoes

Prep time: 10 minutes | Cook time: 4 minutes | Serves 2

1 (7-ounce / 198-g) can tuna in water, drained
2 tablespoons nonfat Greek yogurt
1 tablespoon chopped fresh basil
1 tablespoon diced red bell pepper
1 tablespoon diced red onion
Pinch freshly ground black pepper
2 large tomatoes
¼ cup shredded low-fat Mozzarella, divided
2 pinches crushed red pepper, divided

1. Preheat the broiler to high. In a small bowl, use a fork to mix the tuna, yogurt, basil, bell pepper, onion, and black pepper until well blended.
2. Slice off the top of each tomato with a sharp knife, and use a spoon to hollow out the tomatoes.
3. Stuff the tuna mixture into the tomato cups, and press down firmly with a fork.
4. Place the stuffed tomatoes in a loaf pan or baking dish. Top each with 2 tablespoons of shredded Mozzarella and a pinch of crushed red pepper.
5. Broil 6 to 8 inches from the heat for 3 to 5 minutes, until the cheese melts and slightly browns.
6. Serve immediately. The stuffed tomatoes go well with salad greens or a veggie side dish.

Per Serving
calories: 189 | fat: 3.5g | carbs: 9.6g | protein: 31.1g

Dijon Mustard Baked Scallops

Prep time: 5 minutes | Cook time: 20 minutes | Serves 1

4 jumbo sea scallops (about 4-ounce / 113-g)
1½ teaspoons Dijon mustard
1½ teaspoons real maple syrup

1. Preheat the oven to 350°F (180°C).
2. Place the scallops on a foil-lined baking sheet 1½ inches apart.
3. In a small bowl, mix the mustard and maple syrup. Spoon the mixture evenly over the scallops, and spread to coat the top.
4. Bake for 20 to 30 minutes, depending on size, until opaque.
5. Enjoy warm.

Per Serving
calories: 125 | fat: 0.9g | carbs: 10.1g | protein: 17.3g

Chapter 14 Poultry

Homemade Shepherd's Pie

Prep time: 15 minutes | Cook time: 40 minutes | Serves 8

8 large potatoes, peeled and chopped
¼ cup unsweetened coconut milk
2 tablespoons coconut oil
2½ teaspoons sea salt, divided
½ teaspoon freshly ground black pepper, divided
Nonstick cooking spray
2½ pounds (1.1 kg) lean ground turkey
½ tablespoon dried oregano
½ tablespoon dried parsley
½ tablespoon dried basil
2 cups reduced-fat cream of mushroom soup
1 cup frozen corn
1 cup frozen peas

1. Preheat the oven to 370°F (188°C).
2. In a large pot over high heat, cover the potatoes in water and bring to a boil. Boil for 20 minutes, or until easily pierced with a fork.
3. Drain the potatoes and mash them, using a potato masher or fork, along with the coconut milk, coconut oil, 2 teaspoons of salt, and ¼ teaspoon of pepper, until completely combined and smooth.
4. Heat a large skillet over medium-high heat. Spray with cooking spray and add the ground turkey, breaking it apart with a wooden spoon. Add the oregano, parsley, basil, remaining ½ teaspoon of salt, and remaining ¼ teaspoon of pepper and continue to cook until evenly browned and no signs of pink are showing, about 10 minutes.
5. Coat an 11-by-14-inch baking dish with cooking spray. Spread the turkey over the bottom of the dish. Pour the mushroom soup over the top of the turkey, sprinkle the corn and peas on top, then spread evenly with the mashed potatoes.
6. Bake for 30 to 35 minutes, until lightly golden brown on top, then let cool.
7. Divide the shepherd's pie evenly among 8 airtight storage containers and seal.
8. Store the airtight containers in the refrigerator for up to 5 days. To reheat, microwave uncovered on high for 1 to 2 minutes.
9. Store the airtight containers in the freezer for up to 2 months.

Per Serving
calories: 467 | fat: 16.8g | carbs: 47.1g | protein: 34.4g

Chicken Breast Burrito Bowl

Prep time: 15 minutes | Cook time: 22 minutes | Serves 3

Nonstick cooking spray
3 (8-ounce / 227-g) boneless, skinless chicken breasts
1 tablespoon fresh chopped garlic
1 tablespoon ground cumin
1½ teaspoons chili powder
1 tablespoon paprika
Sea salt, to taste
Freshly ground black pepper, to taste
1½ cups cooked rice, divided
1½ cups cooked black beans, divided
¾ cup salsa or pico de gallo, divided
6 tablespoons guacamole, divided
6 tablespoons reduced-fat sour cream (5%) or nonfat Greek yogurt, divided
3 teaspoons minced jalapeño, divided

1. Preheat the oven to 400°F (205°C). Spray an 8-by-10-inch baking dish with cooking spray.
2. Rub the chicken breasts with the garlic, cumin, chili powder, and paprika, and season with salt and pepper.
3. Place the seasoned chicken in the baking dish and bake for 22 to 26 minutes, or until the chicken reaches an internal temperature of 165°F (74°C) and the juices run clear. Allow it to rest briefly, then cut into half-inch-thick strips. Let cool.
4. Into each of 3 airtight storage containers, place ½ cup of rice, ½ cup of black beans, and 1 chicken breast. Top each with ¼ cup of salsa, 2 tablespoons of guacamole, 2 tablespoons of sour cream, 1 teaspoon of jalapeño, 1 scallion, and ½ tablespoon of cilantro, and seal.
5. Store the airtight containers in the refrigerator for up to 5 days. To reheat, microwave uncovered on high for 1 to 2 minutes.

3 scallions, green parts only, sliced, divided
1½ tablespoons fresh chopped cilantro, divided

Per Serving (1 burrito bowl)
calories: 675 | fat: 14.7g | carbs: 47.1g | protein: 90.2g

Salsa Chicken with Red Kale

Prep time: 15 minutes | Cook time: 17 minutes | Serves 4

For the Kale:

2 tablespoons extra-virgin olive oil
3 garlic cloves, sliced
1 pound (454 g) red kale, washed, stemmed, and chopped
½ cup chicken stock
¼ cup red wine vinegar
Sea salt, to taste
Freshly ground black pepper, to taste

For the Chicken:

Nonstick cooking spray
1 pound (454g) chicken tenders
½ teaspoon sea salt
¼ teaspoon freshly ground black pepper
2 garlic cloves, minced
1 vine-ripened tomato, chopped
¼ cup fresh parsley, finely chopped
½ cup salsa
½ cup shredded Cheddar cheese (optional)

Make the Kale

1. In a large skillet over medium-low heat, heat the olive oil and garlic. Add the kale, toss, and add the chicken stock. Cover and cook for 4 to 5 minutes, or until tender.
2. Add the vinegar, and season with salt and pepper. Divide the kale evenly among 4 airtight storage containers.

Make the Chicken

3. Wipe out the same skillet, and heat over medium-high heat. Spray with cooking spray.
4. Season the chicken with the salt and pepper, then sauté for 2 to 3 minutes, or until browned on both sides. Add the garlic, tomato, parsley, and salsa and mix well.
5. Cover, reduce to a simmer, and cook for about 10 minutes, or until chicken is cooked through and the juices run clear.
6. Add the cheese, if using, and cook for another 1 to 2 minutes, until the cheese is melted.
7. In each storage container, place the chicken on top of the kale. Let cool and seal the containers.
8. Store the airtight containers in the refrigerator for up to 4 days. To reheat, microwave uncovered on high for 1 to 2 minutes.

Per Serving (1 container)
calories: 261 | fat: 8.7g | carbs: 17.3g | protein: 31.2g

Chicken Breast with Tomato-Corn Salad

Prep time: 15 minutes | Cook time: 12 minutes | Serves 4

For the Chicken Strips:

½ cup shredded, unsweetened coconut
1 cup cornflakes, crushed
1 tablespoon ranch seasoning
1 cup unsweetened coconut or almond milk
1 tablespoon apple cider vinegar
3 (8-ounce / 227-g) boneless, skinless chicken breasts, cut lengthwise into strips

For the Tomato-Corn Salad:

1½ tablespoons extra-virgin olive oil
1 tablespoon freshly squeezed lemon or lime juice
½ teaspoon dried basil
Sea salt, to taste
Freshly ground black pepper, to taste
1½ cups frozen corn kernels, thawed

Make the Chicken Strips

1. Preheat the oven to 450°F (235°C). Line a large baking sheet with parchment paper.
2. In a medium bowl, mix together the shredded coconut, cornflakes, and ranch seasoning.
3. In another medium bowl, whisk together the coconut milk and the apple cider vinegar and let sit for 5 to 10 minutes.
4. Dip the chicken strips first into the "buttermilk," then into the cornflake mixture, and lay out on the baking sheet, spacing out the chicken strips so that none overlap or touch.
5. Place in the oven and bake for 12 minutes, or until no longer pink inside (and the chicken reaches an internal temperature of at least 165°F / 74°C). Remove from the oven and let cool.

Make the Tomato-Corn Salad

6. Meanwhile, in a small bowl, whisk together the olive oil, lemon juice, and basil. Season with salt and pepper.
7. In a medium bowl, stir together the corn, tomatoes, and red onion. Pour in the olive oil mixture, and stir to combine
8. Into each of the 4 containers, place a quarter of the salad followed by a quarter of the chicken strips and seal.
9. Store for up to 5 days. Serve cold, or to reheat, microwave the chicken strips on high for 1 to 2 minutes.

¾ cup cherry or grape tomatoes, quartered
¼ cup chopped red onion

Per Serving
calories: 603 | fat: 41.9g | carbs: 32.2g | protein: 32.1g

Stuffed Chicken Breast with Broiled Tomatoes

Prep time: 15 minutes | Cook time: 25 minutes | Serves 4

For the Broiled Tomatoes:

2 large tomatoes
2 teaspoons honey
1 tablespoon garlic butter or 2 tablespoons melted butter mixed with 1 crushed garlic clove
2 tablespoons fresh chopped parsley

For the Spinach and Cheese-Stuffed Chicken:

Nonstick cooking spray
3 tablespoons grated Parmesan cheese
6 tablespoons grated Mozzarella cheese
1 garlic clove, minced
1 teaspoon dried basil
2 cups baby spinach, roughly chopped
Sea salt, to taste
Freshly ground black pepper, to taste
4 (6-ounce / 170-g) skinless, boneless chicken breasts
1 tablespoon extra-virgin olive oil or avocado oil

Make the Broiled Tomatoes
1. Preheat the broiler to high. Core and halve the tomatoes.
2. Place the tomatoes on a small sheet pan cut-side up, drizzle with honey, and broil until tender, 10 to 15 minutes.
3. Drizzle with the garlic butter, and garnish with the parsley.
4. In each of the 4 containers, place 1 tomato half and set aside.

Make the Spinach And Cheese-Stuffed Chicken
5. Preheat oven to 375°F (190°C). Coat a baking sheet with cooking spray.
6. In a medium bowl, mix together the cheeses, garlic, and basil. Stir in the spinach, and season with salt and pepper to taste.
7. Cut the breasts lengthwise to create a small pocket in each chicken breast, trying not to pierce through the breast if possible.
8. Begin filling the chicken breasts with 1 teaspoon of cheese-spinach mixture at a time, until all of the mixture has been distributed evenly. Season the chicken breasts with salt and pepper on both sides.
9. In a large, nonstick skillet over medium-high heat, heat the olive oil. Add the chicken breasts and sear for about 2 to 3 minutes per side, or until golden brown.
10. Transfer the chicken to the prepared baking sheet. Bake for 15 to 20 minutes, or until the chicken reaches an internal temperature of 165°F (74°C) and the juices run clear. Let the chicken cool.
11. Into each container, place 1 chicken breast on top of the tomatoes. Serve with cooked vegetable or grain of your choice.
12. Store for up to 5 days. To reheat, microwave uncovered on high for 1 to 2 minutes.

Per Serving
calories: 345 | fat: 14.8g | carbs: 8.1g | protein: 44.2g

Mustard Almond-Crusted Chicken Breast

Prep time: 10 minutes | Cook time: 20 minutes | Serves 4

¼ cup liquid egg whites
3 tablespoons Dijon mustard
1 cup almond flour
½ teaspoon paprika
½ teaspoon dried tarragon
½ teaspoon ground black pepper
½ teaspoon salt
1 pound (454 g) boneless, skinless chicken breasts, cut into 2-inch (5cm) strips

1. Preheat the oven to 400°F (204°C). Line a large baking sheet with aluminum foil.
2. In a small bowl, whisk together the egg whites and mustard. In a separate shallow baking dish, combine the almond flour, paprika, tarragon, black pepper, and salt.
3. Dip the chicken strips in the egg white mixture, then dredge in the almond flour mixture, making sure to evenly coat the strips with the breading. Place the strips on the baking sheet.
4. Bake for 20 to 22 minutes, or until the juices run clear and the internal temperature reaches 165°F (74°C). Allow the chicken strips to rest for 5 minutes. Serve hot.

Per Serving
calories: 278 | fat: 13.8g | carbs: 5.1g | protein: 34.2g

Roasted Whole Chicken with Apple

Prep time: 5 minutes | Cook time: 1 hour | Serves 8

1 teaspoon salt
1 teaspoon garlic powder
1 teaspoon ground black pepper
1 small chicken, approximately 2½ to 3 pounds (1.2- to 1.4-kg), giblets removed
1 medium Granny Smith apple
Coconut oil cooking spray

1. Preheat the oven to 350°F (177°C). Make the rub by combining the salt, garlic powder, and black pepper in a small bowl.
2. Place the chicken in a large roasting pan. Insert the apple into the cavity, and season the outside of the chicken with half of the rub. Place the chicken in the oven and roast for 45 minutes.
3. After 45 minutes, increase the oven temperature to 400°F (204°C). Remove the chicken from the oven, lightly spray with coconut oil spray, and season with the remaining rub.
4. Bake for an additional 15 minutes, or until the internal temperature reaches 165°F (74°C) and the juices run clear when the chicken is pierced with a sharp knife. Slice and serve hot.

Per Serving

calories: 151 | fat: 4.2g | carbs: 0g | protein: 26.4g

Greek Chicken Skewers

Prep time: 10 minutes | Cook time: 12 minutes | Serves 4

1 tablespoon minced garlic
2 teaspoons dried oregano
1 teaspoon crushed red pepper flakes
1 teaspoon ground black pepper
½ teaspoon salt
½ cup low-sodium chicken broth
¼ cup lemon juice
1 pound (454 g) boneless, skinless chicken breasts

1. Preheat the broiler to low. Spray a 9 x 13in (23 x 33cm) baking pan with non-stick cooking spray.
2. Make the marinade by combining the garlic, oregano, red pepper flakes, black pepper, salt, chicken broth, and lemon juice in a large glass bowl. Mix well to combine.
3. Using a fork, pierce the chicken breasts on all sides, then cut the breasts into ½-inch (1.25cm) cubes. Add the cubes to the bowl with the marinade, tightly cover with plastic wrap, and place in the refrigerator to marinate for 30 minutes.
4. Carefully thread the chicken cubes onto metal skewers, and place the skewers in the baking pan.
5. Broil for 12 to 16 minutes, flipping the skewers halfway through the cooking process. The chicken is done when the juices run clear and the internal temperature reaches 165°F (74°C). Serve hot.

Per Serving

calories: 145 | fat: 3.1g | carbs: 1.7g | protein: 25.9g

Traditional Chicken Cacciatore

Prep time: 10 minutes | Cook time: 35 minutes | Serves 8

1 (16-ounce / 454-g) jar no-sugar-added tomato sauce
½ cup bone broth
1 cup cherry tomatoes, sliced into halves
½ white onion, diced
1 (8-ounce / 227-g) can sliced mushrooms
4 tablespoons minced garlic
1 teaspoon salt
½ teaspoon dried oregano
½ teaspoon ground black pepper
2 pounds (907 g) boneless, skinless chicken breasts
2 teaspoons chopped fresh basil

1. Preheat the oven to 400°F (204°C). Spray a 9 x 13in (23 x 33cm) baking dish with non-stick cooking spray.
2. In a large bowl, combine the tomato sauce, bone broth, cherry tomatoes, onion, mushrooms, garlic, basil, salt, oregano, and black pepper. Mix well. Pour approximately one third of the sauce into the baking dish.
3. Add the chicken to the baking dish in a single layer. Pour the remaining sauce over the chicken, cover tightly with aluminum foil, and bake for 20 minutes.
4. Remove the foil and bake for an additional 15 to 20 minutes. Sprinkle the basil over top. Serve hot.

Per Serving

calories: 161 | fat: 4.2g | carbs: 4.2g | protein: 26.5g

Chicken Hobo

Prep time: 10 minutes | Cook time: 23 minutes | Serves 4

1 pound (454 g) boneless, skinless chicken breasts, cut into 1-inch strips
2 large bell peppers, ribs and seeds removed, sliced into ½-inch strips
1 red onion, sliced crosswise and into ½-inch slices
1 teaspoon chili powder
1 teaspoon ground cumin
1 teaspoon garlic powder
1 teaspoon salt

1. Preheat the oven to 400°F (204°C). Lightly spray four 12 x 12in (30 x 30cm) squares of aluminum foil with non-stick cooking spray. In a large bowl, combine the chicken strips, peppers, and onions. Set aside.
2. Make the seasoning mix by combining the chili powder, cumin, garlic powder, and salt in a small bowl. Mix well.
3. Add the seasoning mix to the chicken, peppers, and onions. Toss thoroughly to coat the chicken and peppers with the seasoning.
4. Place equal amounts of the chicken, peppers, and onions onto each foil square. Grasp the corners of the squares, gather the edges at the middle, and crimp tightly together to form pouches.
5. Place the pouches on a large baking sheet and bake for 23 to 25 minutes, or until the juices from the chicken run clear and the internal temperature reaches 165°F (74°C).
6. Remove the pouches from the oven and allow to cool for 10 minutes before serving. (Use caution when opening the pouches, as the steam will be very hot.)

Per Serving

calories: 173 | fat: 3.1g | carbs: 8.3g | protein: 26.9g

Jerk Chicken Breast Grill

Prep time: 10 minutes | Cook time: 8 minutes | Serves 4

1 small jalapeño pepper, stem and seeds removed
½ medium red onion, roughly chopped
2 teaspoons minced garlic
2 teaspoons fresh thyme
1 teaspoon ground allspice
1 teaspoon ground ginger
⅛ teaspoon ground cloves
2 teaspoons light soy sauce
2 teaspoons lime juice
1 pound (454 g) boneless, skinless chicken breasts

1. Combine the jalapeño, onion, garlic, thyme, allspice, ginger, cloves, soy sauce, and lime juice in a blender. Pulse until the mixture resembles a uniform paste.
2. Spoon the mixture into a large zipper lock bag. Add the chicken breasts, and squeeze the bag to massage the seasonings into the chicken. Place in the refrigerator to marinate for 4 to 6 hours.
3. Preheat a grill to medium. Grill the chicken for 4 to 6 minutes per side. The chicken is done when the juices run clear and the internal temperature reaches 165°F (74°C). Allow the cooked chicken to rest for 5 minutes before serving.

Per Serving

calories: 145 | fat: 3.1g | carbs: 0.8g | protein: 26.8g

Aussie Chicken Breast

Prep time: 10 minutes | Cook time: 21 minutes | Serves 4

4 (6-ounce / 170-g) boneless, skinless chicken breasts, trimmed of fat and pounded to ½-inch thickness
2 teaspoons seasoning salt
6 slices bacon, cut in half
¼ cup yellow mustard
¼ cup honey
2 tablespoons light mayonnaise
1 tablespoon dried onion flakes
1 tablespoon vegetable oil
1 cup sliced white mushrooms
½ cup reduced-fat shredded Monterey Jack cheese
2 tablespoons chopped fresh parsley

1. After pounding chicken breasts, rub them with seasoning salt. Cover and refrigerate for 30 minutes.
2. Preheat the oven to 350°F (180°C).
3. Cook bacon in a large skillet over medium-high heat until crisp. Transfer bacon to a paper towel-lined plate and set aside. Leave bacon fat in skillet.
4. In a medium bowl, mix mustard, honey, mayonnaise, and onion flakes.
5. Warm bacon fat over medium heat. Add chicken and cook until browned, about 3 to 5 minutes per side.
6. Transfer chicken to a 9-inch by 13-inch baking dish. Brush chicken with honey-mustard sauce, followed by adding a layer of mushrooms and bacon. Sprinkle with cheese.
7. Bake until cheese melts and the chicken juices run clear, about 15 minutes. Garnish with parsley and serve.

Per Serving

calories: 399 | fat: 14.2g | carbs: 21.3g | protein: 46.5g

Chicken and Broccoli with Red Wine

Prep time: 10 minutes | Cook time: 5 minutes | Serves 4

2 tablespoons red wine
1 tablespoon less-sodium soy sauce
½ teaspoon cornstarch
1 tablespoon granulated sugar
1 teaspoon salt
2 cups broccoli florets
1 red bell pepper, seeded and chopped
½ onion, sliced
4 (6-ounce / 170-g) boneless, skinless chicken breasts, trimmed of fat and cut into thin strips

1. In a small bowl, combine red wine, soy sauce, cornstarch, sugar, and salt. Whisk well with a fork until cornstarch has dissolved.
2. Coat a large nonstick skillet with cooking spray and warm over medium-high heat. Sauté broccoli, bell pepper, and onion until tender.
3. Add chicken and stir-fry until browned, about 2 to 3 more minutes.
4. Pour soy sauce mixture over chicken and vegetables. Continue to stir-fry until sauce thickens and chicken is cooked through, about 2 to 4 minutes. Remove from heat and serve.

Per Serving

calories: 233 | fat: 2.9g | carbs: 10.2g | protein: 41.5g

Nice Chicken Cacciatore

Prep time: 10 minutes | Cook time: 42 minutes | Serves 4

1 tablespoon extra-virgin olive oil
4 (6-ounce / 170-g) boneless, skinless chicken breasts, trimmed of fat and cut into strips
½ medium onion, chopped
½ cup thinly sliced mushrooms
1 clove garlic, peeled and minced
1 (28-ounce / 794-g) can plum tomatoes with juice
½ cup dry red wine
1 teaspoon dried oregano
1 bay leaf
Salt, to taste
6 ounces (170 g) quinoa rotelle pasta
½ cup chopped fresh parsley

1. Warm oil in a large deep skillet over medium-high heat. Add chicken and brown, cooking about 3 minutes per side. Add onion, mushrooms, and garlic; sauté until vegetables are tender.
2. Add tomatoes with juice, wine, oregano, and bay leaf. Reduce the heat to medium-low and cover with a lid. Stirring occasionally, simmer until chicken is cooked through and sauce thickens, about 30 to 35 minutes.
3. Meanwhile, bring a large pot of lightly salted water to a boil over high heat. Cook rotelle pasta according to package instructions. Drain the pasta, reserving ¼ cup of pasta water.
4. Add both the pasta and reserved pasta water to the chicken. Cook 1 to 2 minutes, mixing until sauce sticks to pasta.
5. Remove bay leaf and discard it. Garnish with fresh parsley and serve.

Per Serving

calories: 440 | fat: 6.9g | carbs: 44.1g | protein: 44.2g

Chicken Fettuccine with Shiitake Mushrooms

Prep time: 10 minutes | Cook time: 14 minutes | Serves 4

Salt and ground black pepper, to taste
8 ounces (227 g) whole-grain fettuccine
2 tablespoons extra-virgin olive oil
2 (6-ounce / 170-g) boneless, skinless chicken breasts, trimmed of fat and cut into strips
3 cloves garlic, peeled and minced
2 ounces (57 g) stemmed and sliced shiitake mushrooms
2 teaspoons lemon zest
2 tablespoons lemon juice
½ cup grated Parmesan cheese
½ cup chopped fresh basil

1. Bring a large pot of lightly salted water to a boil over high heat. Cook fettuccine according to package instructions. Drain the pasta, reserving ½ cup of pasta water.
2. Meanwhile, warm oil in a large nonstick skillet over medium heat. Add chicken strips, sautéing for 3 to 4 minutes.
3. Add garlic and mushrooms. Cook, stirring occasionally, until mushrooms are tender, 4 to 5 minutes. Stir in lemon zest, lemon juice, salt, and pepper. Remove from the heat.
4. Into the skillet, add pasta, reserved pasta water, Parmesan, and basil. Toss well and serve.

Per Serving

calories: 444 | fat: 12.8g | carbs: 43.1g | protein: 33.3g

Chicken Breast Pesto Pasta

Prep time: 10 minutes | Cook time: 20 minutes | Serves 2

Salt and ground black pepper, to taste
4 ounces (113 g) whole-grain ziti
25 fresh basil leaves, finely chopped
1 clove garlic, peeled and minced
1 tablespoon warm water
2 tablespoons pine nuts, crushed
1 tablespoon extra-virgin olive oil
1 (6-ounce / 170-g) boneless, skinless chicken breast, trimmed of fat and cut into small cubes
2 tablespoons grated Parmesan cheese

1. Bring a medium pot of lightly salted water to a boil over high heat. Cook pasta according to package instructions. Drain and reserve.
2. Meanwhile, in a bowl, make pesto mixture: add basil, garlic, water, pine nuts, and oil; mix to combine.
3. Coat a medium pan with cooking spray and warm over medium heat. Add chicken and cook about 7 minutes per side.
4. When chicken is almost cooked through, reduce the heat to low. Stir in salt, pepper, pesto, and cheese. Cook until chicken is no longer pink inside.
5. Add pasta into the pan, stir to combine, and serve.

Per Serving

calories: 412 | fat: 16.7g | carbs: 38.1g | protein: 31.4g

Japanese Chicken Yakitori

Prep time: 10 minutes | Cook time: 3 minutes | Serves 4

½ cup less-sodium soy sauce
½ cup sherry or white cooking wine
½ cup low-sodium chicken broth
½ teaspoon ground ginger
Pinch of garlic powder
½ cup chopped scallions
4 (6-ounce / 170-g) boneless, skinless chicken breasts, trimmed of fat and cut into 2-inch cubes

7. If using bamboo skewers versus metal skewers, soak in water for 30 minutes to prevent the wood from burning.
8. Into a small pot, add soy sauce, sherry, chicken broth, ginger, garlic powder, and scallions. Bring ingredients to a boil over medium-high heat and immediately remove from heat. Reserve.
9. Preheat the oven's broiler. Start threading chicken onto skewers.
10. Coat a broiler pan with cooking spray and place chicken skewers on the pan. Brush each skewer with sherry sauce.
11. Place the pan under the broiler until chicken is browned, about 3 minutes. Remove the pan from the oven to turn each chicken skewer over, brushing sauce onto chicken again.
12. Return the pan to the broiler until chicken is cooked through and nicely browned. Serve.

Per Serving

calories: 225 | fat: 1.9g | carbs: 4.1g | protein: 41.3g

Cheddar Chicken Quesadilla

Prep time: 10 minutes | Cook time: 12 minutes | Serves 2

1 (6-ounce / 170-g) boneless, skinless chicken breast, trimmed of fat
1 tablespoon low-fat sour cream
2 (8-inch) whole-wheat tortillas
⅓ cup salsa
1 cup shredded lettuce
⅓ cup shredded low-fat Cheddar cheese

1. Coat a medium nonstick skillet with cooking spray and warm over medium heat. Add chicken and cook for 3 to 5 minutes per side. Once fully cooked, transfer chicken to a cutting board.
2. Spread sour cream onto 1 tortilla. Slice chicken breast and layer it over sour cream, topping with salsa and lettuce. Sprinkle with cheese and top with the other tortilla.
3. Recoat skillet with cooking spray and warm over low heat. Cook quesadilla until golden, about 3 minutes per side, using a large spatula to carefully flip it. Remove from the skillet, slice, and serve.

Per Serving

calories: 315 | fat: 8.7g | carbs: 28.5g | protein: 30.2g

Curried Chicken

Prep time: 15 minutes | Cook time: 17 minutes | Serves 4

1 small onion, chopped
1 clove garlic, peeled and minced
3 tablespoons curry powder
1 teaspoon sweet paprika
1 bay leaf
1 teaspoon ground cinnamon
½ teaspoon peeled and grated fresh ginger
Salt and ground black pepper, to taste
4 (6-ounce / 170-g) boneless, skinless chicken breasts, trimmed of fat and cut into 1-inch cubes
1 tablespoon tomato paste
½ cup water
Juice of ½ lemon
½ teaspoon Indian chili powder
1 cup 2% Greek yogurt

1. Coat a large skillet with cooking spray and warm over medium heat. Sauté onion until translucent, about 5 minutes.
2. Into the skillet, add garlic, curry powder, paprika, bay leaf, cinnamon, ginger, salt, and pepper; stir for 2 minutes.
3. Add chicken to the pan, along with tomato paste and water; stir to combine. Bring liquid to a boil, reduce the heat to low, and simmer for 10 minutes.
4. Stir in lemon juice and chili powder. Simmer until chicken is cooked through, about 5 more minutes. Take off the heat and remove and discard bay leaf. Stir in yogurt and serve.

Per Serving
calories: 213 | fat: 2.9g | carbs: 6.8g | protein: 40.3g

Chapter 15 Salads

Greek Chicken Breast Salad

Prep time: 15 minutes | Cook time: 14 minutes | Serves 4

2 (10-ounce / 283-g) boneless, skinless chicken breasts
Sea salt and black pepper, to taste
2 tablespoons extra-virgin olive oil
2½ teaspoons freshly squeezed lemon juice
2½ teaspoons red wine vinegar
1½ tablespoons chopped fresh oregano
1 English cucumber, chopped
8 ounces (227 g) red and green peppers, chopped
8 ounces (227 g) kalamata olives
2 tomatoes, cut into slices
½ cup chopped fresh parsley
½ cup red onion
1 cup crumbled feta cheese, divided
½ head romaine lettuce, chopped, divided

1. Heat a grill to medium-high or preheat the broiler to high.
2. Season the chicken breasts with salt and pepper. Grill for 7 to 10 minutes on each side, or broil in a broiler pan 6 inches from the heat for 10 minutes on each side. Let cool completely, and cut into strips.
3. In a small bowl, whisk together the olive oil, lemon juice, vinegar, and oregano.
4. In a medium bowl, toss to combine the cucumber, peppers, olives, tomatoes, parsley, and onion, and season with pepper.
5. Into each of 4 mason jars, place about 2 teaspoons of dressing, one-quarter of the veggie mixture, ¼ cup of crumbled feta, and one-quarter of the lettuce and seal. To serve, shake to distribute the dressing and eat directly from the jar, or invert the jar's contents into a bowl.
6. Store the airtight jars in the refrigerator for 3 to 5 days.

Per Serving
calories: 443 | fat: 21.8g | carbs: 17.9g | protein: 46.1g

Turkey, Walnut, and Fruit Salad

Prep time: 10 minutes | Cook time: 0 minutes | Serves 2

4 cups chopped kale
½ avocado, cubed
¼ red onion, finely chopped
¼ cup blueberries
2 tablespoons chopped and toasted walnuts
½ medium apple, cubed
8 ounces (227 g) roasted turkey, sliced
6 tablespoons Greek yogurt and honey dressing

1. In a medium bowl, combine the kale and avocado and massage the avocado into the kale with your hands. Add the onion, blueberries, walnuts, apple, and turkey, and toss well.
2. In each of 2 airtight storage containers or jars, place about 2 cups of salad. In 2 small airtight storage containers, place 3 tablespoons of Greek Yogurt and Honey Dressing. To serve, mix the salad and dressing.
3. Store the airtight containers in the refrigerator for 3 to 5 days.

Per Serving (1 container)
calories: 419 | fat: 13.1g | carbs: 33.7g | protein: 44.2g

Tuna and Avocado Salad

Prep time: 10 minutes | Cook time: 0 minutes | Serves 2

1 (6-ounce / 170-g) can flaked tuna, packed in water, drained
1 avocado, finely chopped
¼ red bell pepper, chopped
1 celery stalk, chopped
¼ red onion, chopped
1 lemon wedge
Sea salt, to taste
Freshly ground black pepper, to taste
4 rice cakes or 4 large romaine lettuce leaves

1. In a medium bowl, mix the tuna, avocado, bell pepper, celery, and onion. Season with a squeeze of lemon juice, salt, and pepper.
2. Divide the tuna salad evenly between 2 airtight storage containers and seal. To serve, spread on the rice cakes or serve wrapped in 2 lettuce leaves. (If taking this meal on the go, store the rice cakes or lettuce leaves separately in a resealable plastic bag.)
3. Store the airtight containers in the refrigerator for up to 1 week.

Per Serving (2 rice cakes)
calories: 332 | fat: 15.9g | carbs: 24.7g | protein: 28.2g

Egg Salad on Rice Crackers

Prep time: 10 minutes | Cook time: 0 minutes | Serves 4

1 (3½-ounce / 99.2-g) package rice crackers (about 45 crackers), divided
6 hard-boiled eggs, peeled and chopped
½ cup finely chopped celery
¼ cup finely chopped onion
½ cup plain nonfat Greek yogurt
1 teaspoon Dijon mustard
1 tablespoon finely chopped fresh dill
Sea salt, to taste
Freshly ground black pepper, to taste

1. Divide the crackers evenly among 4 resealable plastic bags, placing about 10 to 12 per bag, and seal. Store in the pantry.
2. In a medium bowl, combine the hard-boiled eggs, celery, onion, yogurt, mustard, and dill. Season with salt and pepper.
3. Divide the salad evenly among 4 airtight storage containers. Serve with the crackers.
4. Store the airtight containers in the refrigerator for up to 5 days.

Per Serving
calories: 201 | fat: 7.9g | carbs: 20.1g | protein: 15.3g

Rotisserie Chicken Cobb Salad

Prep time: 10 minutes | Cook time: 0 minutes | Serves 2

4 cups (60g) baby spinach, divided
6 ounces (170g) rotisserie chicken, shredded, divided
2 large hard-boiled eggs, sliced, divided
½ cup diced avocado, divided
½ cup chopped beefsteak tomatoes, divided
¼ cup chopped red onion, divided
¼ cup crumbled cooked bacon, divided
¼ cup crumbled blue cheese or feta cheese, divided
¼ cup light ranch salad dressing, divided

1. Into each of 2 large, airtight storage containers, put 2 cups of spinach, 3 ounces of chicken, 1 hard-boiled egg, ¼ cup of avocado, ¼ cup of tomatoes, 2 tablespoons of red onion, 2 tablespoons of bacon, and 2 tablespoons of blue cheese. Toss, if desired.
2. Into each of 2 small airtight storage containers, place 2 tablespoons of dressing. Add the dressing to the salad just before serving.
3. Store the airtight containers in the refrigerator for up to 5 days.

Per Serving (1 salad with 2 tablespoons dressing)
calories: 483 | fat: 27.8g | carbs: 13.2g | protein: 46.1g

Lemony Tuna Nicoise Salad

Prep time: 10 minutes | Cook time: 0 minutes | Serves 3

¼ cup freshly squeezed lemon juice
¾ cup extra-virgin olive oil
6 fresh basil leaves, minced
Sea salt, to taste
Freshly ground black pepper, to taste
1½ cups cherry or grape tomatoes, halved
8 ounces (227 g) waxy potatoes, cooked and sliced
½ cup frozen shelled edamame, thawed
3 hard-boiled eggs, peeled and cut into wedges
3 canned artichoke hearts, halved
2 (6-ounce / 170-g) cans flaked or solid tuna, in water
¼ cup pitted kalamata olives

1. In a small bowl, whisk together the lemon juice, olive oil, basil, salt, and pepper. Set aside.
2. In a medium bowl, toss the tomatoes, potatoes, edamame, eggs, artichoke hearts, tuna, and olives.
3. Divide the salad evenly among 3 airtight storage containers. Drizzle each salad with 2 tablespoons of the dressing. Store any remaining dressing in a separate airtight container in the refrigerator for up to 1 week.
4. Store the airtight containers in the refrigerator for up to 5 days.

Per Serving (1 salad with 2 tablespoons dressing)
calories: 667 | fat: 35.8g | carbs: 45.8g | protein: 46.2g

Orange Kale Salad

Prep time: 10 minutes | Cook time: 0 minutes | Serves 4

2 cups kale, washed, ribs removed, and chopped into ½-inch (1.25cm) strips
½ naval orange, peeled, separated into wedges, and cut into thirds
¼ medium onion, thinly sliced
1 teaspoon canola oil
2 to 3 drops liquid stevia
1 teaspoon lime juice
1 teaspoon apple cider vinegar
⅛ teaspoon salt
1 teaspoon poppy seeds

1. In a large bowl, combine the kale strips, orange segments, and onion slices. Set aside.
2. In a medium bowl, combine the canola oil, stevia, lime juice, vinegar, salt, and poppy seeds. Whisk to combine.
3. Pour the dressing over the salad and gently toss to coat. Serve immediately.

Per Serving
calories: 43 | fat: 1.4g | carbs: 5.3g | protein: 1.6g

Coconut-Crusted Chicken Breast Salad

Prep time: 15 minutes | Cook time: 25 minutes | Serves 2

For the Vinaigrette:
1 tablespoon extra-virgin olive oil
1 tablespoon honey
1 tablespoon white vinegar
2 teaspoons Dijon mustard
For the Chicken Salad
6 tablespoons shredded unsweetened coconut
¼ cup panko breadcrumbs
2 tablespoons crushed cornflakes
Salt and ground black pepper, to taste
3 egg whites, lightly beaten, or ½ cup liquid egg white substitute
1 (6-ounce / 170-g) boneless, skinless chicken breast, trimmed of fat

6. Preheat the oven to 375°F (190°C). Line a baking sheet with parchment paper.
7. In a small bowl, whisk together oil, honey, vinegar, and mustard. Reserve.
8. In a small, shallow dish, mix coconut, panko, cornflakes, salt, and pepper. In another bowl large enough to fit the chicken, add egg whites and lightly beat them with a fork.
9. Season chicken with salt and pepper. Dip chicken in egg whites followed by the coconut-panko mixture, using your fingers to press coconut mixture onto the chicken if needed. Place chicken onto the prepared baking sheet, lightly coat with cooking spray, and bake for 15 minutes. Flip chicken and bake until cooked through, about 10 to 15 more minutes.
10. To serve, add 3 cups baby greens to each plate. Top with carrots, cucumber, and tomato. Slice chicken diagonally and divide evenly between each salad. Drizzle with dressing.

Chapter 15 Salads • 125

6 cups mixed baby greens
¾ cup shredded carrots
1 cucumber, sliced
1 tomato, sliced

Per Serving
calories: 454 | fat: 20.6g | carbs: 36.1g | protein: 31.5g

Hot Santa Fe Taco Salad

Prep time: 25 minutes | Cook time: 24 minutes | Serves 4

For the Topping:

½ pound (227 g) 93% lean ground turkey
½ cup canned black beans, rinsed and drained
1 tablespoon minced jalapeño pepper
2 beefsteak tomatoes, chopped
1 clove garlic, peeled and minced
3 tablespoons chopped scallions
2 tablespoons chopped fresh cilantro, plus more for garnish
¾ cup frozen corn kernels
Salt and ground black pepper, to taste
1¼ teaspoons ground sweet paprika

For the Avocado Dip:

¼ cup 2% Greek yogurt
¼ cup water
1 medium avocado, peeled, pitted, and chopped, divided
1½ tablespoons chopped fresh cilantro
½ teaspoon cayenne pepper
Salt and ground black pepper, to taste

For the Salad:

5 cups shredded iceberg lettuce
½ cup shredded Mexican cheese blend
1 beefsteak tomato, chopped
2 tablespoons chopped fresh cilantro
2 tablespoons crushed tortilla chips

1. Warm a large nonstick skillet over medium-high heat. Add ground turkey to the skillet, using a wooden spoon to break the meat into small pieces. Cook for 4 to 5 minutes, stirring frequently, until the meat is no longer pink.
2. Stir in beans, jalapeño, tomatoes, garlic, scallions, cilantro, corn, salt, pepper, and paprika. Cover, reduce heat to low, and cook for 15 minutes. Remove the lid from the skillet and simmer until the liquid reduces, about 5 more minutes.
3. Meanwhile, make the avocado dip: into a blender, add yogurt, water, half the avocado, cilantro, cayenne, salt, and pepper. Process until smooth; reserve.
4. Divide the lettuce between 4 plates. Top with turkey mixture, cheese, tomatoes, cilantro, and remaining chopped avocado. Spoon the avocado dip over the top and garnish with crushed tortilla chips.

Per Serving
calories: 347 | fat: 17.6g | carbs: 28.1g | protein: 22.2g

Chickpea and Baby Spinach Salad

Prep time: 10 minutes | Cook time: 0 minutes | Serves 1

3 cups roughly chopped baby spinach
2 cups cooked chickpeas
1 cup chopped mushrooms
1 tomato, chopped
1 avocado, peeled, pitted, and chopped
⅛ teaspoon pink Himalayan salt
⅛ teaspoon freshly ground black pepper
Juice of 1 large lemon
1 tablespoon sunflower seeds, for topping (optional)
1 teaspoon hulled hemp seeds, for topping (optional)

1. In a large bowl, combine the spinach, chickpeas, mushrooms, tomato, and avocado. Add the salt, pepper, and lemon juice. Mix thoroughly so all the flavors combine and the avocado is mixed in well.
2. Top with the seeds (if using). Enjoy immediately or store in a reusable container in the refrigerator for up to 5 days.

Per Serving
calories: 944 | fat: 33.1g | carbs: 139.8g | protein: 34.2g

Black Bean and Corn Salad

Prep time: 5 minutes | Cook time: 0 minutes | Serves 2

2 cups cooked black beans
1 avocado, pitted, peeled, and chopped
½ cup corn
1 small tomato, chopped
2 scallions, chopped
2 tablespoons diced jalapeños
⅛ cup chopped fresh cilantro
1 tablespoon freshly squeezed lime juice
Pink Himalayan salt, to taste (optional)

1. In a large bowl, combine the beans, avocado, corn, tomato, scallions, jalapeños, and cilantro and mix well with a wooden spoon. Sprinkle with the lime juice and a pinch of salt (if using) and enjoy.

Per Serving

calories: 854 | fat: 30.1g | carbs: 123.2g | protein: 38.3g

Baby Spinach Caprese Salad

Prep time: 5 minutes | Cook time: 0 minutes | Serves 1

1½ cups baby spinach
½ cup cherry tomatoes, quartered
1 ounce (28 g) fresh Mozzarella, cubed
2 tablespoons chopped fresh basil
4½ teaspoons extra-virgin olive oil
1 tablespoon balsamic vinegar
Salt, to taste
Freshly ground black pepper, to taste

1. In a salad bowl, sprinkle the cherry tomatoes, Mozzarella, and basil over the baby spinach.
2. Drizzle the olive oil and balsamic over the top, season with salt and pepper, and enjoy.

Per Serving

calories: 181 | fat: 11.7g | carbs: 8.2g | protein: 19.4g

Lime Cucumber Salad

Prep time: 5 minutes | Cook time: 0 minutes | Serves 5

2 seedless cucumbers
1 medium red onion
1 bunch fresh cilantro, chopped
½ cup granulated stevia
½ cup rice vinegar
2 tablespoons freshly squeezed lime juice
½ cup unsalted roasted cashews, whole or chopped, divided (optional)

1. Slice the cucumber into thin rounds using a mandoline slicer, or knife.
2. Quarter the onion, and thinly slice with a mandoline slicer, or knife.
3. In a large bowl, toss the cucumber, onion, and cilantro.
4. In a small bowl, mix the stevia, vinegar, and lime juice until the stevia is dissolved.
5. Add the dressing to the salad, and toss to coat.
6. Divide the salad among five salad plates, garnish each with about 1½ tablespoons of cashews (if using), and serve.

Per Serving

calories: 103 | fat: 5.8g | carbs: 10.6g | protein: 3.2g

Easy Tuna Salad

Prep time: 10 minutes | Cook time: 0 minutes | Serves 1

1 (7-ounce / 198-g) can tuna in water, drained
1 tablespoon finely diced red onion
1 tablespoon finely diced dill pickle

1. In a small bowl, use a fork to mix the tuna, onion, pickle, yogurt, lemon juice, olive oil, dill, and pepper until well combined.
2. Drizzle the balsamic vinegar over the top and enjoy.

1 tablespoon nonfat Greek yogurt
1½ teaspoons freshly squeezed lemon juice
1½ teaspoons extra-virgin olive oil
¼ teaspoon dried dill
Pinch freshly ground black pepper
2 tablespoons balsamic vinaigrette

Per Serving
calories: 285 | fat: 7.5g | carbs: 7.1g | protein: 48.3g

Chicken and Chickpeas Pasta Salad

Prep time: 20 minutes | Cook time: 8 minutes | Serves 6

Salt, to taste
8 ounces (227 g) whole-grain bow-tie pasta
3 (6-ounce / 170-g) chicken breasts, trimmed of fat, cooked, and shredded
½ (15-ounce / 425-g) can chickpeas, drained and rinsed
1 (2¼-ounce / 63.8-g) can sliced black olives, drained
2 stalks celery, chopped
2 cucumbers, chopped
½ cup shredded carrots
½ yellow onion, finely chopped
2 tablespoons shredded Parmesan cheese
3 tablespoons extra-virgin olive oil
¼ cup red wine vinegar
½ teaspoon Worcestershire sauce
½ teaspoon spicy brown mustard
½ clove garlic, peeled and minced
2 tablespoons chopped fresh Italian parsley
1 tablespoon chopped fresh basil or 1 teaspoon dried basil
¼ teaspoon ground black pepper

1. Bring a large pot of lightly salted water to a boil over high heat. Cook pasta according to package instructions. Drain and run pasta under cold water for about 30 seconds or until it is completely cool.
2. Transfer pasta to a large bowl and add remaining ingredients. Use tongs to mix thoroughly to combine.
3. Cover the bowl with plastic wrap and refrigerate for at least 4 hours or up to overnight. Toss the salad prior to serving.

Per Serving
calories: 371 | fat: 12.1g | carbs: 40.8g | protein: 28.3g

Chapter 16 Snacks and Power Bars

Nuts Energy Balls

Prep time: 10 minutes | Cook time: 0 minutes | Makes 12 balls

2 cups Medjool dates, pitted
½ cup walnuts
½ cup almonds
½ cup shredded unsweetened coconut
½ scoop vanilla vegan protein powder
2 tablespoons cocoa powder
1 tablespoon coconut oil
1 teaspoon vanilla extract
½ teaspoon ground cinnamon
Pinch sea salt

1. In a food processor, combine the dates, walnuts, almonds, coconut, protein powder, cocoa powder, coconut oil, vanilla, cinnamon, and salt. Process until crumbly.
2. Remove from the food processor and roll into 1½-inch balls.
3. Transfer to an airtight container, or if using individual serving bags, place 2 balls per bag, and seal.
4. Store the airtight container or bags in the refrigerator for up to 1 week.

Per Serving
calories: 165 | fat: 7.6g | carbs: 25.3g | protein: 4.2g

Cinnamon Peanut Butter and Banana Nice Cream

Prep time: 5 minutes | Cook time: 0 minutes | Serves 4

For the Nice Cream Packs:

4 fresh or frozen bananas, chopped, divided
4 tablespoons creamy peanut butter, divided
4 pinches ground cinnamon, divided

For the Nice Cream:

4 to 8 tablespoons almond or coconut milk, divided
2 teaspoons vanilla extract, divided

Make the Nice Cream Packs
1. Into each of 4 resealable freezer bags, place 1 frozen banana, 1 tablespoon of peanut butter, and a pinch of cinnamon. Lay the bags flat and remove as much air as possible before sealing. Store in the freezer until ready to use.

Make the Nice Cream
2. In a blender, combine 1 to 2 tablespoons of almond milk, ½ teaspoon of vanilla, and the contents of 1 smoothie pack, and blend until smooth.
3. Store the airtight bags in the freezer for up to 2 weeks.

Per Serving
calories: 213 | fat: 8.6g | carbs: 31.3g | protein: 6.4g

Quick Lemon Drop Energy Balls

Prep time: 5 minutes | Cook time: 0 minutes | Makes 12 to 14 energy balls

1¼ cups raw cashews
10 Medjool dates, pitted
½ cup shredded, unsweetened coconut, divided
1 tablespoon coconut oil
Zest of 1 lemon
1 tablespoon freshly squeezed lemon juice

1. In a food processor, process the cashews until roughly ground so that only tiny pieces remain. Remove from the food processor and set aside.
2. In the food processor, combine the dates, ¼ cup of coconut, and the coconut oil and lemon zest, and process until the dates are mashed.
3. Add the ground cashews and lemon juice, and process until a ball of dough starts to form.
4. Remove the dough from the food processor and, with your hands, roll into 1½-inch balls.
5. In a shallow bowl, place the remaining ¼ cup of coconut and roll the balls in the shredded coconut until well covered.
6. Into each of 6 resealable storage bags (freezer bags if freezing), place 2 energy balls, and seal.
7. Store the airtight bags in the refrigerator for up to 2 weeks.
8. Store the airtight bags in the freezer for up to 3 months.

Per Serving (2 energy balls)
calories: 265 | fat: 13.7g | carbs: 35.2g | protein: 5.4g

Cherry and Nuts Energy Bites

Prep time: 10 minutes | Cook time: 0 minutes | Serves 12

¾ cup rolled oats
½ cup almonds
¼ cup cashews
¼ cup walnuts
¼ cup dried cherries
1 tablespoon ground flaxseed
1 tablespoon hemp seeds
6 large Medjool dates, pitted and chopped
2 tablespoons honey
½ teaspoon vanilla extract
Pinch sea salt

1. In a food processor, combine the oats, almonds, cashews, walnuts, cherries, flaxseed, and hemp seeds. Pulse a few times, until they are a coarse meal.
2. Add the dates, honey, vanilla, and salt, and continue to pulse until a dough begins to form or the ingredients stick together. Shape into 12 (1¼-inch) balls.
3. Place in an airtight container, or if using individual resealable storage bags, place 2 balls in each, and seal.
4. Store the airtight container or bags in the refrigerator for up to 1 week.

Per Serving
calories: 137 | fat: 5.7g | carbs: 19.6g | protein: 3.2g

Beef Cheeseburger Bites

Prep time: 10 minutes | Cook time: 20 minutes | Serves 4

1 pound (454 g) lean ground sirloin
2 teaspoons coconut flour
2 large eggs
2 teaspoons no-sugar-added ketchup
2 teaspoons spicy brown mustard
½ cup low-fat shredded Mozzarella cheese
¼ cup diced white onion

1. Preheat oven to 350°F (177°C). Spray an 8-cup muffin tin with non-stick cooking spray.
2. In a large bowl, combine the ground sirloin, coconut flour, eggs, ketchup, mustard, Mozzarella cheese, and onion. Mix the ingredients until just incorporated. (Do not over mix, as the burgers can become tough.)
3. Spoon equal amounts of the mixture into the muffin cups. Bake for 20 minutes, or until the internal temperature reaches 160°F (71°C). Serve hot.

Per Serving
calories: 242 | fat: 12.8g | carbs: 3.1g | protein: 28.4g

Protein Pumpkin and Oat Bars

Prep time: 10 minutes | Cook time: 20 minutes | Serves 6

1 cup oat flour
½ cup vanilla whey protein powder
1 teaspoon baking powder
½ teaspoon salt
2 teaspoons ground cinnamon
½ teaspoon allspice
½ teaspoon ground ginger
⅓ cup powdered stevia
⅓ cup liquid egg whites
1 cup canned pumpkin purée (not pumpkin pie mix)
1 teaspoon vanilla extract

1. Preheat the oven to 350°F (177°C). Spray an 8 x 8in (20 x 20cm) baking pan with non-stick cooking spray.
2. In a large bowl, combine the oat flour, protein powder, baking powder, salt, cinnamon, allspice, ginger, and stevia. Mix well.
3. In a separate large bowl, combine the egg whites, pumpkin purée, and vanilla extract. Mix well.
4. Make the batter by adding the wet ingredients to the dry ingredients. Mix well to combine.
5. Pour the batter into the baking pan. Bake for 20 to 25 minutes, or until a toothpick inserted in the middle comes out clean. Slice into 6 equal-sized bars.

Per Serving

calories: 153 | fat: 0.5g | carbs: 24.7g | protein: 11.9g

Honey Lean Rice Crispy Treats

Prep time: 5 minutes | Cook time: ½ minute | Serves 12

⅔ cup natural almond butter
½ cup raw honey
½ cup vanilla whey protein powder
1 tablespoon ground cinnamon
3 cups toasted brown rice cereal

1. In a large glass bowl, combine the almond butter and honey. Warm in the microwave on medium for 30 to 45 seconds, stir, then add the protein powder and cinnamon. Stir well.
2. Add the brown rice cereal and gently fold it into the mixture. Pour into a 9 x 13in (23 x 33cm) baking dish and use a spoon to flatten the mixture and form a uniform surface.
3. Place in the refrigerator to harden for 15 minutes before cutting into 12 equal-sized squares.

Per Serving

calories: 183 | fat: 8.4g | carbs: 20.1g | protein: 8.6g

Oats and Almond Milk Bars

Prep time: 5 minutes | Cook time: 0 minutes | Serves 12

2 cups quick oats
3 scoops whey protein powder
½ cup creamy almond butter
⅔ cup almond milk
1 teaspoon vanilla extract
2 teaspoons powdered stevia

1. In a large bowl, combine the oats, protein powder, almond butter, almond milk, vanilla extract, and stevia. Mix well until the ingredients form a dough.
2. Press the dough into a 9 x 13in (23 x 33cm) baking pan. Place the pan in the refrigerator for 30 minutes to harden the bars.
3. Cut into 8 equal-sized bars, and individually wrap in parchment paper. Seal the wrapped bars in a plastic storage bag.

Per Serving

calories: 215 | fat: 10.1g | carbs: 17.3g | protein: 14.3g

Iced Pumpkin and Pecan Bars

Prep time: 15 minutes | Cook time: 22 minutes | Serves 9

For the Bars:

4 large eggs
1 cup pumpkin purée
¼ cup pure maple syrup
2 tablespoons unsweetened almond milk
1 teaspoon vanilla extract
⅓ cup coconut flour
2 scoops vanilla whey protein powder
2 tablespoons ground flaxseed
2 teaspoons ground cinnamon
¼ teaspoon baking soda
½ teaspoon ground nutmeg
¼ teaspoon sea salt
⅛ teaspoon ground cloves

For the Topping:

1 scoop vanilla protein powder
Room temperature water, as needed
¼ cup chopped pecans

1. Preheat the oven to 375°F (190°C). Prepare a baking sheet by lining with parchment paper or a silicone mat.
2. In a large bowl, add eggs, pumpkin, maple syrup, almond milk, and vanilla. Use a fork to whisk together until combined.
3. In a medium bowl, add coconut flour, protein powder, flaxseed, cinnamon, baking soda, nutmeg, salt, and cloves, stirring together to combine.
4. Slowly stir dry ingredients into the pumpkin mixture until well combined; let sit for 2 to 3 minutes.
5. Separate batter into 8 parts, about ⅓ cup each. Form batter into rectangular bars by hand (like Clif bars) and place onto the prepared baking sheet.
6. Bake bars until golden brown on the bottom with a top just beginning to crack, about 22 to 25 minutes. Let bars cool for 5 minutes and then transfer to a wire rack.
7. Once bars have fully cooled, prepare the icing. Add protein powder to a small bowl, slowly stirring in water until mixture is thick and smooth.
8. Transfer icing into a small Ziploc bag and use scissors to cut off a small piece of the corner. Squeeze icing out of the cut corner, drizzling evenly over the top of the bars. Sprinkle chopped pecans over the bars.
9. For best results, let icing set for 1 hour or more. Store bars in an airtight container.

Per Serving

calories: 143 | fat: 5.7g | carbs: 12.1g | protein: 12.4g

Simple Dough Oats

Prep time: 5 minutes | Cook time: 0 minutes | Serves 2

½ cup quick or rolled oats
1 tablespoon flaxseeds
2 scoops vanilla flavor vegan protein powder
1 cup unsweetened almond milk
1 tablespoon peanut butter
1 tablespoon carob chips (optional)
1 tablespoon maple syrup (optional)

15. Take a lidded bowl or jar and add the oats, flaxseed, protein powder, and almond milk.
16. Stir until everything is thoroughly combined and the mixture looks runny; if not, add a little more almond milk.
17. Blend in the peanut butter with a spoon until everything is mixed well.
18. Place or close the lid on the bowl or jar and transfer it to the refrigerator.
19. Allow the jar to sit overnight or for at least five hours, so the flavors can set.
20. Serve the dough oats, and if desired, topped with the optional carob chips and a small cap of maple syrup.
21. Serve immediately.

Per Serving

calories: 317 | fat: 11.4g | carbs: 22.8g | protein: 30.8g

Avocado and Strawberry Toast

Prep time: 5 minutes | Cook time: 0 minutes | Serves 4

1 avocado, peeled, pitted, and quartered
4 whole-wheat bread slices, toasted
4 ripe strawberries, cut into ¼-inch slices
1 tablespoon balsamic glaze or reduction

1. Mash one-quarter of the avocado on a slice of toast. Layer one-quarter of the strawberry slices over the avocado, and finish with a drizzle of balsamic glaze. Repeat with the remaining ingredients, and serve.

Per Serving

calories: 151 | fat: 8.2g | carbs: 17.1g | protein: 5.3g

Pistachio Energy Balls

Prep time: 5 minutes | Cook time: 0 minutes | Makes 18 balls

½ cup old-fashioned oats
½ cup almond butter
¼ cup maple syrup
⅓ cup oat bran
⅓ cup flaxseed meal
⅓ cup pistachios, ground
1 tablespoon raw shelled hempseed

1. Add all the ingredients to a large bowl and mix well.
2. Roll into eighteen balls. Serve.

Per Serving (2 balls)
calories: 163 | fat: 12.1g | carbs: 11.3g | protein: 7.1g

Coconut Lemon Protein Balls

Prep time: 5 minutes | Cook time: 0 minutes | Makes 24 balls

1¾ cups cashews
¼ cup coconut flour
¼ cup unsweetened shredded coconut
3 tablespoons raw shelled hempseed
3 tablespoons maple syrup
3 tablespoons fresh lemon juice

1. Place the cashews in a food processor and process until very fine. Add the rest of the ingredients and process until well blended. Dump the mixture into a large bowl.
2. Take a clump of the dough and squeeze it into a ball. Keep squeezing and working it a few times until a ball is formed and solid.
3. Serve.

Per Serving (2 balls)
calories: 158 | fat: 11.4g | carbs: 11.3g | protein: 5.0g

Chapter 17 Desserts and Shakes

Oat and Chia Seeds Muffins

Prep time: 10 minutes | Cook time: 35 minutes | Serves 12

2½ cups rolled oats
3 tablespoons coconut sugar
2 tablespoons chia seeds
2½ scoops vanilla vegan protein powder
1 tablespoon ground cinnamon
Pinch sea salt
2 cups unsweetened vanilla almond milk
½ cup unsweetened applesauce
½ cup egg whites
1 tablespoon vanilla extract
2 tablespoons coconut oil, melted
2 cups peeled and finely chopped apples

1. Preheat the oven to 375°F (190°C). Line a 12-cup muffin tin with silicone baking cups.
2. In a large bowl, mix together the oats, coconut sugar, chia seeds, protein powder, cinnamon, and salt.
3. In a medium bowl, whisk together the almond milk, applesauce, egg whites, and vanilla.
4. Pour the wet ingredients into the dry ingredients, then stir in the coconut oil and the apples.
5. Divide the batter evenly among the prepared muffin cups.
6. Bake for 35 minutes, or until a toothpick inserted into a muffin center comes out clean, and remove from the oven.
7. Remove the muffin cups from the pan and let cool on a wire rack for 30 minutes. Store in a large airtight storage container or individually portioned bags at room temperature for 3 days.
8. Wrap the muffins individually in plastic wrap and store in the freezer for up to 3 months. Thaw at room temperature for 2 hours when ready to serve.

Per Serving (1 muffin)
calories: 151 | fat: 5.7g | carbs: 21.2g | protein: 7.4g

Banana-Peanut Butter Mug Muffins

Prep time: 10 minutes | Cook time: 2 minutes | Serves 3

Nonstick cooking spray
1 ripe banana, mashed
¾ cup egg whites
¾ cup quick oats
3 tablespoons peanut butter
1½ teaspoons vanilla extract
1½ teaspoons ground cinnamon
3 tablespoons mini chocolate chips (optional)

1. Spray 3 large mugs with nonstick cooking spray.
2. In a medium bowl, combine the banana, egg whites, oats, peanut butter, vanilla, and cinnamon. Mix well, then fold in the chocolate chips (if using).
3. Divide the batter equally among the 3 mugs.
4. Microwave each mug on high for 2 minutes, or until the muffin is cooked through and the top is firm to the touch.
5. Remove from the microwave. Free the sides of the muffins from the mugs with a butter knife, and turn the mugs upside down to shake onto a plate. Let cool.
6. Into each of 3 airtight storage containers, place 1 muffin and seal.
7. Store the airtight containers in the refrigerator for up to 1 week.

Per Serving (1 muffin)
calories: 325 | fat: 14.7g | carbs: 35.1g | protein: 15.4g

Blueberry-Almond Milk Shake

Prep time: 5 minutes | Cook time: 0 minutes | Serves 1

1 cup blueberries (fresh or frozen)
¼ cup vanilla whey protein powder
½ cup fat free plain Greek yogurt
½ teaspoon vanilla extract
½ cup unsweetened almond milk
1 cup crushed ice

1. Combine the blueberries, protein powder, Greek yogurt, vanilla extract, almond milk, and ice in a blender. Pulse for 15 second intervals until the ingredients are well incorporated.
2. Scrape the sides of the blender with a rubber spatula. Blend on high for 1 additional minute, or until the ice is crushed and the shake is smooth and creamy. Transfer to a glass and serve immediately.

Per Serving

calories: 266 | fat: 1.3g | carbs: 32.1g | protein: 32.5g

Carrot and Banana Shake

Prep time: 10 minutes | Cook time: 0 minutes | Serves 1

1 cup shredded carrots
½ cup unsweetened vanilla almond milk
½ cup plain nonfat Greek yogurt
3 tablespoons vanilla whey protein powder
½ medium frozen banana
⅛ teaspoon ground cardamom
¼ teaspoon ground ginger
¼ teaspoon ground cinnamon
1 teaspoon powdered stevia

1. Place the carrots in a microwave-safe dish, cover with a damp paper towel, and microwave on high for 1 minute. Allow to cool for 5 minutes.
2. Combine all ingredients in a blender. Blend on high for one minute. Scrape the sides of the blender with a rubber spatula, and blend on high for 1 additional minute. Transfer to a glass and serve immediately.

Per Serving

calories: 290 | fat: 1.7g | carbs: 37.2g | protein: 33.4g

Chocolate Mousse

Prep time: 5 minutes | Cook time: 0 minutes | Serves 4

2 medium avocados, halved lengthwise, seeds removed
⅓ cup unsweetened cocoa powder
1 teaspoon vanilla extract
Pinch of salt
¼ cup powdered stevia
½ cup unsweetened coconut milk

1. Using a spoon, scoop the avocado flesh into a blender. Add the cocoa powder, vanilla extract, salt, and stevia.
2. With the lid off, begin blending the ingredients on low while simultaneously adding the coconut milk in a steady stream. Continue blending until all ingredients are well incorporated.
3. Scrape the sides of the blender with a rubber spatula. Cover, and blend on high for an additional 30 seconds to 1 minute, or until a smooth and creamy texture is achieved. Serve chilled.

Per Serving

calories: 142 | fat: 11.5g | carbs: 7.1g | protein: 3.2g

Cloud Bread Bake

Prep time: 5 minutes | Cook time: 20 minutes | Serves 3

4 large eggs, warmed to room temperature
½ teaspoon cream of tartar
Pinch of salt
4 tablespoons light cream cheese, softened and warmed to room temperature

Per Serving
calories: 119 | fat: 8.1g | carbs: 1.5g | protein: 8.3g

1. Preheat the oven to 350°F (177°C). Line two 9 x 13in (23 x 33cm) baking sheets with parchment paper.
2. Separate the egg yolks from the egg whites, placing the yolks in a medium bowl and the whites in a large glass or metal mixing bowl. (Do not use a plastic bowl for the egg whites.)
3. Add the cream of tartar to the egg whites. Using a hand mixer, beat the egg whites on high speed until they form stiff peaks that don't collapse when the mixer blade is lifted from the bowl.
4. Add the salt and cream cheese to the egg yolks, and whisk until all ingredients are well incorporated. Use a rubber spatula to gently fold the egg yolk mixture into the egg whites.
5. Use a ½ cup measuring cup to measure the batter into individual mounds on the baking sheet, maintaining at least 1 inch between each mound.
6. Bake for 20 to 25 minutes, rotating the baking sheets halfway through the baking process to ensure the bread bakes evenly. Allow the bread to cool on the baking sheets.

Chocolate Almond Shake

Prep time: 5 minutes | Cook time: 0 minutes | Serves 1

1 cup unsweetened vanilla almond milk
¼ cup chocolate whey protein powder
1 tablespoon almond butter
1 tablespoon unsweetened cocoa powder
2 teaspoons unsweetened shredded coconut
3 teaspoons powdered stevia
1 tablespoon slivered almonds

Per Serving
calories: 328 | fat: 20.9g | carbs: 9.5g | protein: 30.6g

1. Combine the almond milk, protein powder, almond butter, cocoa powder, coconut, and stevia in a blender. Blend on high for 30 seconds.
2. Scrape the sides of the blender with a rubber spatula, and blend on high for 1 additional minute.
3. Transfer to a glass and top with the slivered almonds. Serve immediately.

Citrus Creamsicle Shake

Prep time: 10 minutes | Cook time: 0 minutes | Serves 1

1 teaspoon orange zest
1 orange, peeled and cut into segments, seeds and pith removed
¼ cup vanilla whey protein powder
½ cup nonfat plain Greek yogurt
½ cup unsweetened vanilla almond milk
½ teaspoon vanilla extract
2 teaspoons powdered stevia
½ cup crushed ice

Per Serving
calories: 247 | fat: 1.3g | carbs: 26.9g | protein: 32.7g

1. Combine the orange zest, orange segments, protein powder, Greek yogurt, almond milk, vanilla extract, stevia, and ice in a blender. Blend on low for 30 seconds.
2. Scrape the sides of the blender with a rubber spatula. Blend on high for an additional 1 to 2 minutes, or until the shake is smooth and creamy. Transfer to a glass and serve immediately.

Elvis Milkshake

Prep time: 10 minutes | Cook time: 0 minutes | Serves 1

½ medium banana
¼ cup powdered peanut butter
1 cup unsweetened almond milk
¼ cup vanilla whey protein powder
½ teaspoon vanilla extract
½ teaspoon powdered stevia
1 cup crushed ice

1. Combine the banana, powdered peanut butter, almond milk, protein powder, vanilla, stevia, and ice in a blender. Blend on low for 30 seconds.
2. Scrape the sides of the blender with a rubber spatula. Blend on high for an additional 30 seconds to 1 minute, or until the ice is crushed and the shake is smooth and creamy. Transfer to a glass and serve immediately.

Per Serving

calories: 260 | fat: 4.9g | carbs: 23.1g | protein: 34.2g

Orange and Beet Protein Shake

Prep time: 5 minutes | Cook time: 0 minutes | Serves 2

2 cups water
2 cups beet greens
2 beets, peeled and diced
2 oranges, peeled
2 scoops vanilla protein powder
Juice of ½ lemon

1. Into a blender, add water, greens, beets, oranges, protein powder, and lemon juice.
2. Blend the ingredients until smooth. Pour shake into 2 glasses and serve.

Per Serving

calories: 192 | fat: 0g | carbs: 24.6g | protein: 25.2g

Banana-Chai Tea Protein Shake

Prep time: 10 minutes | Cook time: 0 minutes | Serves 1

1 cup water
2 chai tea bags
⅓ cup 2% milk
⅓ cup 2% Greek yogurt
½ banana, preferably frozen, peeled and sliced
½ scoop vanilla protein powder
2 teaspoons maca powder (optional)
6 ice cubes
Ground cinnamon, to taste

1. In a small pot, add water and bring to a boil over high heat. Remove from heat, add tea bags, and let tea steep for 30 minutes to fully infuse with chai flavor. Place tea in the fridge or freezer to fully chill.
2. Once tea is cool, add milk, yogurt, banana, protein powder, and (optional) maca powder into a blender. Process until smooth.
3. Pour in cold tea and blend until smooth. Add ice and continue puréeing until ice is crushed.
4. Pour shake into a glass, garnish with cinnamon, and enjoy.

Per Serving

calories: 243 | fat: 3.2g | carbs: 30.1g | protein: 24.3g

Baked Protein Swirl Brownies

Prep time: 15 minutes | Cook time: 20 minutes | Serves 10

For the Batter:

1 (15-ounce / 425-g) can garbanzo beans, drained and rinsed
2 large eggs
2 tablespoons unsweetened cocoa powder
¼ cup coconut sugar
½ teaspoon salt
2 tablespoons peanut butter
2 teaspoons vanilla extract
1 scoop unflavored whey protein
6 ounces (170 g) dark chocolate, chopped, or 1 cup dark chocolate chips

For the Topping:

½ cup 2% Greek yogurt
2 tablespoons egg whites or liquid egg white substitute
1 teaspoon vanilla extract
2 tablespoons peanut butter
1 scoop unflavored whey protein
1 teaspoon honey

1. Preheat the oven to 350°F (180°C). Prepare an 8-inch by 8-inch baking pan by coating with cooking spray.
2. Into a blender or food processor, add garbanzo beans, eggs, cocoa powder, coconut sugar, salt, peanut butter, vanilla, and whey protein. Blend the ingredients until smooth. Transfer brownie batter to a medium bowl.
3. Using either a microwave or double boiler on the stove, gently stir the chocolate until melted. Stirring constantly, slowly pour the melted chocolate into the brownie batter. Use a spatula to evenly spread into the prepared pan. Set aside.
4. In a small bowl, add the topping ingredients and mix to combine. Pour topping over the brownie batter. Gently drag the tip of a knife through the mixture to create brownie swirls.
5. Bake brownies until topping is set and edges are golden brown, about 20 to 25 minutes. Let cool slightly and cut into 10 pieces. Store in an airtight container.

Per Serving

calories: 234 | fat: 10.8g | carbs: 25.1g | protein: 12.3g

Almond-Soy Protein Shake

Prep time: 5 minutes | Cook time: 0 minutes | Serves 2

1½ cups soy milk
3 tablespoons almonds
1 teaspoon maple syrup
1 tablespoon coconut oil
2 scoops chocolate or vanilla flavor vegan protein powder
2 to 4 ice cubes
1 teaspoon cocoa powder (optional)

1. Add all the ingredients to a blender.
2. Blend for 2 minutes.
3. Transfer the shake to a large cup or shaker.
4. Serve immediately.

Per Serving

calories: 341 | fat: 17.1g | carbs: 15.3g | protein: 31.7g

Oatmeal-Almond Protein Shake

Prep time: 5 minutes | Cook time: 0 minutes | Serves 3

1 cup dry oatmeal
3 scoops chocolate or vanilla flavor vegan protein powder
½ teaspoon cinnamon
½ teaspoon maple syrup
¼ cup almonds
1 cup oat milk
2 ice cubes
2 tablespoons peanut butter (optional)

1. Add the ingredients to a blender.
2. Blend for 2 minutes.
3. Transfer to a large cup or shaker.
4. Serve immediately.

Per Serving

calories: 299 | fat: 9.1g | carbs: 24.8g | protein: 29.4g

Fruit Crisp

Prep time: 5 minutes | Cook time: 40 to 60 minutes | Serves 12

1 cup firmly packed brown sugar
1 cup whole-wheat flour
2 cups rolled oats
2 teaspoons ground cinnamon
½ cup canola oil
4 to 5 cups fresh or frozen fruit
1 teaspoon lemon juice
1 teaspoon grated lemon peel

1. Preheat the oven to 350°F (180°C). Lightly grease a 9-inch square baking pan, and set aside.
2. In a small bowl, stir together sugar, flour, oatmeal, and cinnamon. With a pastry blender or fork, cut in oil until mixture is crumbly.
3. Chop fruit and place in baking dish. Sprinkle with lemon peel and lemon juice.
4. Sprinkle crumb mixture evenly over the top.
5. Bake, uncovered, for 40 to 60 minutes until fruit is soft and bubbly. Let cool about 15 minutes before serving.

Per Serving
calories: 276 | fat: 11.2g | carbs: 44.8g | protein: 3.6g

Chocolate Cranberry Quinoa Bars

Prep time: 10 minutes | Cook time: 25 minutes | Makes 12 bars

1½ cups uncooked quinoa
½ cup ground almonds
½ cup grated or shredded dried coconut
½ cup dried cranberries
½ cup dried apples or other dried fruit, chopped
¼ teaspoon salt
½ cup almond or peanut butter
2 tablespoons coconut oil
¼ cup agave
½ cup chocolate chips or dark chocolate pieces

1. Preheat the oven to 350°F (180°C).
2. Spread the quinoa on a cookie sheet and toast for 7 to 8 minutes.
3. In a large bowl, combine the toasted quinoa, almonds, coconut, and dried fruit.
4. In a saucepan, combine the remaining ingredients, except for the chocolate chips. Bring to a simmer over medium heat for 2 minutes.
5. Pour over quinoa mixture and combine until dry ingredients are evenly coated.
6. Mix in chocolate chips.
7. Spoon into a greased baking dish. Press mixture into pan. Bake for 15 minutes.
8. Let cool and then cut and serve or store in an airtight container.

Per Serving
calories: 299 | fat: 16.9g | carbs: 31.8g | protein: 6.9g

Chapter 18 Soup

Curry Red Lentil Soup

Prep time: 15 minutes | Cook time: 26 minutes | Serves 4

2 tablespoons coconut oil
¾ cup finely chopped white onion
½ cup finely chopped carrots
Pinch sea salt
2 garlic cloves, minced
1½ tablespoons curry powder
1 teaspoon ground cumin
1 teaspoon ground cinnamon
5 cups vegetable stock, divided
1 cup canned red lentils, rinsed and drained
¾ cup chopped potato
1 dried bay leaf
1 tablespoon freshly squeezed lemon juice
¼ cup finely chopped fresh parsley
Sea salt and black pepper, to taste

1. In a large stockpot, melt the coconut oil. Add the onion, carrots, and salt. Stir, and sweat over medium heat until the onion is translucent, 5 to 7 minutes.
2. Stir in the garlic, curry powder, cumin, and cinnamon until combined. Continue cooking for about 1 minute more, or until fragrant, then add ½ cup of vegetable stock and cook for about 5 more minutes, or until the vegetables have softened and the liquid has reduced slightly.
3. Add the remaining 4½ cups of stock and the lentils, potato, and bay leaf, and stir to combine. Increase the heat to high and bring to a boil, then reduce the heat to medium-high and simmer, uncovered, for 15 to 20 minutes, until the potatoes are cooked through. Make sure to stir regularly so the lentils don't burn.
4. Turn off the heat, and stir in the lemon juice and parsley. Remove the bay leaf. Season with salt and pepper. Let cool completely.
5. Divide the soup evenly among containers and seal.
6. Store for up to 1 week. To reheat, microwave at 30-second intervals, stirring in between, or on low on the stovetop.

Per Serving
calories: 287 | fat: 9.7g | carbs: 42.3g | protein: 14.7g

Carrot-Coconut Milk Soup

Prep time: 10 minutes | Cook time: 35 minutes | Serves 4

1 teaspoon extra-virgin olive oil
1 medium onion, chopped
10 carrots, unpeeled and sliced
3 cloves garlic, minced
2 teaspoons peeled and grated fresh ginger
4 cups low-sodium chicken broth
1 (14-ounce / 397-g) can lite coconut milk
Chopped fresh cilantro, to taste
Salt and ground black pepper, to taste

1. In a medium pot, warm olive oil over medium-high heat. Add the onion and sauté for about 3 minutes. Add carrots, garlic, and ginger; stirring frequently, cook for about 5 minutes.
2. Stir in broth and coconut milk. Bring soup to a boil over high heat; reduce heat to low and simmer until carrots until tender, about 30 minutes.
3. Remove soup from the heat and stir in cilantro. Carefully use an immersion blender to purée soup until very smooth; or, transfer the soup in batches into a blender or food processor to purée. Season with salt and pepper. Serve immediately.

Per Serving
calories: 170 | fat: 6.8g | carbs: 21.2g | protein: 6.5g

Hearty Spicy Chili

Prep time: 25 minutes | Cook time: 2¼ hours | Serves 12

2 tablespoons canola oil
2 red bell peppers, seeded and chopped
2 jalapeño peppers, finely chopped
3 Anaheim chiles, roasted, peeled, seeded, and chopped
3 poblano chiles, roasted, peeled, seeded, and chopped
2 yellow onions, chopped
1 pound (454 g) boneless chuck steak, trimmed of fat and cut into ¼-inch cubes
2 pounds (907 g) 92% lean ground beef
1 pound (454 g) lean Italian sausage
¼ cup minced garlic
2 teaspoons granulated onion
2 teaspoons garlic powder
3 tablespoons chili powder
2 teaspoons ground hot paprika
2 teaspoons ground cumin
2 teaspoons ground cayenne pepper
2 teaspoons ground coriander
2 teaspoons salt
2 teaspoons ground black pepper
1 cup tomato paste
2 cups tomato sauce
12 ounces lager beer
1 cup low-sodium chicken broth
2 (15½-ounce / 439.4-g) cans pinto beans, undrained
2 (15½-ounce / 439.4-g) cans kidney beans, undrained
½ cup thinly sliced scallions

1. Warm a large stockpot or Dutch oven over high heat and add oil. Cook bell peppers, jalapeños, Anaheim chiles, poblano chiles, and onions until tender, about 5 minutes.
2. Add cubed beef chuck and brown on all sides. Mix in ground beef, sausage, and garlic. Gently stir, trying not to break meat up too much. Cook until meat is browned and cooked through, about 7 to 10 minutes.
3. Stir in granulated onion, garlic powder, chili powder, paprika, cumin, cayenne, coriander, salt, and pepper. Cook for 1 minute and then stir in the tomato paste and tomato sauce. Cook for 2 minutes.
4. Pour in beer, chicken broth, pinto beans, and kidney beans. Thoroughly mix and reduce the heat to medium-low. Simmer for 2 hours, stirring occasionally. Top with scallions and serve.

Per Serving
calories: 460 | fat: 17.8g | carbs: 35.6g | protein: 37.1g

Cheesy Chicken Enchilada Soup

Prep time: 15 minutes | Cook time: 4 hours | Serves 4

2 teaspoons extra-virgin olive oil
½ cup chopped onion
3 cloves garlic, minced
1 (8-ounce / 227-g) can tomato sauce
3 cups low-sodium chicken broth
1 to 2 teaspoons chopped canned chipotle chilies in adobo sauce
1 (15-ounce / 425-g) can black beans, rinsed and drained
1 (14½-ounce / 411-g) can diced tomatoes
2 cups frozen corn
1 teaspoon ground cumin, plus more to taste
½ teaspoon dried oregano
2 (8-ounce / 227-g) boneless, skinless chicken breasts, trimmed of fat
Salt, to taste
¼ cup chopped scallions
¾ cup shredded reduced-fat Cheddar cheese
¼ cup chopped fresh cilantro

1. Place a medium pot over medium-low heat and add oil. Sauté onion and garlic until soft, about 3 to 4 minutes. Slowly stir in tomato sauce, chicken broth, and chipotles. Once soup comes to a boil, carefully transfer it to the bowl of a slow cooker.
2. Into the slow cooker bowl, add beans, tomatoes, corn, cumin, and oregano; stir to combine. Add chicken breasts to the slow cooker. Cover with a lid and cook on low heat for 4 hours.
3. Transfer chicken from the slow cooker to a small bowl. Let cool for a few minutes and then use forks to shred the meat. Return to the soup, along with salt and cumin to taste.
4. To serve, ladle the soup into the bowls and top with scallions, cheese, and cilantro.

Per Serving
calories: 429 | fat: 9.7g | carbs: 41.4g | protein: 42.1g

Green Split Pea Soup

Prep time: 5 minutes | Cook time: 45 minutes | Serves 6

1 (16-ounce / 454-g) package dried green split peas, soaked overnight
5 cups low-sodium vegetable broth or water
2 teaspoons garlic powder
2 teaspoons onion powder
1 teaspoon dried oregano
1 teaspoon dried thyme
¼ teaspoon freshly ground black pepper

1. In a large stockpot, combine the split peas, broth, garlic powder, onion powder, oregano, thyme, and pepper. Bring to a boil over medium-high heat.
2. Cover, reduce the heat to medium-low, and simmer for 45 minutes, stirring every 5 to 10 minutes. Serve warm.

Per Serving
calories: 298 | fat: 2.1g | carbs: 48.2g | protein: 23.3g

Carrot, Tomato, and Spinach Soup

Prep time: 10 minutes | Cook time: 13 minutes | Serves 4

6 multicolored carrots, cut into 1-inch pieces
½ cup barley
1 (15-ounce / 425-g) can diced tomatoes
2 garlic cloves, minced
4 cups no-sodium vegetable broth
2 cups water
4 cups fresh spinach
¼ cup chopped fresh basil leaves, plus more for garnish
2 tablespoons chopped fresh chives, plus more for garnish
1 (15-ounce / 425-g) can cannellini beans, rinsed and drained
1 tablespoon balsamic vinegar
Freshly ground black pepper, to taste

1. In a large pot over medium heat, combine the carrots, barley, tomatoes with their juices, garlic, vegetable broth, and water. Bring to a simmer. Cover the pot and cook for 10 minutes, or until the barley is chewy and not hard.
2. Place spinach, basil, and chives on top of the water but do not stir. Cover the pot, reduce heat to low, and cook for 3 minutes to soften the leaves.
3. Stir the pot and add the cannellini beans and vinegar. Remove the pot from the heat and let sit, covered, for 5 minutes. Garnish with chives, basil, and a pinch of pepper to serve.

Per Serving
calories: 262 | fat: 2.2g | carbs: 49.8g | protein: 12.3g

Red Lentils and Asparagus Soup

Prep time: 10 minutes | Cook time: 27 to 37 minutes | Serves 4

2 leeks
1 tablespoon water
2 garlic cloves, minced
¾ teaspoon dried tarragon
1 cup dried red lentils
1 pound (454 g) asparagus, cut into 1-inch pieces, including the ends
6 cups no-sodium vegetable broth
Juice of 1 lemon
Fresh ground black pepper, to taste

1. Cut off the leeks' root ends and the dark green portion of the stalks. Slit the remaining white and light green portion lengthwise down the center and run the leeks under cool water, using your fingers to remove any dirt between the layers. Thinly slice the leeks.
2. In a large pot over medium-high heat, combine the leeks and water. Sauté for 5 minutes. Add the garlic and tarragon. Cook for 2 minutes more.
3. Add the lentils, asparagus, and vegetable broth. Bring the soup to a boil, cover the pot, reduce the heat to medium-low, and cook for 20 to 30 minutes until the lentils are tender.
4. Remove some of the cooked lentils, leeks, and asparagus if you'd like some larger pieces in your soup. Using an immersion blender, purée the soup until smooth, or slightly chunky if preferred. Stir in the ingredients removed, if using.
5. Serve with a light drizzle of fresh lemon juice and season with pepper.

Per Serving
calories: 244 | fat: 2.2g | carbs: 44.9g | protein: 16.3g

Lush Minestrone Soup

Prep time: 10 minutes | Cook time: 25 to 35 minutes | Serves 6 large bowls

1 tablespoon olive oil
1 large onion, chopped,
5 stalks celery, thinly sliced
3 cloves garlic, minced
2 bay leaves
10 cups water
1 to 2 teaspoons iodized salt
2 cups fresh tomato purée
3 (15-ounce / 425-g) cans beans (combination of kidney, garbanzo, cannellini, butter, or lima beans)
3 cups chopped seasonal or frozen vegetables (such as carrots, green beans, potatoes, corn, zucchini, and okra), cut in ½-inch pieces
½ cup TVP
2 cups fresh or frozen kale, cut in ½-inch strips
2 cups cooked small shaped pasta
3 tablespoons pesto

1. Sauté onions, garlic, and celery in large soup pot with olive oil.
2. Add water, salt, bay leaves, tomato purée, beans, mixed vegetables, and TVP. Simmer over low for 15 to 20 minutes until all vegetables are tender.
3. Add pasta and kale. Simmer for another 10 to 15 minutes. Stir in the pesto. Note that pasta can also be cooked separately and added at end with the pesto if a firmer texture is desired.
4. Serve warm.

Per Serving
calories: 422 | fat: 9.9g | carbs: 64.8g | protein: 21.2g

Potato and Brown Lentil Soup

Prep time: 10 minutes | Cook time: 45 minutes | Serves 4

2 medium onions, chopped
3 garlic cloves, chopped
4 cups water, divided
3 small potatoes, chopped
1 cup dried brown lentils
3 cups chopped kale
4 celery stalks, chopped
3 medium carrots, chopped
1 teaspoon turmeric
½ teaspoon freshly ground black pepper
½ teaspoon pink Himalayan salt

1. In a large nonstick pot over medium-high heat, sauté the onions and garlic in ¼ cup of water for 5 minutes, or until softened.
2. Add the remaining 3¾ cups of water, the potatoes, lentils, kale, celery, carrots, turmeric, pepper, and salt and stir well. Reduce the heat to medium low, cover, and simmer for 40 minutes, or until the potatoes are soft.
3. Serve warm.

Per Serving
calories: 333 | fat: 1.2g | carbs: 66.2g | protein: 19.3g

White Bean Soup with Turkey Sausage

Prep time: 10 minutes | Cook time: 27 minutes | Serves 4

2 teaspoons extra-virgin olive oil
1 onion, chopped
1 clove garlic, minced
1¼ pounds (567 g) lean turkey sausage, casings removed
6 cups low-sodium chicken broth
1 cup canned white beans, drained and rinsed
1 cup roughly chopped kale (stems removed)
Salt and ground black pepper, to taste

1. In a medium heavy-duty pot, warm oil over medium-high heat. Add onion and garlic, sautéing for 2 to 3 minutes. Add sausage, using a wooden spoon to break the meat into small pieces. Sauté for 5 to 6 minutes, stirring frequently, until the meat is cooked through.
2. Stir in chicken broth and beans. Cover with a lid and simmer on low heat for 10 minutes.
3. Add the kale and continue simmering with the pot covered for another 10 minutes.
4. Season with salt and pepper, and divide soup into 4 bowls to serve.

Per Serving
calories: 351 | fat: 15.8g | carbs: 20.1g | protein: 34.4g

Chapter 19 Sandwich and Wraps

Breakfast Burritos

Prep time: 5 minutes | Cook time: 11 minutes | Serves 1

4 (10-ounce / 283-g) slices lean deli ham (97% fat free, preferably)
2 large eggs
10 thin asparagus stalks, ends trimmed, and chopped into ½-inch pieces
¼ cup shredded Cheddar cheese

1. Preheat the oven to 400°F (204°C). Spray a small non-stick frying pan with non-stick cooking spray and place over medium heat.
2. Crack the eggs into the pan and add the asparagus pieces. Cook for 4 to 5 minutes, stirring occasionally, until the eggs just begin to set. Sprinkle the cheese over top of the eggs and cook for 1 additional minute, or until the cheese is melted. (Do not stir.)
3. Make the wraps by placing two slices of ham side-by-side on a plate, overlapping the edges just slightly. Repeat with the remaining slices. Divide the filling into two equal portions and spoon onto each of the wraps. Grasp the ends of each wrap and gently roll into bundles.
4. Spray an 8 x 8in (20 x 20cm) baking dish with non-stick cooking spray, and place the wraps in the dish. Bake for 6 to 8 minutes, or until the ham is lightly browned and the cheese starts to bubble. Serve hot.

Per Serving
calories: 318 | fat: 20.5g | carbs: 2.2g | protein: 29.7g

Egg and Avocado Sandwiches

Prep time: 10 minutes | Cook time: 2 minutes | Serves 4

8 egg whites or 1½ cups liquid egg white substitute
Salt and ground black pepper, to taste
Ground cayenne pepper, to taste
1 tablespoon extra-virgin olive oil
¼ cup diced red bell pepper
¼ cup chopped scallions
¼ cup seeded and diced tomatoes
8 slices whole-grain bread, toasted
1 medium avocado, peeled, pitted, and sliced

1. In a medium bowl, add egg whites and use a fork or whisk to beat together. Stir in the salt, pepper, and cayenne.
2. Add the olive oil to a small nonstick skillet and warm over medium-high heat. Add 1 tablespoon each of bell peppers, scallions, and tomatoes. Stirring constantly, sauté for 1 minute; mix in ¼ of the egg whites. Cover with a lid, reduce heat to low, and cook until eggs have set, about 1 to 2 minutes. Use a spatula to fold eggs over themselves (in half) and then fold in half again. Remove eggs from pan and reserve. Repeat process 3 more times until all the egg whites and vegetables have been used.
3. Lay eggs onto 4 pieces of toasted bread and layer avocado slices on top. Close with top half of bread, cut each sandwich in half, and serve.

Per Serving
calories: 289 | fat: 13.1g | carbs: 29.7g | protein: 16.5g

Turkey Lettuce Wraps

Prep time: 15 minutes | Cook time: 15 minutes | Serves 4

1 tablespoon extra-virgin olive oil or avocado oil
1 pound (454g) extra-lean ground turkey
½ sweet onion, chopped
2 garlic cloves, minced
¼ cup marinara pasta sauce
¼ cup chicken broth
1 tablespoon chili powder
1 teaspoon ground cumin
½ teaspoon dried oregano
½ teaspoon sea salt
¼ teaspoon freshly ground black pepper
½ cup cooked black beans
½ cup frozen yellow corn kernels, thawed
½ cup shredded Cheddar cheese, divided
½ cup chopped red bell pepper, divided
1 avocado, cubed, divided
4 romaine lettuce leaves

1. In a large skillet over medium-high heat, heat the oil. Add the ground turkey and cook until browned, 8 to 10 minutes.
2. Add the onion and sauté for a few more minutes, until softened, then add the garlic and sauté for another minute.
3. Add in the marinara sauce and chicken broth, and stir to combine.
4. Season with chili powder, cumin, oregano, salt, and pepper, and cook until the stock is absorbed, 5 to 7 minutes.
5. Stir in the black beans and corn and cook for another minute to heat through. Remove from the heat and let cool.
6. Into each of 4 airtight storage containers, place a quarter of the turkey filling. Divide the cheese, red bell pepper, and avocado evenly among the containers and seal. Into each of 4 resealable storage bags, place 1 romaine leaf and seal. Serve the warmed filling in a lettuce leaf.
7. Store the airtight containers and bags in the refrigerator for up to 5 days. To reheat, microwave the turkey filling on high for 1 to 2 minutes.

Per Serving (1 container)
calories: 410 | fat: 26.7g | carbs: 16.7g | protein: 29.2g

Italian-Style Sloppy Joe

Prep time: 10 minutes | Cook time: 4 hours | Serves 4

1 pound (454 g) lean Italian turkey sausage, casings removed
½ cup chopped onion
3 cloves garlic, minced
1 red bell pepper, seeded and chopped in ½-inch pieces
1 green bell pepper, seeded and chopped in ½-inch pieces
1⅓ cups canned crushed tomatoes
½ teaspoon dried rosemary
Salt and ground black pepper, to taste
4 whole-wheat 100-calorie potato rolls
4 slices reduced-fat provolone cheese
1 cup baby spinach

1. Warm a large nonstick skillet over medium-high heat. Add sausage, using a wooden spoon to break the meat into small pieces. Sauté for 5 to 6 minutes, stirring frequently, until the meat is cooked through.
2. Stir in onion and garlic. After cooking about 2 minutes, transfer sausage mixture to the slow cooker bowl. Add peppers, tomatoes, rosemary, salt, and pepper. Stir to combine.
3. Cover the slow cooker with a lid and set the heat to low. Cook for 4 hours.
4. To serve, fill a roll with a heaping ½ cup of meat. Top with cheese and baby spinach.

Per Serving
calories: 373 | fat: 14.8g | carbs: 31.2g | protein: 32.4g

Spiced Turkey Taco Lettuce Wraps

Prep time: 10 minutes | Cook time: 24 minutes | Serves 4

1 pound (454 g) 93% lean ground turkey
1 teaspoon garlic powder
1 teaspoon ground cumin
1 teaspoon chili powder
1 teaspoon ground sweet paprika
½ teaspoon dried oregano
Salt and ground black pepper, to taste
½ small onion, chopped

1. Warm a large nonstick skillet over medium-high heat. Add ground turkey to the skillet, using a wooden spoon to break the meat into small pieces. Cook for 4 to 5 minutes, stirring frequently, until the meat is no longer pink.
2. Stir in garlic powder, cumin, chili powder, paprika, oregano, salt, and pepper. Add onion, bell pepper, and tomato sauce. Cover the skillet with a lid, reduce the heat to low, and simmer for 20 minutes.
3. To serve, place 2 lettuce leaves on each plate. Divide filling between lettuce leaves, placing in the center of each leaf. Garnish with cilantro and serve.

¼ red bell pepper, seeded and chopped
½ cup canned tomato sauce
8 large iceberg lettuce leaves, washed and dried
½ cup chopped fresh cilantro

Per Serving
calories: 196| fat: 7.8g | carbs: 3.9g | protein: 21.8g

Classic French Dip Sandwiches

Prep time: 10 minutes | Cook time: 9 hours | Serves 8

1 tablespoon minced garlic
1 tablespoon chopped fresh rosemary
1 tablespoon chopped fresh thyme leaves
Salt and ground black pepper, to taste
2 pounds (907 g) lean beef round roast, trimmed of fat
1 teaspoon Worcestershire sauce
2 (14½-ounce / 411-g) cans low-sodium beef broth, plus more if needed
3 large onions, sliced
1 large red bell pepper, seeded and sliced into strips
1 large green bell pepper, seeded and sliced into strips
2 (8-ounce / 227-g) baguettes
8 slices reduced-fat Mozzarella

1. In a small bowl, mix together garlic, rosemary, thyme, salt, and pepper. Rub roast entirely with the spice mix and place it in the slow cooker.
2. Add Worcestershire sauce and enough broth to cover the meat. Cover with the lid and cook on low until the meat is fork-tender, 9 to 12 hours, depending on roast thickness.
3. An hour before the meat is done, add onions and bell peppers into the slow cooker. When roast is tender, transfer the meat to a cutting board and shred with a fork or slice with a knife.
4. Using a slotted spoon, remove the onions and peppers from the broth. Use a gravy separator to remove any fat from broth or leave it in the fridge overnight to skim off the solidified fat.
5. To serve, preheat the broiler. Slice baguette and top with 2 ounces beef, plus onions, peppers, and cheese. Place under the broiler until cheese melts and serve with ramekins of broth for dipping.

Per Serving
calories: 324 | fat: 10.1g | carbs: 24.5g | protein: 35.2g

Perfect Vegan BLT Sandwich

Prep time: 5 minutes | Cook time: 15 minutes | Serves 2

1 (7-ounce / 198-g) pack tempeh, thinly sliced
½ cup BBQ sauce
2 large tomatoes, sliced
4 lettuce leaves
4 whole wheat buns

Optional Toppings:
Guacamole
BBQ sauce
Red onion

1. Add the tempeh slices and the BBQ sauce to an airtight container.
2. Close the airtight container, shake well and put it in the fridge, allowing the tempeh to marinate for 1 hour, up to 12 hours.
3. Preheat the oven to 375°F (190°C) and line a baking sheet with parchment paper.
4. Transfer the tempeh slices onto the baking sheet and bake for about 15 minutes or until the tempeh is browned and crispy.
5. Bake the buns with the tempeh for the last 5 minutes if you want crispy and browned bread.
6. Spread the guacamole on the bottom half of each bun and add a lettuce leaf on top.
7. Put a quarter of the BBQ tempeh slices on top of the lettuce on each bun and top with 2 slices of tomato on each bun.
8. Cover with the top halves of the buns and serve immediately.

Per Serving
calories: 259 | fat: 9.8g | carbs: 14.7g | protein: 24.2g

Chickpea Mustard Salad Sandwich

Prep time: 5 minutes | Cook time: 0 minutes | Serves 2

2 cups cooked chickpeas
½ block firm tofu, chopped
1 celery stalk, chopped
1 scallion, chopped
3 tablespoons vegan mayonnaise
1 tablespoon yellow mustard
⅛ teaspoon freshly ground black pepper
Pink Himalayan salt, to taste (optional)
4 slices whole wheat bread

1. In a large bowl, mash the chickpeas.
2. Add the tofu, celery, scallion, mayo, mustard, pepper, and salt (if using) and mix well.
3. Spread the salad equally on 2 slices of bread and top with the remaining slices to make 2 sandwiches.
4. Serve immediately.

Per Serving

calories: 618 | fat: 14.8g | carbs: 93.9g | protein: 33.1g

Speedy Tofu Club Wrap

Prep time: 10 minutes | Cook time: 3 to 5 minutes | Serves 1

¼ block firm tofu, sliced
3 slices tempeh
1 large gluten-free tortilla wrap
1 tablespoon vegan mayonnaise
1 small avocado, pitted, peeled, and chopped
1 romaine lettuce leaf, chopped
1 small tomato, sliced
¼ small red onion, sliced
⅛ teaspoon freshly ground black pepper

1. Preheat a nonstick pan over medium heat. Place the tofu slices and tempeh in the pan and cook for 3 to 5 minutes, until both sides are lightly browned.
2. Place the tortilla on a plate and spread with the mayo. Layer on the avocado, lettuce, tomato, and onion. Top with the tofu and tempeh and sprinkle with the pepper. Wrap the tortilla and serve.

Per Serving

calories: 577 | fat: 29.8g | carbs: 60.2g | protein: 23.3g

Chapter 20 Sauces, Dressings and Rub

Lime Avocado Dressing

Prep time: 10 minutes | Cook time: 0 minutes | Makes 3 cups

1 large ripe avocado, halved, pitted, and peeled
Sea salt, to taste
Ground white pepper, to taste
2 tablespoons white wine vinegar
1¼ cups avocado oil
¼ cup freshly squeezed lime juice
Pinch ground cayenne pepper
1 tablespoon honey

1. In a blender or food processor, place the avocado flesh. Add the salt, white pepper, vinegar, avocado oil, lime juice, cayenne pepper, and honey. Process until smooth.
2. Store in an airtight container in the refrigerator for 5 to 7 days.

Per Serving (2 tablespoons)
calories: 122 | fat: 13.2g | carbs: 2.1g | protein: 0g

Light Ranch Salad Dressing

Prep time: 10 minutes | Cook time: 0 minutes | Makes 1¼ cups

¾ cup nonfat plain Greek yogurt
¼ cup reduced-fat sour cream (5%)
1 tablespoon freshly squeezed lemon juice
2 tablespoons chopped fresh chives
1 teaspoon garlic powder
½ teaspoon onion powder
½ teaspoon dried parsley
Sea salt, to taste
Freshly ground black pepper, to taste
2 to 3 tablespoons water

1. In a small bowl or measuring cup, whisk together the yogurt, sour cream, lemon juice, chives, garlic powder, onion powder, and parsley. Season with salt and pepper. Whisk in the water as needed to achieve desired thickness.
2. Store in an airtight container in the refrigerator for up to 1 week.

Per Serving (2 tablespoons)
calories: 24 | fat: 0.9g | carbs: 2.1g | protein: 3.3g

Tangy Maple-Tahini Sauce

Prep time: 10 minutes | Cook time: 0 minutes | Makes 1 cup

½ cup tahini
Juice of 1 lime
1 tablespoon pure maple syrup
1 tablespoon extra-virgin olive oil

1. In a small bowl, whisk the tahini, lime juice, maple syrup, olive oil, mustard, and water. Season with salt. Taste and adjust flavor as desired, using maple syrup for sweetness, lime juice for acidity, or salt for more saltiness.
2. Store in an airtight container in the refrigerator for up to 5 days.

1 teaspoon Dijon mustard
½ cup water
Sea salt, to taste

Per Serving (2 tablespoons)
calories: 112 | fat: 9.9g | carbs: 5.1g | protein: 3.2g

Best Guacamole

Prep time: 10 minutes | Cook time: 0 minutes | Makes 2 cups

2 ripe avocados, halved, pitted, peeled, and mashed
Juice of 1 large lime
1 garlic clove, minced
2 tablespoons finely chopped red onion
1 tablespoon finely chopped fresh cilantro
20 grape tomatoes, finely chopped (optional)
½ teaspoon sea salt
Freshly ground black pepper, to taste

1. In a medium bowl, mix the avocados, lime juice, and garlic. Stir in the onion, cilantro, and tomatoes (if using). Season with salt and pepper. Refrigerate for at least an hour before serving.
2. Store in an airtight container in the refrigerator for up to 3 days.

Per Serving (¼ cup)
calories: 84 | fat: 6.8g | carbs: 6.1g | protein: 1.3g

Easy Homemade Hummus

Prep time: 10 minutes | Cook time: 0 minutes | Makes 3 cups

1 (15-ounce / 425-g) can chickpeas, drained and rinsed
¼ cup nonfat or low-fat plain Greek yogurt
Juice of 1 lemon
¼ cup tahini
2 tablespoons extra-virgin olive oil
2 garlic cloves, peeled
½ teaspoon sea salt
½ teaspoon ground cumin
2 to 4 tablespoons water, as needed

1. In a high-speed blender or food processor, combine the chickpeas, yogurt, lemon juice, tahini, olive oil, garlic, salt, and cumin. Blend until smooth. Add the water as needed to reach your desired consistency.
2. Store in an airtight container in the refrigerator for up to 7 days.

Per Serving (2 tablespoons)
calories: 46 | fat: 2.9g | carbs: 5.1g | protein: 1.3g

Fresh Berry Sauce

Prep time: 5 minutes | Cook time: 5 minutes | Makes 1¾ cups

3 cups frozen mixed berries, slightly thawed
¼ cup water
3 to 4 tablespoons pure maple syrup or honey (maple syrup if vegan)
½ tablespoon freshly squeezed lemon juice
¼ teaspoon ground cinnamon
Pinch sea salt
1 tablespoon chia seeds

1. In a medium pot, combine the berries and water. Bring to a boil over high heat, stirring occasionally.
2. Lower to a simmer and add in the maple syrup, lemon juice, cinnamon, salt, and chia seeds.
3. Cook for 5 to 7 more minutes, stirring, until the sauce reduces slightly and thickens.
4. Remove from the heat, let cool briefly, then purée with an immersion blender until smooth.
5. Store in an airtight container in the refrigerator for up to 2 weeks.
6. Store in an airtight container in the freezer for up to 3 months. To reheat, microwave, heat over low heat in a saucepan on the stovetop, or let thaw in the refrigerator.

Per Serving (2 tablespoons)
calories: 33 | fat: 0.9g | carbs: 7.1g | protein: 1.3g

Low-Fat Tzatziki Sauce

Prep time: 5 minutes | Cook time: 0 minutes | Serves 16

1 small cucumber
¾ cup 2% Greek yogurt
¾ teaspoon Worcestershire sauce
2 tablespoons finely chopped fresh mint
Salt, to taste

1. Peel the cucumber, cut it lengthwise, and use a spoon to remove and discard the seeds. Into a blender or food processor, add half of the cucumber. Purée until smooth and transfer to a small bowl.
2. Add yogurt, Worcestershire sauce, mint, and salt to the cucumber purée in the bowl, and mix well. Finely chop remaining cucumber half and stir it into the tzatziki sauce. Use within 2 days.

Per Serving
calories: 12 | fat: 0g | carbs: 1.1g | protein: 1.3g

Spicy Cilantro Dressing

Prep time: 10 minutes | Cook time: 0 minutes | Serves 7

½ cup low-fat buttermilk
¼ cup light mayonnaise
¼ cup 2% Greek yogurt
1 small jalapeño pepper, seeded
¼ cup chopped fresh cilantro
1 tomatillo, husked, rinsed, and chopped
1 clove garlic
1 scallion, sliced
Juice of ½ lime
⅛ teaspoon cumin
Salt and ground black pepper, to taste

1. Add all the ingredients into a blender. Pulse until smooth. Use immediately or refrigerate until needed.

Per Serving
calories: 38 | fat: 1.9g | carbs: 3.1g | protein: 2.4g

Green Salsa Verde

Prep time: 10 minutes | Cook time: 0 minutes | Serves 4

2 poblano peppers, halved and seeded
2 serrano peppers, halved and seeded
1 avocado, peeled, pitted, and diced
1 clove garlic, peeled
1 cup chopped fresh cilantro
½ green bell pepper, seeded and chopped
½ medium sweet onion, chopped
¼ head iceberg lettuce, chopped
½ cup water
Juice of 2 limes
1 (15-ounce / 425-g) can diced tomatoes, drained

1. Into a blender or food processor, add all the ingredients except canned tomatoes. Blend until mostly smooth with a slight chunky consistency. (Do this in batches, if needed, depending on the size of blender or food processor.)
2. Transfer the mixture into a large bowl. Stir in drained canned tomatoes and mix well. Serve.

Per Serving
calories: 128 | fat: 6.8g | carbs: 15.1g | protein: 2.3g

Strawberry-Peach Vinaigrette

Prep time: 5 minutes | Cook time: 0 minutes | Makes 1¼ cups

1 peach, pitted
4 strawberries
¼ cup water
2 tablespoons balsamic vinegar

1. In a blender, combine the peach, strawberries, water, and vinegar. Blend on high for 1 to 2 minutes, or until the dressing has a smooth consistency.
2. Store in a refrigerator-safe container for up to 3 days.

Per Serving (2 tablespoons)
calories: 10 | fat: 0g | carbs: 2.0g | protein: 0g

Pine Nuts-Basil Pesto Sauce

Prep time: 5 minutes | Cook time: 0 minutes | Makes 24 tablespoons

3 cups packed fresh basil leaves
3 to 4 cloves garlic
⅓ cup pine nuts, lightly toasted
⅓ cup olive oil
¼ cup nutritional yeast
¼ teaspoon salt
⅛ teaspoon cayenne pepper
Cooked pasta, for serving

1. Place the basil leaves and garlic in a blender or food processor and mince well.
2. Add the pine nuts and continue to blend until nuts and basil are ground.
3. Drizzle in the olive oil, as you keep the machine running, until mixture becomes a fine paste.
4. Transfer to a bowl and stir in the nutritional yeast. Season with salt and pepper.
5. Toss over hot pasta and serve immediately.

Per Serving (1 tablespoon)
calories: 45 | fat: 4.4g | carbs: 1.2g | protein: 1.1g

Maple Peanut Butter Sauce

Prep time: 5 minutes | Cook time: 0 minutes | Serves 4

½ cup peanut butter
1 to 2 tablespoons soy sauce
2 teaspoons rice vinegar
1 tablespoon maple syrup
2 to 4 cloves garlic
1 tablespoon-sized piece of fresh ginger or 1 teaspoon powdered ginger
Sriracha or other hot sauce, to taste (optional)
½ cup low-sodium vegetable broth

1. Combine all the ingredients, except for the broth, in a blender and blend until smooth. Add the vegetable broth until desired consistency is reached.

Per Serving
calories: 217 | fat: 17.2g | carbs: 12.3g | protein: 8.3g

Balsamic Raspberry Dressing

Prep time: 5 minutes | Cook time: 0 minutes | Serves 5

1 cup fresh raspberries
2 tablespoons raspberry vinegar
1 tablespoon regular or golden balsamic vinegar
2 tablespoons water
2 teaspoons liquid sweetener
2 teaspoons Dijon mustard
Freshly ground pepper, to taste

1. Combine all the ingredients in a food processor and blend well.

Per Serving
calories: 23 | fat: 0g | carbs: 5.1g | protein: 0.6g

The Best Beef Rub

Prep time: 10 minutes | Cook time: 0 minutes | Makes 5 tablespoons

2 tablespoons finely ground coffee
4½ teaspoons granulated garlic
4½ teaspoons salt
1 heaping teaspoon freshly ground black pepper
¼ teaspoon ground cayenne pepper
¼ teaspoon ground cinnamon
¼ teaspoon ground cloves

1. In a small bowl, mix well to combine the coffee, garlic, salt, black pepper, cayenne pepper, cinnamon, and cloves.
2. Store in a sealed storage container.

Per Serving
calories: 0 | fat: 0g | carbs: 0g | protein: 0g

Appendix : Measurement Conversion Chart

MEASUREMENT CONVERSION CHART

VOLUME EQUIVALENTS(DRY)

US STANDARD	METRIC (APPROXIMATE)
1/8 teaspoon	0.5 mL
1/4 teaspoon	1 mL
1/2 teaspoon	2 mL
3/4 teaspoon	4 mL
1 teaspoon	5 mL
1 tablespoon	15 mL
1/4 cup	59 mL
1/2 cup	118 mL
3/4 cup	177 mL
1 cup	235 mL
2 cups	475 mL
3 cups	700 mL
4 cups	1 L

WEIGHT EQUIVALENTS

US STANDARD	METRIC (APPROXIMATE)
1 ounce	28 g
2 ounces	57 g
5 ounces	142 g
10 ounces	284 g
15 ounces	425 g
16 ounces (1 pound)	455 g
1.5 pounds	680 g
2 pounds	907 g

VOLUME EQUIVALENTS(LIQUID)

US STANDARD	US STANDARD (OUNCES)	METRIC (APPROXIMATE)
2 tablespoons	1 fl.oz.	30 mL
1/4 cup	2 fl.oz.	60 mL
1/2 cup	4 fl.oz.	120 mL
1 cup	8 fl.oz.	240 mL
1 1/2 cup	12 fl.oz.	355 mL
2 cups or 1 pint	16 fl.oz.	475 mL
4 cups or 1 quart	32 fl.oz.	1 L
1 gallon	128 fl.oz.	4 L

TEMPERATURES EQUIVALENTS

FAHRENHEIT(F)	CELSIUS(C) (APPROXIMATE)
225 °F	107 °C
250 °F	120 °C
275 °F	135 °C
300 °F	150 °C
325 °F	160 °C
350 °F	180 °C
375 °F	190 °C
400 °F	205 °C
425 °F	220 °C
450 °F	235 °C
475 °F	245 °C
500 °F	260 °C

Printed in Great Britain
by Amazon